To Alan Donagan *and* Moltke Gram,
in gratitude *for* their stimulus,
their encouragement, *and*
their friendship

Henry B. Veatch
Two Logics
The Conflict Between Classical and Neo-analytic Philosophy

editiones scholasticae

Henry B. Veatch

Two Logics

The Conflict Between Classical
and Neo-analytic Philosophy

Bibliographic information published by Deutsche Nationalbibliothek
The Deutsche Nationalbibliothek lists this publication in the Deutsche Nationalbibliographie;
detailed bibliographic data is available in the Internet at http://dnb.ddb.de

Reprint of the First Edition, Evanston 1969

©2019 editiones scholasticae
53819 Neunkirchen-Seelscheid
www.editiones-scholasticae.de

ISBN 978-3-86838-222-8

Printed on acid-free paper

Printed in Germany
by CPI Buchbücher.de GmbH

Acknowledgments

IT IS NOT INFREQUENT nowadays for the acknowledgment page of a philosophy book to resemble nothing quite so much as a page of self-advertisement. Paraded before the astonished eyes of openmouthed readers, there is likely to be the most prestigious list of indebtednesses to Guggenheim, to Fulbright, to Rockefeller, to Ford, to the A.C.L.S., to the N.S.F., etc., etc. Unhappily, the present writer has no such acknowledgments to make. And while he cannot but be humbled by the realization that neither his grantsmanship nor his professional competence has been such as to win him the usual foundation largesse, he at the same time recognizes that one need not be of the stature of a Dr. Johnson to resent having to wait, application blank in hand, in the anterooms of those contemporary supercilious and philosophically purblind Lord Chesterfields who today preside over our money-dispensing foundations and government agencies.

Instead of being thus nationally prestigious, this writer's indebtedness is merely to his own university, Northwestern, for having generously granted him a leave of absence during the spring quarter of 1966 for work on this book. Also, but in a somewhat different vein, he is indebted to the Rev. Joseph Owens, C.Ss.R., of the Pontifical Institute of Mediaeval Studies, for having read the entire book in manuscript and for having made invaluable suggestions, both stylistic and philosophical. Likewise, to two colleagues at Northwestern, Professor Gram of the Philosophy Department and Professor Graff of the English Department, he would like to express his warm and personal thanks for their expert discussion and criticism of several chapters when these were still in their formative stages. A very particular sin of omission, however, would be to pass over in silence the singular help and encouragement that have come from Northwestern University Press, and particularly from Mrs. Joy Neuman, the copyeditor, whose deft and tactful corrections, while they could hardly suffice to make the style interesting, may still be credited with having alleviated not a little of its gall.

Contents

vii

TWO LOGICS

Introduction

The Battle *of the* Books Renewed

A NEW BATTLE OF THE BOOKS? But who would ever conceive of such a thing in this nuclear day and age? The very words
suggest "old, forgotten, far-off things and battles long ago." In one sense,
of course, battles of books we shall always have with us. And yet Swift's
"full and true account of the battle fought last Friday . . . in Saint James'
Library" had to do with issues and controversies around "the year 1697,
when the famous dispute was on foot between ancient and modern learning." [1] Surely, no such quarrel between the ancients and the moderns any
longer agitates either the academies or the literary and intellectual circles,
to say nothing of the libraries of today. Far from it, for the poor ancients,
if they are able any longer to speak to us at all, can hardly speak to us even

---

1. Jonathan Swift, *A Tale of a Tub to which is added the Battle of the Books and the
Mechanical Operation of the Spirit*, ed. A. C. Guthkelch and D. Nichol Smith, 2nd ed.
(Oxford: Clarendon Press, 1958), p. 213.

in their own languages. So how could they possibly stand party to any imagined contemporary literary or philosophical dispute?

Still, even though one no longer hears loud noises of quarrels between ancients and moderns, one does sometimes hear, whether inside or outside academic walls, faint mutterings and grumblings about the respective educational values of the humanities and the sciences. It is true that these noises are sporadic and very largely muted, it now being the case that science, and particularly physics, is to the present academic scene pretty much what Bonaparte once was to the French political scene after the Eighteenth Brumaire: the bickerings and inefficiencies of a would-be republic had all been put behind; a Caesar was now in control! And just as Bonaparte did not deign to justify his domination of the scene through much in the way of explanation and argument — for who needs reason as an arbiter, when he has an army — so the scientists of today don't have to worry about educational theories — for who needs a theory in justification, when he has government grants, foundation support, social prestige, yes, everything that a man could want whose only devotion is, of course, to the truth and nothing else. Indeed, if by some stretch of the imagination one were to envisage a serious challenge being aimed at the present-day educational hegemony of the scientists, all the challenged need do would be to raise the hue and cry of "Sputnik!", "Nuclear arms race!", etc., and the challengers would at once voluntarily and ignominiously retire from the field.

To be sure, we have not forgotten what the history books tell us about Bonaparte, who, though he had securely ensconced himself in the consulate and did not really need to bother with such concerns of the intellect as discussion and argument, did nevertheless take the trouble to make a few gestures of condescension toward what might be labeled "informed public opinion." And so today, Sir Karl Popper has, on at least one occasion and in a manner not unreminiscent of a condescending Bonaparte, deigned to observe that in his judgment our educational curricula should be revised so as to give the student more of a firsthand acquaintance with scientific problems. True, Sir Karl's recommendation does not involve in so many words a downgrading of the humanities in favor of the sciences, but rather a downgrading of what he calls "the prima facie method of teaching philosophy."[2] And what does such a prima facie method of teaching philosophy consist of? Apparently, it consists of "giving the beginner (whom

2. *Conjectures and Refutations* (New York: Basic Books, 1962), p. 72.

4

we take to be unaware of the history of mathematical, cosmological, and other ideas of sciences as well as of politics) the works of the great philosophers to read; the works, say, of Plato and Aristotle, Descartes and Leibniz, Locke, Berkeley, Hume, Kant and Mill." [3]

Now, quite patently, such a method of teaching philosophy might be roughly comparable to the traditional method of teaching literature and the humanities, i.e., a teaching via the so-called classics, it being through familiarizing himself with these that the student is supposed to become educated, and his taste and judgment and understanding to become cultivated and informed. But Sir Karl is skeptical of the results of such a method. Why? Because as he sees it, "genuine philosophical problems are always rooted in urgent problems outside philosophy, and they die if these roots die away." [4] Moreover, the extraphilosophical problems in which most genuine philosophical problems are rooted tend, Sir Karl thinks, to be problems deriving from science and mathematics. Accordingly, the way to discover the particular extraphilosophical problems that "inspired the great philosophers" is by "studying the history of, for example, scientific ideas, and especially the problem situation in mathematics and the sciences during the period in question." [5]

Alas, what a fate for philosophy! For have we not all been brought up to believe that the bankruptcy of philosophy is due precisely to the fact that all of the special sciences developed one by one out of philosophy, and thus poor philosophy was eventually left with no capital of its own. Yet now along comes the eminent Sir Karl Popper and tells us that it is not the sciences that have sprung from philosophy, so much as it is philosophy that owes all of its genuine problems to science; therefore the present bankruptcy of philosophy is due not to its having given its all to science, but rather to its owing its all to science and not being willing to acknowledge the debt. Either way philosophy is made to appear in a sorry light and strikes everyone as being a most woebegone, if not actually disreputable, competitor alongside its stunning and seemingly omnicompetent rival, science.

More seriously, though, just what is one to say to the more substantive part of Sir Karl's contention, viz., that whether we like it or not all really serious philosophy has its roots in problems arising out of science and mathematics? Apparently Sir Karl is prompted to make this claim partly on the general ground that philosophical problems always tend to be rooted in

3. *Ibid.*   4. *Ibid.*   5. *Ibid.*, p. 73.

5

problems that are extraphilosophical.[6] And in a way this is quite true — indeed, even a truism. For who would wish to deny that philosophy is a sort of discipline that should not, and cannot, operate in any sheer cultural vacuum? On the contrary, one might even go so far as to say that any and all human problems and human issues, of whatever sort and of whatever origin, may well become matters of philosophic concern. And, for that matter, Sir Karl Popper himself in one of his more incautious moments lets it slip that such extraphilosophical problems as provide grist for the mill of philosophy may just as well be moral or political problems as mathematical or scientific ones.[7] Not only that, but suppose that Sir Karl had been rather less arbitrarily selective in his list of "the great philosophers." Suppose that he had included Plotinus, Scotus, Ockham, or Spinoza — then surely he would have had to recognize that religious and theological problems would need to be added to his list of extraphilosophical problems that have a peculiar relevance for philosophy. And if he had gone on to include the names of St. Augustine, Hegel, Bradley, Croce, and Collingwood in his roster of the great in philosophy (and, after all, why not include them, if even John Stuart Mill could make the grade?), then it would have to be further conceded that problems of history and of literature and the arts could with equal justice be said to give rise to philosophical problems.

So, on the very grounds adduced by Sir Karl to show that science and mathematics are somehow the true and proper breeding grounds of philosophy, it turns out that science and mathematics, far from having any privileged position in this regard, are in no better position, or even in no other position, than are religion, politics, morals, art, history, law, or heaven knows what else. With this, though, Sir Karl's ponderously considered thesis — that in the future our young philosopher-trainees should begin their study of philosophy only after a prior training in the problems of science and mathematics — falls flat on its face, simply from the encumbrance of its own (that is to say, Sir Karl's) argument.

What is more, as regards the question of the more general cultural and

6. We say "partly on the general ground," because in this particular essay of Sir Karl's, "The Nature of Philosophical Problems and Their Roots in Science," the greater part of the argument is directed toward providing quite specific evidence for the thesis that philosophical problems are rooted in scientific and mathematical problems. Sir Karl's evidence consists of an elaborate and learned exploitation of two examples, Plato's theory of ideas and Kant's *Critique of Pure Reason*. In each of these cases, Sir Karl maintains that the relevant philosophical doctrines simply "cannot be properly understood" except in the context of the scientific (and hence extraphilosophical) situation of the time.

7. *Ibid.*, p. 73.

6

intellectual concerns out of which philosophy arises, would it not seem that the case of philosophy might not be so unlike that of other areas in the humanities — literature or painting or music or history? Consider: just what would the work of a Dante or a Milton have been without the background of what we might loosely designate as Christian theology? Or how is the achievement — supposing it to be an achievement — of a painter like Dali even to be conceived of apart from the impact upon contemporary culture of Freudian psychology? And as for Gibbon, can one imagine his being the historian he was in complete abstraction, not just from the Renaissance, but more particularly from the peculiar way in which the ideal of classical antiquity continued to live on in eighteenth-century England?

Yet merely because poetry or art or history or the novel has its roots in what might be called extrapoetical or extra-artistic or extraliterary concerns, we surely would not require that our would-be poets and artists and writers first put themselves through a course in psychology or theology or economics or mathematics or what not before addressing themselves to economic or social or theological issues in their paintings or novels or poetry. Why might not the case be at least analogous with respect to philosophers? For even supposing that, as Sir Karl Popper would have it, philosophy does sometimes have its roots in scientific or mathematical problems, it would scarcely seem to follow that in order to be a good philosopher, one must first be something of a scientist or a mathematician. This could be as ridiculous as demanding of a Kafka or a Faulkner that merely because he happens to be concerned as a novelist with problems that are undeniably psychological or sociological in character he must first become a psychologist or a sociologist. For might not the point be that when a philosopher addresses himself to problems that originally were of concern to the scientist or the mathematician, he nonetheless does so as a philosopher, with the result that the problems themselves then cease to be properly scientific or mathematical problems and become, instead, much more broadly based human problems — that is to say, they become philosophical problems, and as such require for their solution a philosopher's competence and not a scientist's or a mathematician's competence at all?

Some Confusions Confounded

Alas, though, the very ease with which we might thus fancy ourselves to score points on Popper really only serves to point up the superficiality and triviality of our own discussion. For in trying to expose the fatuousness of

Sir Karl's recommendations in regard to philosophical pedagogy, we have doubtless succeeded in doing little more than displaying the somewhat splenetic character of our own antiscientific bias and prejudice. Nor would the trouble appear to be traceable to any other source than that both we and Sir Karl have only been bandying about various fulsome contrasts between "scientific problems" on the one hand and "philosophical problems" on the other, or between humanistic learning as over against scientific knowledge. What more precisely, though, is the difference between a philosophical problem and a scientific one? Indeed, is there any significant distinction between them at all? Until such prior questions are dealt with, how can one possibly shed much light on the issue of whether or not the proper way to study philosophy is through a prior acquaintance with scientific and mathematical problems? As for all the fuss and feathers of science vs. the humanities, this will never amount to anything more than fuss and feathers, unless and until we succeed in determining just what is to be understood by the term "humanistic learning" and how it differs from its supposed opposite number, viz., "scientific knowledge." That the study of seventeenth-century English poetry somehow leads to a different sort of knowledge from that arising from the study of the physics of fluids, we all recognize readily enough. But just what is the difference? Or again, that Aristotle's discussion of the infinite seems to be of a noticeably different character from Cantor's, or even from Russell's somewhat popular exploitation, is obvious enough. But just what is the nature of this difference? Is it that Aristotle speaks to this issue as a philosopher, and Cantor as a mathematician? And if so, just what does this mean? Or is it rather the case that in this instance there is no very significant difference between the philosophical problem and the mathematical one?

Accordingly, having raised these prior and more fundamental questions, let us now see how some of the recognized authorities have undertaken to answer them. And no sooner does one speak of recognized authorities than, of course, the ever recurrent figure of Sir Karl Popper again obtrudes itself upon the scene. Unfortunately, however, when Sir Karl's particular ruminations on the subject of the difference between science and philosophy are exhibited for public view, it is just possible that the public may find itself at once surprised and disappointed. We say "surprised," because in his earlier days everybody thought of Professor Popper as the man who distinguished himself before all others in an almost schoolmasterish in-

sistence upon the importance of what he was wont to call "the line of demarcation" separating those disciplines whose assertions are susceptible
of an empirical test by way of falsification from those disciplines whose assertions are in principle not empirically falsifiable. Such a line of demarcation, he maintained, would surely serve to distinguish scientific questions
from philosophical, or at least from metaphysical, ones.[8] But, curiously
enough, it would now appear that Sir Karl in his most recent book has
gone a long way toward replacing his own earlier line of demarcation
with something that would seem to be little better than a smudge. Thus he
confidently declares that "there exist not only genuine scientific problems,
but genuine philosophical problems."[9] And how are we to distinguish
them? The answer seems to be: "Even if, upon analysis, these problems
[i.e., the philosophical problems] turn out to have factual components, they
need not be classified as belonging to science. And even if they should be
soluble by, say, purely logical means, they need not be classified as purely
logical or tautological."[10] Alas, though, this only makes the question still
more pressing: how are we to know when we have a scientific problem on
our hands and when a philosophical one? This time the answer comes
through in much greater detail, even if in rather more confusion:

. . . a problem may rightly be called "philosophical" if we find that although
originally it arose in connection with, say, atomic theory it is more closely connected with problems and theories which have been discussed by philosophers
than with theories now-a-days treated by physicists. And again, it does not matter in the least what kind of methods we use in solving such a problem.
Cosmology, for example, will always be of great philosophical interest even
though in some of its methods it has become closely allied with what is perhaps
better called "physics." To say that since it deals with factual issues it must belong to science rather than to philosophy is not only pedantic but clearly the

---

8. Cf. *The Logic of Scientific Discovery* (New York: Science Editions, 1961). See especially Pt. 1, Chap. 1, § 4. In fairness to Popper, it should perhaps be said that his original
notion of demarcation may have been thought of as serving to distinguish science only from
metaphysics, not from philosophy generally. In any case, in his Preface to the English edition
of 1958 (reprinted in the edition cited above), Popper says flatly that "there is no method
peculiar to philosophy" and that philosophy, quite as much as science, is interested in "the
problem of cosmology: the problem of understanding the world" (p. 15). Still, all this would
seem to make for more, rather than less, confusion when it comes to the question of just how
we are to know when we are dealing with a scientific problem and when with a philosophical
one.

9. *Conjectures and Refutations*, p. 73.   10. *Ibid.*

result of an epistemological, and thus of a philosophical, dogma. Similarly, there is no reason why a problem soluble by logical means should be denied the attribute "philosophical." It may well be typically philosophical, or physical, or biological.[11]

Somehow, one reads these lines with an astonishment amounting almost to bafflement. For is Professor Popper really telling us no more than that the way to recognize a philosophical problem is to consider whether it is the kind of problem that philosophers have been accustomed to treat of, just as the way to recognize a scientific problem is to consider whether it is the kind of problem that scientists occupy themselves with? Surely, though, if this isn't a downright tautology, at least it doesn't tell us anything that all of us did not already know.

As for the distinction that we were promised between the peculiar character of scientific problems as contrasted, say, with those of philosophy, this would now appear to have emerged in the guise of that most subtle of all distinctions, a distinction without a difference.

Nor are we helped much if, forsaking Sir Karl, we turn to that other and otherwise more perceptive and illuminating authority Lord Snow. For while C. P. Snow certainly brings home to us the fact that ours is an age of two cultures, not one — and oh, what a shame it is too! — he does not seem to occupy himself too much with the question of just what sort of knowledge or wisdom is characteristic of those whom he calls "the literary intellectuals" on the one hand, as over against the knowledge that is characteristic of the scientists, "and as the most representative, the physical scientists,"[12] on the other.

Oh, it's true he succeeds in pointing out many of the *propria* of the representatives of the two cultures, and yet without ever really getting at the *differentiae*. Thus the nonscientists tend to think of the scientists as "shallowly optimistic" and "unaware of man's condition," whereas "the scientists believe that the literary intellectuals are totally lacking in foresight, peculiarly unconcerned with their brother men, in a deep sense anti-intellectual, anxious to restrict both art and thought to the existential movement."[13] Likewise, the scientists have little real feeling for "the traditional culture." Instead, "they have their own culture," and it is a culture which "doesn't

11. *Ibid.*, p. 74.
12. *The Two Cultures and the Scientific Revolution* (New York: Cambridge University Press, 1959), p. 4.
13. *Ibid.*, pp. 5–6.

contain much art, with the exception, an important exception, of music. Verbal exchange, insistent argument. Longplaying records. Color-photography. The ear, to some extent the eye. Books, very little. . ." [14] And "what about the other side? . . . They still like to pretend that the traditional culture is the whole of 'culture' as though the natural order didn't exist." [15] Not only that, but "the intellectuals, in particular literary intellectuals, are natural Luddites," [16] etc., etc.

All this, no doubt, is most illuminating; it is also for the most part unhappily true. The only trouble is that it still does not succeed in disclosing what, for want of a better term, we might call the logic of the sciences as contrasted with the logic of philosophy or of the humanities. How, indeed, are knowledge and understanding achieved in science as contrasted with the way they are effected in philosophy and in humanistic studies generally? [17] And what are the respective types of knowledge that are so achieved? Might it not be that what is decisive, so far as the answer to this question is concerned, is that there are two logics [18] operative here and not just one? Moreover, if this is so, might it not account for the fact of our having two cultures, in Lord Snow's sense, and not just one — two radically different modes of learning and knowledge, and therewith two radically different types of cultured human personalities?

Two Logics: One for Bees and One for Spiders

Very well, then, suppose we try to fix what the differences are between these two apparently alternative logics. And if neither Sir Karl nor Lord Snow seems able to shed much light on this matter of the respective logics of the sciences and the humanities, then perhaps we might try turning to Swift for help — although it must be conceded at the outset that poor Swift was one who in his time fell so far short of the accomplishments of either Sir Karl or Lord Snow in theirs, that he could not even win a bishopric from his queen, much less a knighthood or a peerage. Hope-

---

14. *Ibid.*, p. 14.   15. *Ibid.*, p. 15.   16. *Ibid.*, p. 23.

17. Throughout this Introduction we have simply assumed, quite without explanation or justification, that philosophy is to be classified with the humanities, and that insofar as we are able to differentiate a humanistic type of knowledge from scientific knowledge we have thereby also succeeded in differentiating philosophical knowledge from scientific knowledge. Unfortunately, the argument for this will have to await the conclusion of our book as a whole.

18. It goes without saying that "logic" here means not simply formal logic, but rather the far broader discipline of the sort that the Scholastics called "material logic" or that Kant called "transcendental logic."

11

fully, though, if we can but keep ourselves from being corrupted by the Englishman's inveterate pursuit and pride of place, we can perhaps listen sympathetically to what Swift has to say concerning the logic of the sciences and of the humanities. It's true that Swift in the seventeenth century did not speak to the issue in quite these words. Yet there is the well-known passage in *The Battle of the Books* where he develops the amusing, if, be it admitted, at times rather scurrilous, fable of the spider and the bee.[19] Now it was the spider whom Swift put forward as a sort of allegorical figure or prototype of "the modern," as the bee was of "the ancient." Why choose the spider as typifying modern culture and learning? Because, as Swift remarks, it has so often been "urged by those who contended for the excellence of modern learning" that it is precisely with respect to "improvements in the Mathematics" and in architecture that modern learning has so far advanced over that of the ancients.[20] And what is the characteristic boast of the mathematician? It is that he "spins and spits wholly from himself, and scorns to own any obligation or assistance from without." [21] Yes, thinks the spider-mathematician — or at least so Swift depicts him — that's just the trouble with all these so-called humanists and lovers of the classics, as typified in the person and character of the bee:

What art thou but a vagabond without house or home, without stock or inheritance? born to no possession of your own, but a pair of wings and a drone-pipe. Your livelihood is a universal plunder upon nature; a free booter over fields and gardens. . . . Whereas I am a domestic animal, furnished with a native stock within myself.[22]

To which the bee replies:

The question comes all to this; whether is the nobler being of the two, that which, by . . . an overweening pride, feeding and engendering on itself, turns all into excrement and venom, producing nothing at all but fly bane and a cob-web; or that which by a universal range, with long search, much study, true judgment, and distinction of things, brings home honey and wax.[23]

19. Swift, pp. 228–35. Having thus cited Swift's fable, we shall proceed to interpret it more or less to suit our own purposes and not necessarily in accordance with the most recent opinions of historical scholars as to what Swift himself must have had in mind in devising the fable. For example, we have construed the antagonism between the spider and the bee as going beyond any mere seventeenth-century quarrel between ancients and moderns and as typifying the still current and contemporary issue between the sciences and the humanities. If Swift did not have the larger issue in mind, then he was indeed more prophetic than he knew.

20. *Ibid.*, pp. 231, 232.   21. *Ibid.*, p. 234.
22. *Ibid.*, p. 231.   23. *Ibid.*, p. 232.

Accordingly, the humanists, or those whom Swift calls the ancients, are only too happy to accept the simile of the bee as applied to themselves:

As for us the ancients, we are content, with the bee, to pretend to nothing of our own beyond our wings and our voice: that is to say, our flights and our language. For the rest, whatever we have got has been by infinite labor and search, and ranging through every corner of nature; the difference is that, instead of dirt and poison, we have chosen rather to fill our hives with honey and wax; thus furnishing mankind with the two noblest of things, sweetness and light.[24]

And what was the spider-mathematician's response to all this? Swift's only comment is that it "left the spider, like an orator, collected in himself, and just prepared to burst out." [25]

Now supposing that we cut through Swift's satire and invective, it is interesting, and to many of us perhaps even curious, to note the two chief points which Swift appeals to in his justification of the study of literature and the humanities. One is that their method might be considered thoroughly empirical, in the sense of being always open to and receptive of what is presented to one's view and what one finds in one's investigations. And indeed, in this connection he notes that one's search must be "long," of "universal range," and with no preconceptions of one's own, to wit, with "no possession of [one's] own, but a pair of wings and a drone-pipe." The second point which Swift makes in his defense of the humanities is that, in addition to their discipline being one which requires a person to be ever open to what he finds everywhere, both in literature and in life, their pursuit should eventually bring one to the point of "true judgment, and distinction of things." [26] In other words, Swift is here saying no less a thing than that it is precisely through the study of literature, the classics, if you will, that we come to know what's what, what the score is, so far as our very existence as human beings is concerned — what, in short, the truth is about ourselves and about the world in which we find ourselves. By implication, too, Swift seems to be suggesting that this same world — of which we are a part, and which we allow ourselves to become tutored and instructed in regard to by submitting to the discipline of the classics — is none

24. *Ibid.*, pp. 234–35. It might be remarked that Swift wrote these words at the very end of the seventeenth century, and hence long before "sweetness and light" had become all "sicklied o'er with the pale cast" of nineteenth-century sentimentality.

25. *Ibid.*, p. 233.

26. We have here altered slightly the order and sense of Swift's words, but we scarcely think the distortion a serious one.

other than the everyday world of men and things, of sights and sounds, of animals and plants, of summer and winter, of night and day, of life and death, of change and permanence, etc. Thus it isn't anything on the order of that fantastically wrought universe such as the modern spider-scientist is wont to spin out — a universe of not three, but multiple, dimensions, of strange quanta of energy, of distances measured in light years, of fissionable atoms, of curved space, etc. All of these, so far from being things which we meet with in experience, are things which are not even intelligible save in mathematical equations — a spider-universe, in short, and not a bee's world at all.

Oh, but you will say, this is all so wrongheaded. It is Swift himself who has got it all wrong, and little wonder, since after all he had the misfortune to be born some two and three-quarter centuries too soon, poor man. For what could he mean by supposing that the method of the humanities is empirical? Don't all of us nowadays know that a reliance upon observation and experiment is the hallmark of science and not of the humanities? And as for the study of literature bringing us to a true judgment and distinction of things, this is not the point of the study of literature at all. No, it's aesthetic enjoyment and the cultivation of our tastes that we may hope to derive from such things as a reading and study of the classics. But when it comes to true judgments of fact and of things, of the way the world is, of the causes and natures of things, that is ultimately and in principle the domain of science. For where may you find statements of fact — and in this sense "true judgments and distinctions of things" — which are not under obligation, as it were, to submit themselves to scientific verification and falsification? And whoever heard of a mode of verification or falsification that could be said to be not scientific, but literary or humanistic? Even considered as a mere manner of speaking, the thing sounds ridiculous.

Very well, let us consider ourselves duly chastened by this outburst of sober contemporary opinion. And let Swift also stand chastened — or at least we may imagine him chastened if he may justly be supposed to have intended that his fable of the bee should apply not just to the seventeenth-century opposition of modern and ancient, but to the twentieth-century opposition of scientist and humanist as well.

All the same, was it really so farfetched for Swift to have thought the true empiricist to be the student of the humanities rather than of the sciences? Consider the recently expressed opinion of a certain Professor Atkinson, a contemporary psychologist and disciple of the late Kurt Lewin, who wishes to exploit Lewin's plea for the elimination of what he (Lewin) calls Aristotelian modes of thought and their replacement with properly Galilean modes of thought. Indeed, we cite this opinion of Atkinson-Lewin not because of its distinction, but rather because of its being so commonplace, just the sort of thing that it is now fashionabe for scientists and philosophers of science to say about that currently most mighty and revered of human activities, viz., "modern science."

Now according to this view, the trouble with Aristotle — at least as judged by the standards of modern scientific methods — was precisely the fact that he was content to rely upon experience and empirical observation, thus seeking "to abstract from many different instances the general (lawful) tendency which *most frequently* characterizes the behavior of an object." In contrast, Galileo proceeded by way of the *Gedankenexperiment*, i.e., by way of "the disciplined use of the creative imagination," which refuses to accept mere "intuitive conclusions drawn from observation of actual happenings." The author proceeds,

How then may we characterize some of the differences between the Aristotelian and the Galilean modes of thought? In one respect, they differ as the occupations of newspaper reporter and author differ. The one is limited to what has actually happened in the natural flux of daily events. The reporter would be fired if he began to try to make the news himself (by robbing a bank) or of including the possible relevances of some imagined events in his daily copy. The author is not so constrained. He may imagine novel events that have never really happened. In fact, an author is expected to consider *creative imagination a central feature of the job.*[27]

So it would seem that Swift's fable of the spider and the bee is not so wide of the mark after all. For on Lewin's testimony, as cited by Atkinson, is not the modern scientist, with his mathematically elaborated *Gedankenexperimente*, quite strikingly spider-like in his activities? True, Atkinson prefers in this connection to speak of the "creative imagination" of the modern scientist, whereas Swift puts it rather differently:

For pray, gentlemen, was ever anything so modern as the spider in his air, his turns, and his paradoxes? he argues in behalf of you his brethren and himself with many boastings of his native stock and great genius; that he spits and spins wholly from himself, and scorns to own any obligation or assistance from without.

27. John William Atkinson, *An Introduction to Motivation* (Princeton, N. J.: Van Nostrand, 1964), p. 69 and Chap. 4, *passim*.

In other words, what the one calls "creative imagination," the other calls "spitting and spinning wholly from himself." But, then, what's in a name? A scientist by any other name would smell as sweet, call him "a creative genius" or call him "a spider"!

In contrast, as Swift characterizes the work of the humanist in terms of the simile of the bee, it would seem that the sorts of knowledge and understanding which the humanist seeks to achieve, as well as the methods by which he would achieve them, are not altogehter unlike the objectives and methods of the Aristotelian mode of thought, at least as Lewin conceives of the latter. For just as the Aristotelian scientist, Atkinson suggests, simply lets himself be instructed by "the many different instances" of an object, abstracting from them "the general (lawful) tendency which *most frequently* characterizes the behavior of [the] object," so analogously, in Swift's words, the humanist-bee "by infinite labor and search, ranging through every corner of nature," and "pretending to nothing of [his] own beyond [his] wings and [his] voice, that is to say [his] flights and [his] language," thus hopes to arrive eventually at a "true judgment and distinction of things."

Very well, then, may we perhaps not take it for granted that at least a prima facie case has been made out for the relevance of Swift's allegory of the spider and the bee to the present-day issue between the sciences and the humanities, as well as to that between what Lewin calls Galilean as over against Aristotelian modes of thought?

Two Knowledges: Humanistic and Scientific

Nevertheless, there is still much about all of this, we feel sure, that is bound to stick in the reader's craw. For doubtless he will wonder if we can really be serious in our constant implication that the study of what we have called the humanities — literature, history, art, philosophy — can truly be said to mediate a kind of knowledge which, while it is certainly not scientific knowledge in the modern sense, is yet a scientific knowledge in the more traditional sense of being an achieving and an attaining of the universal. For while a reader of today, be he gentle or downright ungentle, might go so far as to concede that the pursuit of the humanities perhaps does bring with it something more than mere aesthetic sensitivity or artistic or literary appreciation (he might quite willingly concede that the study of the humanities actually leads to a genuine and undeniable kind of learning),

16

yet he would insist that such learning is only erudition, not science, a knowledge of particular facts, and not of universal laws and principles. That is the
most, he would say, that can be claimed as the fruit of humanistic, in contrast to scientific, study.

Consider, though, the following passage from the great classical scholar,
C. M. Bowra, in *The Greek Experience*:

... the Greeks allowed reason a large part in poetry, but there is another side
to this, more important and more illuminating. Because the Greeks regarded
poetry as a rational activity, they brought to it a remarkable source of strength.
They put into it their own pondered and serious view of life, and they thought
it their duty to say what they really meant. For this reason they infuse it with
the power which comes from long and intense thought. When Aeschylus constructs a tragedy, he makes his action illustrate the divine laws which operate
through human life. His view of these laws is not only original; it has been
reached by a deep consideration of human affairs, and his presentation of it
comes vastly enriched by all the imaginative and emotional attention which he
has given to it. These are no conventional judgments, lightly adopted and hast-
ily presented. They are what experience has forced on him and in his majestic
and searching treatment of them there is an uncommon power because he is desperately concerned with the truth. Unlike him, Sophocles keeps his own views
in the background, but lets them emerge through the personalities and fortunes
of his characters. But the fortunes of these characters present instances of problems which have long troubled his mind — the vast difference between human error and divine knowledge, the conflict between heroic and merely human
standards of conduct, the illusions which beset those who are unworthily in
power. He sees the issues with extreme clarity and has thought so hard upon
them that they have become part of his consciousness and, when he puts them
into poetry, they are enriched by the associations and the special strength which
come from sustained personal familiarity.
Such honesty and seriousness of purpose show themselves in the concern
which the Greeks felt for the truth of poetry.[28]

No doubt Bowra's prose style might be said to have a flavor that is rather
more post-Matthew Arnold than post-Hemingway. Yet does not the passage give a direct indication of how the study of literature may bring
with it a knowledge that is truly "scientific," at least in the sense of being a
knowledge of the universal — in this case of man and of the human situation? For that matter, is it not just such a knowledge as might be said to
come from the experience of life itself and not merely from the reading of
literature? And indeed, Bowra implies that is the way that such knowledge

28. (New York: World, 1958), p. 144.

17

came to Aeschylus and to Sophocles, and before, so to speak, they transmitted it to their verses and plays for all to read.

Moreover, from what Bowra says of the knowledge possessed by an Aeschylus or a Sophocles, it is clear that theirs was quite unmistakably a scientific knowledge in the sense of being a knowledge of that which is universal, and yet that it was just as unmistakably not a scientific knowledge in the modern sense of proceeding spider-like from mathematical constructions and *Gedankenexperimente*. For consider how absurd it would be to try to picture a modern science, be it physics or psychology, physiology or sociology, or whatever, as disclosing to us such things as "the divine laws which operate through human life," or as setting forth for us "the vast difference between human error and divine knowledge, the conflict between heroic and merely human standards of conduct, the illusions which beset those who are unworthily in power."

Nor do we necessarily have to read Professor Bowra in order to see the contrast between what might be called a humanistic and a scientific way of knowing. On the contrary, we are confronted with the contrast on almost every hand in the contemporary scene. For example, suppose we ask ourselves what we mean today by psychological knowledge. Is it the sort of knowledge that a Plato or a Shakespeare or a Hogarth might be said to have possessed and that is discussed and formulated rather more "scientifically" in, say, Plato's *Republic*, or in Aristotle's *Ethics*, or in Augustine's *Confessions*, or in the various seventeenth- and eighteenth-century treatises on the passions, or even in Sartre's *Being and Nothingness*? Or is it the sort of knowledge that proceeds from countless experiments upon rats and pigeons, that talks only in the language of technical terms such as "SR," "learning theory," etc., and that likes nothing better than to deck itself out in elaborate mathematical models by way of theory construction?

Clearly, it is knowledge of the latter sort, and only of that sort, that scientific psychology is nowadays thought to consist of. But does this mean, then, that psychological knowledge of the other sort — of the sort, say, that is involved in Kierkegaard's account of the behavior and motives of "the serious man," or in Clarendon's "characters," or in Plato's discussions of the democratic man and the tyrant, etc. — is just not knowledge at all? Or if it is knowledge, is it to be shuffled off as a mere forerunner of an eventual, truly scientific knowledge of human behavior, which will surely come in time but which for the present must limit itself to more manageable studies on such things as apes, rats, and pigeons, postponing

18

for a much later stage of scientific development the more ambitious sort of undertaking that would perforce be required for a properly scientific treatment of such troublesome phenomena as tyrants, characters, and serious men?

Or is there perhaps still another alternative? Instead of an "either-or" with respect to so-called humanistic knowledge on the one hand and scientific knowledge on the other, might it not be a case of "both-and"? Might it be that the sort of understanding which, say, an Aeschylus achieved of human nature and human life was just as much a matter of knowledge, and indeed in its own way just as "scientific," as, for example, the knowledge of human behavior that proceeds from the researches of a Kurt Lewin? Thus, though both might be instances of genuine knowledge, the nature of the knowledge in the one case, to say nothing of the means and methods of its attainment, must be recognized as being radically different from what it is in the case of the other. Moreover, if there are two different knowledges of man and the world, a humanistic one and a scientific one, then just as it would be quite ridiculous to suppose that the insights of an Aeschylus were such as to render useless and unnecessary the researches of a Lewin, it would be no less ridiculous to suppose that the advances of a scientific psychology could ever displace and render antiquated the insights of an Aeschylus. Precisely in the matter of knowledge, in other words, and not merely in respect to what they may have to offer in the way of aesthetic enjoyment, the humanities can perfectly well hold their own and need feel under no sentence of eventual banishment in favor of any supposedly omnicompetent sciences.

Consider still another example. Just as there would appear to be a certain ambiguity in what we nowadays understand by the term "psychological knowledge," may we not find things to be in a like case with respect to the present-day notion of "political science"? Indeed, if we limit the incidence of this new example simply to what is presently happening within departments of government and political science in American colleges and universities, the ambiguity in the notion "political science" becomes not merely patent but painful and, some would even say, scandalous. For to put it very bluntly, the spiders are now determined to drive out the bees! In academic psychology, of course, such struggles and disputes are long past, the spiders having now completely taken over: in witness whereof just consider where one may today find a scientifically respectable department of psychology anywhere in the country in which, say, Hume's theory of the passions, or Augustine's account of the restlessness of the human soul, or Nietzsche's theory of the *Übermensch* is regarded as anything more than a curiosity of intellectual history.

But in the field of political science, the situation is not quite the same, or at least not yet. For the time was, and in some old-style departments still is, when the student of political science had to pore over his Plato and Aristotle, his Machiavelli and Bodin, his Hobbes, Locke, and Rousseau. For of such was the very stuff of political science. But not so now; or at least the winds of scientific progress are howling and blowing so hard in the corridors and offices of political science departments that it will not be so for much longer. Instead of Plato, the political scientist of the near future will have to know statistics and the latest computer techniques. Instead of studies on the nature of sovereignty or the rights of man, the new scientist-politico or politico-scientist will bring out studies involving the latest sampling techniques on, say, the voting habits of unmarried women of foreign descent between the ages of 21 and 30 on the Eastern seaboard, or else, perhaps, on the decision procedures of public officials responsible for foreign policy decisions in the newly liberated states of black Africa.[29]

Whether it be in psychology or in political science, in linguistics or in anthropology, indeed even in the domain of history itself, the price of progress would appear to be ultimately the same: spiders everywhere, and bees either nowhere or on their way out. And while, so far as colleges and universities are concerned, the custom of academic tenure may still serve to protect a few scattered bees here and there, the spiders need not be in the least downhearted, for they have only to remember the slogan, "While there is death, there is hope." Nor is that all, for from their impregnable strongholds in redoubts like that of "educational testing services," the spi-

29. In a recent political science textbook, *Simulation in International Relations* by Harold Guetzkow and others (Englewood Cliffs, N. J.: Prentice Hall, 1963), on p. 159 one of the authors, with no little consternation, not to say irritation, quotes the following passage from an address by George F. Kennan, delivered at Princeton University: ". . . let the international affairs course stand as an addendum to basic instruction in the humanities. . . . International relations are not a science. And there is no understanding of international affairs that does not embrace understanding of the human individual. . . . If men on this campus want to prepare themselves for work in the international field, then I would say: let them read their Bible and their Shakespeare, their Plutarch and their Gibbon, perhaps even their Latin and their Greek. . . ." The author, Professor Chadwick Alger, then proceeds to make the following sour comment anent Mr. Kennan: "It is perhaps the writings of such men as Kennan that have perpetuated the notion, held by many undergraduates, that abilities bordering on the mystical are required in order to comprehend the alchemy of the world of the diplomat."

ders can complacently view the landscape o'er and take comfort in the fact that while the present may not belong entirely to them, the future is theirs for certain. Even the mere admission to the groves of academe is rapidly ceasing to depend on such old-fashioned capabilities as the ability to weigh evidence pro and con, to mount a discussion of relevant issues, to make balanced and considered judgments; it is simply an affair of S.A.T., G.R.E., and other such scores. In short, what Lewin would call Aristotelian modes of thought would appear to be systematically discriminated against, with the result that a poor bee hasn't a chance in present-day academia, unless perhaps he can manage to slip in, and then stay in, disguised as a spider.

The Project of the Book

But enough by way of rhetoric — let us come directly to a statement of the strategy of our book as a whole. Following what we take to be Swift's lead, we shall not only want to develop the suggestion that in the present-day intellectual scene there are two very different and competing types of knowledge — the more traditional humanistic or philosophical knowledge on the one hand, and the newer-fashioned scientific knowledge on the other — but in addition, and more specifically, we shall want to try to clarify the nature of the difference between these two "knowledges" in terms of the respective logics that are brought into play as the characteristic means or instruments for effecting each sort of knowledge in turn — logics which for the time being we shall continue to label a bee-logic and a spider-logic. However, we can hardly rest content, as was Swift, merely to point up the contrast between these two logics in the purely figurative terms of a procedure that "spins and spits wholly from himself," scorning for the most part to "own any obligation or assistance from without," as over against a procedure that ranges universally "with long search, much study, true judgment, and distinction of things" and so "brings home honey and wax." Nor can we remain content with such mere labels as "the Galilean mode of thought" in contrast to "the Aristotelian mode of thought." Rather, what we propose is to try to exhibit with respect to several of the key logical tools and devices — propositions, inductive and deductive arguments, scientific and historical explanations, definitions, etc. — how these several instruments are differently conceived, both as to their natures and their functions, in each of these respective logics. To this end, we want to avail ourselves of the results and insights that have been achieved over the years by modern analytic philosophy. For as we interpret the achievement of this particular brand of philosophy, it might be said to consist largely in its having determined both in detail and with some precision the proper requisites of a genuine and unmitigated spider-logic. Moreover, in so doing, neo-analytic philosophers have tended to argue for the superiority of such spider-like means and methods, as contrasted with those of the more traditional bee-logic. Such arguments we shall in large measure be concerned with trying to rebut, seeking to show that a bee-logic has a proper integrity of its own, and that for the kind of humanistic and philosophical knowledge which it aims at bringing about it functions properly and efficiently, just as a spider-logic, for the quite different sort of scientific knowledge which it aims at mediating and bringing about in its turn and in its way, functions with equal propriety and efficiency. In other words, our ultimate purpose will be to show that it is not, or should not be, a case simply of either the one logic or the other, but rather a case of "both-and" — and yet not so as to exclude a possible ordering of the two logics, one with respect to the other, in terms of a certain priority and posteriority. Indeed, in our concluding chapter we shall argue that a scientific type of knowledge, while impressive in its own right and certainly indispensable, is, or at least ought to be, subordinate to the properly architectonic knowledge of the more humanistic and philosophical variety.

Having forewarned our readers that the theme of our book is not just an unfashionable one, but, in the judgment of most, one so utterly wrongheaded as to be well-nigh unspeakable, we must nonetheless compound the offense still further with more warnings. For it is a common assumption nowadays that if one is out to challenge the domination by science of both our intellects and our culture, then one cannot be other than some sort of an existentialist. Thus witness even that passing reference in our earlier quotation from C. P. Snow, where it was suggested that the scientists, in reacting against their opposite numbers in the other culture, tend to write off the literary intellectuals as being "in a deep sense anti-intellectual, anxious to restrict both art and thought to the existential movement."

Alas, we must make a frank and forthright confession at the very outset, for however desperate may be our own philosophical isolation in the present-day philosophical scene, we still are not ready to recognize that our only philosophical salvation must lie in making common cause with the existentialists and phenomenologists. And should one doubt the sincerity of such a disclaimer, insisting that in philosophy nowadays one has no choice but to ride with the analyst hounds or to run with the existentialist hares, then we would reply by once more exhuming poor Dean Swift and pointing to his example. For just think what the consequences for him would be of insisting that in choosing the career of a bee rather than of a spider he had thereby committed himself to being some sort of an existentialist. Imagine Jonathan Swift in the company of the likes of Heidegger and Sartre! To say that he would be like a fish out of water would scarcely be to employ the most apt figure. On the contrary, in Swift's own estimate it would doubtless be rather more like Gulliver among the Lilliputians.

To speak more seriously, we must acknowledge that we cannot in this book address ourselves to the challenge of contemporary phenomenology and existentialism, in the way we intend to do with respect to the challenge of contemporary analytic philosophy. Suffice it to say that as regards the sorts of issues which we have been raising here in the Introduction, the contemporary phenomenologist might well respond with no little sympathy to the thesis that scientific knowledge is not the sole or even the most significant knowledge of which human beings are capable; and for the same reason he might even applaud our project of trying first to understand and then to put in its place the characteristic spider-logic that is so closely associated with the scientific outlook. On the other hand, he would certainly challenge the thesis that there is another knowledge and another logic that simply takes the everyday world of objects as one finds it, and by a straightforward analysis of such given objects eventually achieves a more or less reliable understanding of what these objects are and why they are. Heidegger, for example, simply takes it for granted that modern scientific knowledge with its reliance upon mathematics, far from being opposed to the bee-logic of the more Aristotelian modes of thought, is but a natural extension and development of the latter. This, in turn, is quite in line with Heidegger's overarching concern to contrast the being of mere objects, to which so-called "categories" may apply, with the being of the human subject, *Dasein*, which can be characterized only in terms of "existentials." [30]

Without speaking to the merits of this latter concern, we will merely content ourselves with a direct challenge to Heidegger's particular reading of the history of Western philosophy, a reading which he somehow takes to be ancillary to his main philosophical concern.[31] For while it may be

---

30. Cf. *Sein und Zeit* (Tubingen: Max Niemeyer Verlag, 1953), p. 44.

31. As is well known, Heidegger's radical reinterpretation of the history of Western thought is central to his entire philosophical position. We are not seeking to challenge this reinterpre-

true as a mere matter of history that a bee-logic, or what we shall subsequently call a what-logic, such as is associated with Aristotelian modes of thought, can be shown to have undergone a certain evolution in the direction of more Galilean modes of thought,[32] still any such presumed evolution in fact is quite inconclusive as to there being any reconcilability in principle of the two modes of thought. Since it will be the task of our book as a whole to establish the distinctive difference as well as the decisive autonomy of a bee-logic as over against a spider-logic, our rebuttal of Heidegger and of the existentialists and the phenomenologists can be no more than dogmatic at this stage. It is enough to say that when it comes to finding an alternative to contemporary analytic philosophy with its partiality for Galilean modes of thought, one is by no means constrained to embrace contemporary phenomenology or existentialism. Quite the contrary; a Heidegger, for example, so far from providing an alternative to, would appear pretty much to go right along with, much of contemporary analytic philosophy in its tendency to assume that something on the order of a spider-logic is the one and only proper instrument for achieving an objective knowledge of man and the world. Heidegger, in short, just is not radical enough for our purposes!

Having, though, given fair warning that our subsequent critique of current analytic philosophy is not to be confounded with the kinds of suspicions and disavowals that phenomenologists and existentialists are wont to deliver in regard to the analytic method in philosophy, we must now hasten to scotch yet another snake, which we hope eventually to kill off and dispose of more effectively. For doubtless, in declaring ourselves ready to do battle with the analytic philosophers, we shall at once be put down as just another of those speculative metaphysicians, who are pretty much among the disgruntled has-beens in philosophy nowadays, their activities having been at least fashionably discredited by the currently triumphant analysts.

To this, our response of the moment will be merely to appeal to certain

---

tation in its entirety, but only that part of it which attempts to construe the mathematical methods of modern physical science as being continuous with the bee-like methods of the more traditional Aristotelian modes of thought.

32. Cf. Heidegger's flat statement to the effect that *Funktions-begriffe sind immer nur als formalisierte Substanzbegriffe möglich* (*op. cit.*, p. 88). Cf. also various statements which Heidegger makes concerning Descartes's achievement with respect to *die Umschaltung der Auswirkung der traditionellen Ontologie auf die neuzeitliche mathematische Physik* (*ibid.*, p. 96).

elementary facts of the history of Western philosophy. It is true that in many ways this may not be as easy as it sounds, inasmuch as one sometimes gets the impression from contemporary English philosophers that the history of Western philosophy begins with G. E. Moore. One does, to be sure, occasionally come across references to David Hume, or perhaps even to Bishop Berkeley. But somehow these references are made in such a way as to imply that in this new version of the history of philosophy references to such men are rather like references to the pre-Socratics in the older and more traditional version of the history of philosophy, i.e., a sort of slumming amid the ruins of the archaic and the prephilosophical.

Be this as it may, we should merely like to point out that well before G. E. Moore, and even before Hume and Berkeley, there was a philosopher who wrote a couple of treatises that have come to be known as the *Prior* and *Posterior Analytics*. Moreover, if the use of the word "analytics" is still not a sufficient warrant for calling Aristotle an analytic philosopher, it might be remarked that the actual method of Aristotelian philosophy could perhaps be loosely, but still not improperly, described as a method of simply accepting what we are presented with in our everyday experience and analyzing it with a view to disclosing the principles and elements and causes that are directly there and present in it. In other words, there is no dialectician's discrediting of the world of everyday experience, as if it were somehow no more than appearance as over against Reality — in the manner of, say, a Plato or a Bradley. Nor is there any speculative reconstruction of the everyday world in the manner of, say, a Descartes, or more recently of a Whitehead or even a Russell. No, the method is simply one of analysis, an analysis of things of the world right here before us and present to us.

Such, then, is the clue to the title of our Introduction. For the battle of the books which we wish to relate, and even to join, is not a battle between non-analytic and analytic philosophy, but rather between classical analytic philosophy and neo-analytic philosophy.

Enough, though, by way of preface and apology. Let us move directly to our projected "high argument," which, though it may have little to do with "man's first disobedience," might still have some relevance to "the fruit of that forbidden tree" that could indeed be the source, if not of "all," then surely of some of, "our woe"!

Chapter I

A Logic That Can't Say

What Anything Is

HAS IT NEVER STRUCK ANYONE as passing strange that the logic of *Principia Mathematica*, for all of its elaboration, provides no means either for saying or for thinking what anything is?[1] And if we not only cannot claim to know what things are, but if our very logic debars us from even stating or formulating propositions as to what this, that, or the other thing is, then the very idea of what a thing is, or the very conviction that each thing is what it is, that things are what they are, or indeed that anything is anything becomes simply impossible, or at least logically improper.

So what? Why worry about what things are? Will computers, or deficit

1. Much of this chapter, in somewhat revised form and bearing the title, "A Variation on the Theme of the Hollow Universe," is due to appear in a forthcoming volume, *Mélanges à la mémoire de Charles de Koninck*, to be published by Les Presses de l'Université de Laval, Québec.

26

financing, or atomic explosions, or whatever else this present age esteems be any the less effective merely because people no longer ask the question "What is it?" After all, mathematics and science, as we know them today, seem not to turn on any such question, nor does the present cultural prestige of these disciplines rest on their ability to answer such a question in regard to anything whatever. Rather the logic of all modern knowledge could very properly be said to be a logic of how things work, how they behave, what their relationships are to other things, what verifiable or falsifiable consequences they may have, how they may be manipulated, what uses they may be put to, etc. So why worry about what things are, or even whether they are anything?

Perhaps, though, this is just the point, that modern culture is not merely despairing of ever answering the question "What?" but that it no longer even wants the question to be asked, or at least not seriously. All this might be a commentary, if not actually a reflection, upon modern culture. Still we had better not allow ourselves to get carried away in an entire critique of modern culture — at least not at this stage. Rather we had better concentrate on our limited critique of modern logic. For supposing that modern logic does little more than pander to modern culture and some of its more vulgar errors, our immediate task is to try to explain and sustain the thesis that was laid down in our opening sentence, viz., that so-called modern logic, the logic that has received its most classical and elaborate formulation in *Principia Mathematica*, simply does not allow for, or permit of, one's saying or thinking what anything is.

At first, such a contention must strike the informed reader as little less than obscurantist. For would it not generally be conceded that, so far as Western thought is concerned, the standard logical form in terms of which any what-question is to be answered is the traditional subject-predicate form of Aristotelian logic? Thus to the question "What is x?", the standard form of answer would be "x is such and such," or "x is thus and so." Furthermore, would it not also be conceded that modern symbolic logic, and specifically *PM* logic, so far from repudiating or eliminating the subject-predicate form of the proposition, has actually retained it and taken it over, and then built upon it in ways that never were dreamed of in Aristotelian logic?

Thus everyone knows how Russell explicitly declared that he had nothing against the traditional Aristotelian S-P form of propositions. On the contrary, such a form was admirably suited to expressing the relation of a thing to its property or quality — or, in more strictly Aristotelian terms, of a substance to its accident. For example, in such statements as "Bertrand Russell is a philosopher," or "Winston Churchill is a statesman," or "That spot is pea green," the subject-predicate form of proposition suffices admirably. This much Russell not merely conceded, but insisted upon. However, when it comes to statements that assert not the relation of a thing to its property, but rather the relation of one thing to another, or of several things to each other, then the traditional Aristotelian form needs to be amended. In such statements as "London is below Edinburgh," or "England is inferior to Scotland," it is not just cumbersome, it is downright misleading, to suppose that there is one subject term and one predicate — as if, for instance, in the first example London were the subject, and being below Edinburgh were somehow its property or quality, or as if, in the second example, what was being predicated of England was that it was inferior to Scotland. No, the far more reasonable, to say nothing of more appropriate, way of interpreting such propositions — at least so the modern logicians tell us — would be to consider that they do not represent the relation of anything to its property at all, but rather the relation of two things to each other, viz., London and Edinburgh in the one case, and England and Scotland in the other.

Moreover, the very subject-predicate terminology itself, it is sometimes said, can be adapted to this new way of regarding propositions, as representing relations. Thus with respect to the last two examples, it would be the relation, "below" or "inferior to," that would be the predicate, and the two relata, "London" and "Edinburgh" in the one instance and "England" and "Scotland" in the other, that would be the subjects. More generally, if it were a three-term, instead of a two-term, relation that the proposition represented, then there would be three subjects instead of two; if a four-term relation, then four subjects; if a five-term relation, then five subjects; and so on up to n-term relations.

Quite patently, therefore, the logic of *Principia Mathematica* would not appear to exclude or even to discredit subject-predicate relations, so much as to extend and expand the ancient subject-predicate schema immeasurably. Similarly, it would not seem that the new logic had in any respect failed to provide a means for anyone's saying or thinking what things are. Instead, such a means is still available, but in a mightily expanded version, so that one no longer has to conceive of what things are on the old restricted model of things and their properties, but rather on the now more all-embracing model of things and their relations.

But, unhappily, all this just won't wash! And the reason it won't wash is that the revised subject-predicate schema, or, as the Fregeans would prefer to call it, the function-argument schema, of modern logic does violence to the "logical grammar" of the word "is," or of the "is"-relationship. For there is just no way in which this relationship can be extended beyond the original schema of one predicate–one subject and be made to embrace the whole hierarchy of sentential schemas involving one predicate and many subjects.

For example, if we simply put the matter to the test in terms of some of our earlier examples, we find that we come out with results such as the following:

(1) "Bertrand Russell is a man of some philosophic capacity."

Such a statement can clearly be construed as an answer to a question of the general type of "What is x?" — "What is Bertrand Russell, what sort of a man is he?" Moreover, so construed as an answer to the question "What," (1) can be properly regarded as having the logical form of a predicate with one subject. Or, using more Fregean terminology, we may say that (1) is a statement involving a one-place function, $f(x)$.

But now consider:

(2) "Bertrand Russell is superior both as a man and as a philosopher to A. N. Whitehead."

Clearly, in (2) we have a statement whose form, if we heed the promptings of the new logic, would be not of one subject and one predicate, but rather of two subjects, viz., "Bertrand Russell" and "A. N. Whitehead," and one relational predicate, viz., "being superior as a man and as a philosopher to ———." Or, again, in Fregean terminology, (2) would involve not a one-place but a two-place function, $f(x, y)$.

However, if (2) is regarded as a two-place function, then it is impossible to regard it as a statement in which the predicate provides an answer to the question "What?" with respect to the subjects. In other words, if "Bertrand Russell" and "A. N. Whitehead" are the subjects, then "being superior as a man and as a philosopher to" can hardly be regarded as stating what Russell and Whitehead are.

Or, again, in the statement,

(3) "England is inferior to Scotland,"

it can scarcely be considered that something is being said about England

and Scotland in the same way in which something is being said about England in the statement,

(4) "England is now philosophically effete."

In other words, in (4), being now philosophically effete is what England is said to be, but in (3) one is certainly not saying that what England and Scotland are is inferior to. This last is nonsense.

Put more generally, then, what the test that we have just carried out would seem to indicate is that in any statement or proposition involving a function other than the basic one-place function, it is impossible to regard the function (or predicate) as stating or as representing what the arguments (or subjects) are.[2] Thus to choose a still different example:

(5) "England has exported Wittgenstein to the U.S."

This is clearly a three-place function, $f(a, b, c)$. And just as clearly, it is quite ridiculous to regard the function term in this statement as indicating what the arguments are. For whatever England, Wittgenstein, and the U.S. can meaningfully be said to be, they certainly cannot be said to be exporters of —— to ——.

Of course, it is true that (2), (3), and (5) can all be regarded as stating what something is, and as thus involving an "is"-relationship. Thus (2) does say what Bertrand Russell is: it says that he is superior as a man and as a philosopher to A. N. Whitehead. And (3) certainly says what England is, viz., that it is a country inferior to Scotland. But, clearly, no sooner are (2) and (3) construed in this way than it becomes apparent that they are not being taken, as *PM* logic would require, as two-place functions, but rather as one-place functions, i.e., as subject-predicate propositions of the old-fashioned type.

Apparently, then, there is no escaping the dilemma: (a) either the relation of predicate to subject in traditional S-P propositions is to be regarded as a mere one-place predicate that is simply on all fours with the so-called relation of predicate to subject that is exhibited in the many-place predicates of modern logic — in which case the relation of predicate to subject

2. It might be objected that this pronouncement is too extreme. For if one were to take a symmetrical, rather than an asymmetrical, relation as an example of a relational predicate or many-place function, then it would seem that the function or predicate does indeed state what the arguments or subjects are. For example, "John is a brother of Joe" might be interpreted as saying that what John and Joe are are brothers. But even if it is granted that "John is a brother of Joe" and "John and Joe are brothers" say exactly the same thing, it would indicate no more than that symmetrical relations are but the exceptions which prove the rule about many-place functions not stating or representing what their arguments are.

cannot possibly be construed as involving an "is"-relationship and cannot possibly be used as a device for saying what something is; or (b) the relation of predicate to subject in the case of so-called one-place predicates does involve an "is"-relationship and is a device for expressing what the subject is — in which case it not only is something *sui generis* and in no wise on all fours with so-called many-place predicates, but what is more, it will have the effect of eliminating any and all such many-place predicates simply on the ground that they aren't predicates, because they do not and cannot express what their subjects are.

Subject-Predicate vs. Substance-Accident

This, however, is still no more than a first point in our case against the capabilities of modern logic with respect to statements as to what things are. There is a second point as well. For consider once more just how, in the context of *PM* logic, the relation of a single subject to its predicate is to be understood. We have seen how this is supposed to be understood on the model of Fregean functions, which is but another way of saying that we are to consider that subjects are to their predicates as things related are to the relation that relates them. The upshot of this, though, is that no predicate in a proposition can ever be regarded as stating or expressing what the subject of the proposition is, for the simple reason that no relation ever expresses what its various relata are.

Now we shall see that our second point is very closely related to the first one. We have noted, just in passing, that Russell offered a particular meta-linguistic interpretation of subject-predicate propositions of the old-fashioned type — i.e., of propositions involving one-place predicates. These, he felt, were propositions whose purpose it was to express not the relation of one thing to another thing, or of several things to each other, but rather the relation of a thing to its property.[3] But curiously enough, and despite

---

3. This is perhaps misleading and unfair to Russell. So far as we know, he never says in so many words that a proposition involving a one-place predicate expresses the relation of a thing to its quality. At the same time, inasmuch as Russell does hold — or at least once held — that "in a logically perfect language the words in a proposition would correspond one by one with the components of the corresponding fact," it would seem entirely proper to ask with respect to such corresponding facts just what the "relation" is between a particular and its quality or between several particulars and their relation. For quite clearly Russell seems to feel that the "relation" of a quality to that of which it is a quality is quite comparable to the "relation" of a relation to its relata. Indeed, he even proposes to "call a quality a 'monadic relation,' so as to stress its comparability to dyadic, triadic, tetradic . . . relations." Accordingly, it is our

31

the fact that Russell seems never to have suspected such a thing, this interpretation is tantamount to saying that no subject-predicate proposition can ever involve an affirmation of what something is. And why not? Simply because nothing ever is its property or quality as such. For instance, if one says,

(6) "That leaf is green,"

then on Russell's analysis the subject of such a proposition refers to the particular thing designated, viz., the leaf, while the predicate signifies a certain property of that thing, viz., the color green. But if this is so, then the proposition in question does not really mean what it seems to say. For it seems to say what the leaf is, viz., green. And yet if the predicate signifies a certain property or quality of the leaf, viz., its color, it is quite ridiculous, and indeed impossible, to suppose that what the leaf is is a color, or more specifically that the leaf is itself the color green.[4] After all, a leaf is not a color, but a leaf. Or, more generally, a thing isn't a property; it isn't even its own property — for the simple reason that a thing is a thing and not a property.

Or to take another example, suppose that one were to say what surely no one would ever say,

(7) "Bertrand Russell is senile."

Now on Russell's own interpretation of such a statement, (7) is to be construed as predicating a certain quality, viz., senility, of a certain thing, viz., Bertrand Russell. But immediately it becomes apparent that in one sense at least this is not, and cannot be, the correct interpretation of (7). For if we render this interpretation of what is being predicated of what in (7) into an actual predication of that quality of that thing, we come out with something that is patently ridiculous,

(8) "Bertrand Russell is senility."

---

contention that just as the relation of a relation to its relata is not properly (save possibly in the case of symmetrical relations) an "is"-relationship at all, so analogously the relation of a quality to the particular of which it is a quality is not an "is"-relationship. Cf. "The Philosophy of Logical Atomism," § 2, in Bertrand Russell, *Logic and Knowledge*, ed. A. C. Marsh (New York: Macmillan, 1956), esp. pp. 197–200.

4. Of course, it needs to be noted that color words are curiously ambiguous in this regard. For while one cannot say that the leaf is greenness any more than one can say that the surface of the paper is smoothness, usage does permit the locution "The leaf is the color green," whereas it will not permit "The paper is the quality smooth." Clearly, though, in "The leaf is the color green," the meaning is not that a leaf is a color, but rather that it is of a certain color or is green in color. The point would appear to have been noticed by Aristotle in connection with his effort to distinguish "present in" from "predicable of." Cf. *Categories* 2a 27–33.

It is true that one might be permitted such a locution by way of hyperbole. One might conceivably exclaim, "Russell is now senility itself!", much as in another context and using another example, one might say,

(9) "St. Francis of Assisi was holiness itself."

But the point is that in such cases what would be involved would not be any literal truth, but rather a hyperbole, which achieves its effect of exaggeration by proclaiming what is, in all strictness, something of an impossibility; and the reason it would be an impossibility is that no thing or substance can ever be a quality or a property as such.

In fact, if for purposes of illustration we were to use a scheme of metaphysical classification such as that of Aristotle's categories, it then becomes obvious that what falls under one category, e.g., a substance, cannot possibly be something falling under any other category, e.g., a quality or a quantity or a relation or an activity or a place or what not. Indeed, the whole point of such a scheme of metaphysical or ontological classification is to set forth the basically different kinds of things or entities. Clearly, therefore, one such kind is not to be identified with another such kind, for the very reason that they then would not be different kinds after all.

Accordingly, applying such considerations here, one can readily see that a logical scheme such as that of subject-predicate in the traditional sense ought never to be interpreted simply in terms of an ontological scheme like that of substance and accident, or thing and property. For the subject-predicate scheme turns on the "is"-relationship, whereas in the ontological scheme such a relationship is altogether improper: it can never be said of any substance that it *is* a quality, or of any thing that it *is* a property; indeed if it were, then it wouldn't be a substance or thing at all, but rather something very different, viz., an accident or a property.

Very well, then, if Russell wishes to consider the one-place predicates of *PM* logic as being designed to exhibit not the relation of one thing to another, or of several things to each other, but rather the relation of a thing to its property, then there is no way in which such predicates can be regarded as expressing what their subjects are. And on the other hand, if one wishes to challenge the historical accuracy of Russell's interpretation of the traditional S-P propositions of Aristotelian logic, and to insist that such S-P propositions are not designed to exhibit the relation of a thing to its property, but rather to express the very different relation of a thing (be it anything whatever, a thing in the sense of a substance or a quantity or a quality or an activity or what not) to what it is, or to what is true of it, or to what can be said of it or about it — then one must accept as a consequence that there is no way by which S-P propositions of the traditional sort can be approximated to propositions of the *PM* type involving one-place predicates, and consequently no way whereby these traditional subject-predicate propositions can be integrated into the logic of *Principia Mathematica.*

All this is but another way of saying that *PM* logic, for all of its ponderous elaboration, provides no means for saying even so simple a thing as what a thing is. In short, our second point in the case against *PM* logic can now be seen to reinforce our first point, which was that in *PM* logic one-place predicates are understood on the model of relational predicates generally. Indeed, they are, as it were, to be regarded as a sort of limiting case of relational predicates, it being necessary in any complete scheme of predicates to provide not merely for many-place predicates with five, four, three, or two subjects as the case might be, but also for one-place predicates in which there would be but a single subject.[5] However, if predicates are to be understood on the model of relations, then this is tantamount to acknowledging that no predicate ever expresses what its subject is, simply for the reason that no relation ever expresses what its relata are.

Likewise, our second point is to the effect that if the one-place predicates of *PM* logic are, as Russell says they are, but so many devices for exhibiting the relations of things to their qualities or properties, then this is tantamount to acknowledging that no one-place predicate of the sort envisaged in *PM* logic is ever capable of expressing what its subject is, for the reason that what any given thing or substance is is never its quality or property or accident.

The Example of Logical Atomism

Suppose it be granted, at least for purposes of argument, that the resources, or rather lack of resources, of *PM* logic are such that it cannot properly be used to formulate or express even so simple and rudimentary a truth as that something is thus and so, or that it is what it is. What of it? By way of answering this question, let us proceed right down the high road into metaphysics. For it is indeed a matter of fact and of history that *PM* logic has given rise to certain distinctive types and varieties of metaphysics, the most obvious being Russell's own philosophy of logical atom-

5. See note 3 above.

ism. Or if one hesitates to rely upon the statement of such a metaphysics as formulated by the somewhat volatile and philosophically fickle Russell himself, one can have not the slightest hesitation in relying upon the far tighter and tougher statement of it by that most redoubtable of contemporary American metaphysicians, Professor Gustav Bergmann, and his school.[6]

For our purposes what is so singularly instructive about a metaphysics of the type of logical atomism is that, being a logical atomism that is at the same time an ontological atomism, it manages to exhibit in all of their starkness some of the more remarkable consequences for metaphysics and ontology of a logic that is congenitally incapable of stating what anything is. Of course, it might already be anticipated that those consequences will amount to a metaphysics in which literally nothing is anything. Still, this remains to be seen.

As a beginning, suppose we first consider just what are the logical atoms, which, as the logical atomists see it, are the ultimates in logical analysis. Needless to say, they are those ultimate constituents out of which the simplest and most basic propositions — so-called atomic propositions — are built up. And these constituents, we have already noted, are propositional functions or predicates on the one hand, and arguments or subjects of such functions on the other. Thus for a function such as "to the left of," one might have as arguments or subjects two black spots or dots:

(1) "This dot is to the left of that."

Clearly, this simple, atomic proposition can be analyzed without remainder into its function and two arguments. And so, *mutatis mutandis*, for any and every other atomic proposition as well.

Moreover, to convert such a logical atomism into an ontological atomism, one has but to consider what sorts of things or entities might qualify for the role of subjects or arguments on the one hand and for that of predicates or functions on the other. So far as the latter are concerned, it is apparent that they can only be such things as qualities or relations, of which

6. It goes without saying that in the pages immediately following we make not the slightest pretense of having given anything like a just estimate of the philosophy of logical atomism, particularly in its developed Bergmannian form. Instead, we would focus attention upon but a single facet of that philosophy, viz., the peculiar correlation between logical and ontological structures that is so characteristic of such a philosophy; in fact, we would exploit this correlation simply for a particular purpose of our own — that of showing how, given a logic which does not permit of one's saying what a thing is, this is bound to affect one's entire understanding of the way things are and the way the world is.

the distinctive feature of both is that they are universal. And so far as the former are concerned, what else could they be but particulars or individuals?

Thus, for example, in (1), a relation such as that of "to the left of" certainly does not require as its arguments just those two particular dots and no others. On the contrary, any two particulars might function equally well — not just those two dots, but two others; and not necessarily two dots at all, but two patches, or two trees, or two stars, or two people, or two houses. Of each of these pairs it is perfectly conceivable that the same identical relation might hold, i.e., that the one member might be to the left of the other. Consequently, so far as any quality or relation is concerned, the only sort of thing or entity that could fill such a role would be a universal.

In contrast, just as the only things that can serve as functions or predicates of propositions have to be universals, so also the only things that can fill the bill so far as arguments of functions go are particulars. Indeed, if qualities and relations, in the very nature of the case, can only be universal, so likewise anything that comes to be so qualified or related can only be particular — at least in the final analysis. And the way such a final analysis is effected is itself instructive.

For suppose one says,

(2) "Man never is, but always to be, blest."

Here, clearly, it is not the universal quality of being a man to which the further quality of never being blessed is said to attach; a quality doesn't attach to another quality. Rather it is only individual men that may be thought to have the quality of never being blessed. And not even individual men are really fit candidates for the role of the ultimate unanalyzable arguments or subjects in a proposition, for further analysis promptly reveals that being a man is itself a quality, and as such is universal. But if universal, then its role in the proposition can only be that of a function term or a predicate; it is not and cannot properly be an argument or a subject at all. Accordingly, analyzing out of the subject, or subjects, of the proposition all properly predicative or universal elements, we come out with a proposition in the familiar form of:

(2a) "For anything x, if x is a man, then x never is, but always to be, blest."

And what does x stand for here? It can stand for nothing other than pure or, as they are usually called, bare, particulars as such. And to say they are bare means that they are bare of all qualities or relations; they are utterly characterless, in short. Indeed, if they had any sort of characteristics at all, then such characteristics could only be qualities or relations; and qualities and relations being perforce universal, they are in need of being analyzed out and removed from the subject place of the proposition altogether and assigned to their proper place and role as predicates or functions.

For that matter, even in the case of (1) above, one might legitimately question whether it has after all been analyzed to such a point as to render out all of the unanalyzable logical atoms that compose it, and only such ultimate atoms or elements. For to speak of this dot or that dot is surely to consider things that have at least a certain character, however minimal that may be. At least they can be characterized as being dots, if nothing else; and that surely is something.

Accordingly, to complete the analysis, one would need to render (1) in such fashion as,

(1a) "This *x* is a dot and is to the left of that *y*, which is also a dot."

In other words, a complete logical analysis of a proposition cannot stop short of such absolutely ultimate elements as bare particulars in the role of subjects, and universals (be they qualities or relations) in the role of predicates. What is more, such a logical analysis of the proposition can also be regarded as being equally and concurrently an ontological analysis of the real facts of the world. For as we have seen, the question as to what are the ultimates in the way of subjects or the ultimates in the way of predicates, out of which basic propositions can be compounded, is at the same time a question as to what sorts of things or entities in the world are competent to play these respective roles of subjects and predicates. And to the latter question the only possible answer would seem to be the one already sketched out: no things or entities other than particulars, and more specifically bare particulars, can perform as subjects, just as nothing save universals (qualities or relations) can function as predicates. In other words, what such an ontological analysis discloses as being the ultimate elements or atoms that comprise, as Russell was wont to put it, "the ultimate furniture of the world" are bare particulars on the one hand and universals on the other.

Given these ultimate ontological atoms of bare particulars and universals, it remains for us to see the curious import, for the entire ontological or metaphysical scheme of so-called logical atomism, of that peculiar disability of *PM* logic which renders it unable to provide any logical means for saying what anything is. For instance, if we take a mere sense presentation or sense datum of a green spot, or of a middle *c* sound — for of such like are "the cloud-capped towers, the gorgeous palaces, the solemn temples, the great globe itself" with which this metaphysics loves to conjure — we can promptly analyze it into its proper logical and ontological elements. For the original sense presentation must be a presentation of a bare particular, to which we may give the logically proper name of *a*, and of a quality or universal, say the color green, which in Bergmann's terminology *a* may be said to "exemplify." Accordingly, expressing our knowledge of this given, presented fact in an atomic proposition, we get:

(3) "*a* is green." $f(a)$

But although in ordinary English we tend to say, and indeed can scarcely help saying, that *a* is green, the relation involved is not, strictly speaking, an "is"-relationship at all. In the preceding section we have seen how the function-argument relation, $f(a)$, does not involve an "is"-relationship: a function of an argument is never what that argument is at all. But still more concretely, and with respect to the very statement itself that *a* is green, one can readily see that for the logical atomist the relation of the bare particular *a* to the color green could not possibly be an "is"-relationship. For one thing, *a* is a bare particular and green is a universal, and a bare particular cannot possibly *be* a universal. Or again, on the sort of logico-ontological analysis which the logical atomists carry out, we have seen that the ultimate atoms or elements which constitute the ultimate furniture of the world are of just two kinds: bare particulars, and qualities or relations. But, obviously, between these two ultimate and irreducible elements no "is"-relationship could possibly hold; a bare particular such as *a* could not possibly be said to be a quality, such as the color green, for that would in effect be to reduce the one such irreducible ontological kind to the other.

For that matter, in the metaphysics of logical atomism the division of things into particulars and universals is at least analogous to what in Aristotelian metaphysics is the division of things into categories — into substances and the accidents of substance. But, clearly, in an Aristotelian context the "is"-relationship can never hold between a substance and one of its accidents. A leaf (substance), for example, may well be green, but it can never be the quality of greenness itself (an accident). Indeed, if it could be, then a substance would in effect cease to be a substance and become what it is not, viz., an accident, or more specifically a quality. Or to put the same thing in a somewhat different way: in the context of Aristotelian philosophy, it is of the utmost importance not to confuse the logical relationship of subject and predicate with the ontological relationship of substance and accident; the former involves an "is"-relationship, the latter does not.

Mutatis mutandis, then, in logical atomism it is just as impossible to suppose that an "is"-relationship holds between particulars and universals as it is in Aristotelian metaphysics to suppose that an "is"-relationship holds between substances and their accidents. To be sure, for an Aristotelian such an "is"-relationship has a quite proper place and function in logic, being simply the subject-predicate relationship. But for an atomist, who acknowledges no distinction between the ontological relation of bare particular to universal and the logical relationship of subject to predicate, the "is"-relationship just drops out altogether.

But, then, if there is no "is"-relationship in logical atomism, and if the logical atoms which make up the ultimate furniture of the world are of just two kinds, bare particulars and universals, then clearly in such a metaphysics nothing can possibly be anything. For if any given entity, call it z, were to be anything, then it should be possible to make z the subject of a proposition and to say of it that it is thus and so. However, from the standpoint of logical atomism, if z is to be the subject of a proposition, it must be a bare particular; but what could a bare particular possibly be? Indeed, as we have already seen, if a bare particular were anything, if it had any sort of nature or character, then it could not be a proper subject of a proposition. Instead, before it could possibly function as a proper subject, any and all characterizing features, any and all features that might constitute it a definite something, must be analyzed out and relegated to the predicate place in the proposition. Moreover, once all such universal elements — qualities and relations — are removed from the subject and fixed in the predicate, then according to the principles of *PM* logic the relation of such a bare particular as subject to the various qualities and relations which are its predicates cannot possibly be an "is"-relationship: the qualities and relations that are predicated of a bare particular nowise represent what that particular is. In other words, z simply could not be anything.

On the other hand, if one turns from bare particulars to those other items in the ultimate furniture of the atomists' world, viz., qualities and relations, these no more than bare particulars can be said to be anything.

In order for them to be something or other, they would have to enter as subjects into propositions. But as we have seen, on the principles of logical atomism, qualities and relations can never be proper subjects of propositions. And even if they could be, the predicates that one might ascribe to them could no more characterize them for what they are than, as we saw in the case of bare particulars, predicates could characterize such particulars for what they are, the reason being that in *PM* logic predicates don't express what their subjects are.

An Inconsistency in Logical Atomism?

Still, you may object that there is one very obvious and very serious reservation that needs to be made with respect to the intended conclusion of this section. For the conclusion is that in a metaphysics such as logical atomism nothing is anything; and the reason for this peculiar consequence in metaphysics is the equally peculiar principle in logic, or at least in the *PM* logic of which the atomists wish exclusively to avail themselves, that there is no way in which anything can be said to be anything. "What"-statements, in short, just aren't proper statements in such a logic. But exception can surely be made to this, and it can be made in terms of the very account which we ourselves have just given of the logic and metaphysics of logical atomism. For does not this entire philosophical position rest upon the foundation of bare particulars and universals? It is entities of these two basic kinds that comprise the ultimate furniture of the world, and surely these entities are of their own respective kinds: bare particulars are just that, viz., bare particulars — that is precisely what such entities are; and similarly, qualities and relations are universals — that is precisely what they are. Not only that, but in order to set forth the philosophical position of logical atomism, we found that we had to pose such direct questions as: What sorts of entities in the world are capable of functioning as subjects of atomic propositions, and what as predicates? These were certainly "what"-questions, and the answers to them certainly involved "what"-statements. Thus to recognize that qualities and relations are universal or that such things as might be designated by logically proper names like *a*, *b*, etc., are bare particulars can only be expressed in "what"-statements involving "is"-relationships.

Now the substance of such an objection is surely true. However, it would seem to constitute a criticism not so much of our account of logical atomism as of logical atomism itself. For Bergmann clearly recognizes that a statement such as "*a* is a bare particular" is of a different type from a statement such as "*a* is green" or "*a* is to the left of *b*." In the two latter cases what is being predicated of *a*, or of *a* and *b*, is in the one case a quality and in the other a relation. On the other hand, being a bare particular is assuredly not a quality of *a* in the way in which being green is: *a* is not related to the character of being a bare particular in the same way it is related to the quality of being green; or, to express the same thing in Bergmann's own terminology, *a* "exemplifies" the color green, but it cannot be said to "exemplify" being a bare particular.[7]

How, then, can we account for this radical difference in types of predicate — "what"-predicates on the one hand, and quality- or relational-predicates on the other? The answer is that Bergmann would seem not to account for the difference at all. Instead, he takes his stand on the fact that in *PM* logic, or in "the ideal language" as he likes to call it, "what"-predicates and "is"-relationships are inadmissible. True, in the everyday language which we use to talk informally about what is set forth in the ideal language, we can and do use "what"-statements — e.g., "*a* is a bare particular." On the other hand, in the ideal language itself, one can do no more than, as it were, exhibit such bare particulars or universals; one cannot say that that is what the entities exhibited are.

But by such a turn does Bergmann really extricate himself from the difficulty? Or is what he does little more than hocus-pocus and sleight of hand? Could it be that in a metaphysics such as logical atomism the exiguous circumstances of its own logic have tended to force it into a position where it is compelled at once to deny and to affirm that things are what they are?

Nevertheless, our present purpose is not to mount a critique of logical atomism, but only to suggest that there may be many logics and not just one, and that it will presumably make no little difference to one's metaphysics whether the logic one employs is one that is tolerant of "what"-statements or intolerant of them. To this simple truth the example of a philosophy like that of logical atomism does seem to bear eloquent, if not disturbing, witness.

7. On this entire issue, see Bergmann's interesting paper, "Ineffability, Ontology, and Method" in *Logic and Reality* (Madison: University of Wisconsin Press, 1964), pp. 45–63. While we hardly think that Bergmann in this paper manages to extricate himself from the difficulty that we have been pressing him with, we would certainly not wish to pretend that our own discussion has done justice to his elaborate and subtle argument.

Chapter II

Alternative Logics: *A* What-Logic

and a Relating-Logic

MAY WE NOT GENERALIZE the results of the preceding chapter, so as to cover more than just the case of certain propositional structures in *PM* logic or certain features of the philosophy of logical atomism? For what difference does it make whether one's logical and philosophical slogan be such as Peirce's, "Our idea of anything is our idea of its sensible effects," or as Wittgenstein's "Look not for the meaning but for the use," or "Treat of the network, not of what the network describes"? In all such cases, is it not possible that what is really being announced and proclaimed is a sort of over-all way of thinking about things or of looking at things — a kind of logic — which seeks to understand things not in terms of what they are, but rather in terms of the contexts they are in or their relations to other things?

For instance, to choose but a single example more or less at random, one might consider Stephen Toulmin's discussion of how in modern geometrical optics light came to be understood on the model of something traveling in straight lines. He remarks on how strange it is to

find that nothing in geometrical optics gives us any occasion to discuss the question *what* it is that "travels." So far as geometrical optics is concerned, it is enough that we have as the grammatical subject of our sentences the bare substantive "light," and it does not matter whether or not we can say any more about it. . . . We know that light starts off from lamps, stars and other shining bodies, and ends up on illuminated surfaces: all we need ask, therefore, in geometrical optics are the questions, "Where from? Where to? And by what path?" The whole of geometrical optics could have been, and much in fact was developed, without there being real backing for any particular answer to the question "What is it that travels?" Even the question "How fast?" was answered by Römer in 1676 from observations on the eclipses of the satellites of Jupiter, before any substance had been given to the bare grammatical substantive "light." [1]

From such an example, one might be tempted to conclude that what concerns the physicist in this instance is not so much what light is, but how it behaves, such "behavior" being understood through being plotted on a conceptual map, as it were, in terms of its "Where from," "Where to," and "By what path." For a rather more precise account of just what is involved in this sort of understanding-through-contexts, as contrasted with an understanding-through-"whats," we perhaps could not do better than to turn to some of C. I. Lewis' luminous formulations. Thus in *Mind and the World Order*, he flatly declares:

Logical analysis is not dissection but relation: the analysis of A into B and C does not divide A into constituents B and C but merely traces a pattern of relations connecting A with B and C. As regards their conceptual meaning, terms are very closely analogous to points in space. A point is nothing whatever apart from its relation to other points; its very essence is relational. Likewise the conceptual meaning of a term is nothing whatever apart from other such meanings. Also it is true that if point A is located by reference to B and C, B and C in turn, and the other points in any spatial array, have their position eventually, in circularwise, in their relation to A and to one another. The positional relationships of any point are internal to its nature and constitute that nature. Likewise, the definitive relations of a term, signifying a concept, are internal to the meaning of that term and constitute it. The nature of a concept as such is its internal (essential or definitive) relationships with other concepts. All points have their positions eventually in terms of the array of all space: no point or set of points has any primal position in any other fashion; we merely choose as an arbitrary

1. *The Philosophy of Science* (London: Hutchinson's University Library, 1953), pp. 36–37.

basis of reference some set which is convenient or marks the place where we happen to be. All terms or concepts similarly have their meaning eventually in the array of all meanings, and no member of this array is intrinsically primal or privileged.[2]

Moreover, earlier in the same book Lewis remarks on what he says is "a general characteristic of logical analysis — that it does not discover the 'substance' or cosmic constituents of the phenomenon whose nature is analyzed but only the constant context of experience in which it will be found." [3]

To be sure, in such passages Lewis may have been rather carried away by his own partialities. For what he describes as a general characteristic of logical analysis he might more accurately have termed a characteristic of *one particular kind* of logical analysis; and similarly, rather than to say that logical analysis simply is relation and not dissection, it might have been at once more accurate and more modest to say that one kind of logical analysis is to relate the *analyzandum* to other things, or phenomena, rather than to dissect it with a view to getting at its own "substance" or its own "what." In any case, whether he explicitly states it or not, or even whether he would have admitted it or not, there is implicit in Lewis' formulation a recognition that there are two logics, that rather than a single organon of understanding there are two — what we might call a relating-logic or a context-logic on the one hand, and a what-logic on the other.

There is another caveat that one perhaps should raise with respect to Lewis' implied contrast between a context-logic or relating-logic and a what-logic or descriptive logic. In the first of the passages quoted above Lewis seems to be saying that what he considers to be the only proper type of logical analysis involves not just a relating-logic, but more specifically a logic of internal relations. Now such a specification may well be an over-specification. For if we are not mistaken, the peculiar genius of a relating-logic or context-logic, such as took definite form and shape in *Principia Mathematica*, or such as we shall try to show has come to have wide use in the practice of modern physical scientists, is that it is at least neutral with respect to, if not actually exclusive of, any such thing as the internality of relations.

Now it may well be, as Lewis suggests by way of analogy, that so far as points in space are concerned the position of any one such point must be

2. Clarence Irving Lewis, *Mind and the World Order* (New York: Dover Publications, n.d.,), pp. 82–83.

3. *Ibid.*, p. 5.

such as to make that point's relations to all other points in space internal to it. And yet we scarcely believe that such an analogy is entirely apposite when it comes to clarifying just how a relating- or contextual-logic seeks to effect an understanding of things (or of terms or concepts) through their relations to other things. For if we recall the discussions of the preceding chapter pertaining to function-argument relations in *PM* logic or to bare particular-universal relations in logical atomism, it should become clear at once that it would be both dubious and misleading to say that functions are somehow "internal to" their arguments, or that the universals and the relations that are exemplified by bare particulars are internal to those particulars. For one thing, in the latter case, if what it exemplified were internal to a bare particular, then alas, such a particular would be bare no longer! True, in ordinary contexts nudity is not necessarily considered to be a virtue per se, but in the context of logical atomism the bareness of a bare particular is, quite literally, its only virtue.

For another thing, if within the context of *PM* logic specifically the functions of arguments were held to be somehow internal to those arguments, then this would be tantamount to considering that the functions of arguments represent simply what those arguments are. And as we have already seen, it is just such a "what"-relationship or "is"-relationship that the function-argument schema vigorously excludes and puts itself forward as an alternative to.

To be sure, all this is not to say that what we have chosen to regard as a general type or kind of logic, viz., a relating-logic or a context-logic in general (of which *PM* logic would be only a particular variety or manifestation), might not be patient of an exploitation in metaphysics somewhat in the manner of a Leibniz or a Whitehead. Indeed, the interesting thing about both of these types of metaphysics is that, *mutatis mutandis*, for Leibniz as well as for Whitehead the relations of things to other things constitute the very being of the things thus related. Or to express the same thing in terms of epistemology rather than of ontology, one might say that just as a Whiteheadean actual occasion is to be understood in terms of its prehensions of the entire past actual world, so also a Leibnizian monad is to be understood in terms of its relations to all the other monads, these "relations" being internal to the substance of the monad in the mode of accidents or attributes of that substance.

But while a relating-logic might in general be patient of such a use and implementation in metaphysics, still it is clear that such an employment

45

would reflect seriously on the purity of this type of logic as over against the contrasting type of a what-logic or descriptive logic. Indeed, it would be untrue to say that, for Leibniz, what Lewis would call logical analysis would surely be aimed at discovering the "substance" or the "cosmic constituents" of the monads analyzed. In a way, for Leibniz the "substance" of a monad simply is its relations to all the other monads; or to use our terminology, what any monad is is simply its relations to other monads. And no sooner does one say this much, than in effect one has subsumed a relating-logic under a what-logic after all, the "what" of a thing being now held to be simply its relationships to other things. But this is indeed to confound alternative logics rather than to see them as alternatives and to think them through as genuinely alternative ways of seeing and understanding things.

Differing Logics, Differing Knowledges

Supposing, then, that we now consider these alternative logics, respecting so far as possible the purity of each as over against the other, may we not then be in a position to see just how, when these logics are employed in the understanding of a common subject matter, they will each effect a patently different understanding of that same subject matter? For that matter, may we not exploit this very difference between a what-logic and a relating-logic so as to make it tend to approximate to that contrast which we suggested earlier between a bee-logic, or logic of the humanities, and a spider-logic, or logic of the sciences? For if we can succeed in making out a case for there being an entirely different logic operative in the enterprise of humanistic learning from what there is in that of science, then it should become much more readily understandable why the sort of knowledge of man and of the nature of things that is achieved in the humanistic disciplines is bound to be a very different sort of knowledge from that which may be achieved through the sciences. More specifically still, and just by way of a sort of preliminary test or trial, let us attempt to counterpose a characteristically humanistic account of human conduct, both in general and in the case of a particular individual, with an imagined scientific account of the same conduct, such as might be put forward by a behavioral scientist.

First, then, in order to illustrate a rather typical use of a what-logic in the context of the humanistic disciplines, let us consider a short passage from Edward Earl of Clarendon's *History of the Rebellion and Civil Wars in England.* The passage, indeed, is an instance of a peculiar sort of literary genre that was much in vogue in the seventeenth century, the so-called character. In this particular case the character set forth is that of the celebrated Thomas Wentworth, Earl of Strafford. It begins with Clarendon giving a brief account of the Earl's being led from his prison in the Tower to the place of execution on Tower Hill. Clarendon then comments as follows:

Thus fell the greatest subject in power, and little inferior to any in fortune, that was at that time in any of the three kingdoms; who could well remember the time, when he led those people, who then pursued him to his grave. . . . a man of great parts, and extraordinary endowments of nature;

There then follows a one-sentence summary of a particular incident in the Earl's early rise to power, after which the character continues:

These successes, applied to a nature too elate and haughty of itself, and a quicker progress into the greatest employments and trust, made him more transported with disdain of other men, and more contemning the forms of business, than happily he would have been, if he had met with some interruptions in the beginning, and had passed in a more leisurely gradation to the office of a statesman. He was, no doubt, of great observation, and a piercing judgment, both in things and persons; but his too good skill in persons made him judge the worse of things: for it was his misfortune to be in a time wherein very few wise men were equally employed with him; and scarce any . . . whose faculties and abilities were equal to his; so that upon the matter he relied wholly upon himself; and discerning many defects in most men, he too much neglected what they said or did. Of all his passions, his pride was most predominant: which a moderate exercise of ill fortune might have corrected and reformed; and which was by the hand of Heaven strangely punished, by bringing his destruction upon him by two things that he most despised, the people and sir Harry Vane. In a word, the epitaph, which Plutarch records that Sylla wrote for himself, may not be unfitly applied to him; that no man did ever exceed him, either in doing good to his friends, or in doing mischief to his enemies; for his acts of both kinds were most notorious.[4]

Such an account, we should like to maintain, is not untypical of the kind of knowledge and understanding that may be presumed to be mediated by the various humanistic disciplines. True, as we have already acknowledged in both an apologetic and an admonitory way in our Introduction, the very suggestion that it is the business of the humanities to purvey a knowledge that could claim to be something rather more than mere historical erudition

4. (Oxford: Clarendon Press, 1826), I, 455–56.

is likely not to set too well even with the present-day practitioners of the humanistic disciplines. However, that our contemporary humanists should thus deliberately prefer to hide their light under a bushel or to stick their heads in the sand, emitting only vague defensive aphorisms, like "a poem should not mean but be," or a poem is "equal to: not true," [5] is not directly our affair. Suffice it to say that there once was a different, not to say more traditional, conception of the humanities according to which it was thought to be their proper and primary business to convey knowledge, and more specifically a knowledge at once theoretical and practical, of what man is and of what it means to be human. Accepting, then, this conception of the humanities as the one we propose to subscribe to in this book, we shall attempt not so much to argue for it, or to defend it, as simply to provide a kind of rationale for it by setting forth what we think to be the proper logic of such a knowledge, as contrasted with the sort of logic that would appear to be proper to modern scientific knowledge.

Might it not be said that Clarendon's character of the Earl of Strafford conveyed a knowledge of just that humanistic sort that we have been talking about? As a character, to be sure, it is a superb achievement of seventeenth-century literary art. It is a portrait in words that could be compared to a portrait in line and color such as a Van Dyck might conceivably have executed. One might go even further and say that, concise though it is, this account of the career and character of the Earl has many of the lineaments prescribed by Aristotle for something no less than a proper tragedy. The hero of the action passes from a condition of high and happy estate to the depths of ill-fortune. He is a man unmistakably noble and better than the average. The action involved is clearly one to excite pity and fear. And in the account which Clarendon gives of his character, it is as if a

5. Both of these dicta, of course, come from Archibald MacLeish, the second being exploited by Austin Warren in his chapter on "The Function of Literature," in R. Wellek and A. Warren, *Theory of Literature*, 3d ed. (New York: Harcourt, Brace & World, 1956), p. 35. In this chapter, Mr. Warren, so far from suggesting that the function of literature is to make for better knowledge and understanding, seems rather to suggest that it is really a poly-function, which to the somewhat baffled reader might almost appear to be equivalent to a non-function.

For an altogether different view of the function of literature, and one more consonant with our own suggestions regarding the proper logic of the humanities, consider the following pronouncement by Yvor Winters: "I believe that the work of literature, in so far as it is valuable, approximates a real apprehension and communication of a particular kind of objective truth" (*In Defense of Reason*, 3d ed. [Denver: Alan Swallow, n.d.], p. 11). A most illuminating discussion of this general way of regarding literature may be found in an article by Gerald E. Graff entitled "Statement and Poetry" in the *Southern Review*, III, No. 3 (Summer, 1967), 499–515.

sort of substitute were being provided for a properly dramatic imitation of an action. Nor is it even too much to say that the pride and arrogance which Clarendon points to in the Earl's character exhibits just the element of *hamartia* that makes it possible to say of the Earl's downfall that it was "a misfortune brought about not by vice or depravity, but by some error or frailty" (*Poetics* 13. 3).

Of course, one can, if one wishes — and perhaps one must, if one is a professor of English literature — let oneself be transported into raptures over the excellence of Clarendon's literary art as displayed in this passage. Yet it would seem that the really significant thing about the piece is not merely that it is so well done, but that it is so undeniably informative and instructive. It tells us something about the man, Thomas Wentworth, as well as something about man and about human life — and what it tells is true, is significant, and is of a sort that any human being needs to know.

Moreover, the means or the vehicle of such knowledge would seem to be none other than a logic of the kind that we have been designating as a what-logic. For it is precisely through bringing us to a better understanding of what kind of man the Earl was that Clarendon thereby brings us to a better understanding of what man is and of what life is. And vice versa, it is through suggesting what is of the essence of human nature and of human existence that Clarendon manages to render peculiarly intelligible the whole of the brilliant, if tragic, career of this same Earl of Strafford. For is it not the characteristic pride and arrogance of the man, Thomas Wentworth, that both illuminate and in turn are illuminated by the nature of human pride and arrogance generally? Thus Wentworth's pride, as Clarendon represents it, was of a sort as to seem almost justified by the man's indisputably great gifts, at the same time that it was the real source of his downfall. It was this same pride that constituted the very flaw or *hamartia* in his character, which in turn served to render his fall from power and his death on the block akin to real tragedy and not a mere instance of ordinary failure or misfortune. Indeed, tragedy being every bit as much a fact of life as the somewhat more everyday phenomena of coming to a bad end through miscalculation or folly or hard luck, any adequate understanding of what man is and of what life holds in store for man cannot do other than take the reality of tragedy into account. And this is precisely what Clarendon's account would appear to do.

Now let us turn abruptly from this humanistic account of a particular man's conduct and career to the very different sort of account that we might imagine could be given of the same conduct and career in the context of the modern behavioral sciences. To simplify the issues, as well as our exposition of them, we shall avail ourselves of one of the current "personality inventories" or "personal preference tests" that are so much in use today,[6] and we shall imagine no less a person than the Earl of Strafford to be the subject of the test. True, even to conjure up the picture of such a thing in imagination is to evoke a spectacle so incongruous as to be almost ludicrous. However, let us imagine the Earl bent over a question paper, the answers to which should provide "a comprehensive survey of an individual from the social interaction point of view."[7]

More specifically still, we might imagine the test to be set up in accordance with the *California Psychological Inventory*, in which the scales to be determined would be grouped under four broad categories:

Class I. Measures of Poise, Ascendancy, and Self-Assurance

1. Do Dominance
2. Cs Capacity for status
3. Sy Sociability
4. Sp Social presence
5. Sa Self-acceptance
6. Wb Sense of well-being

Class II. Measures of Socialization, Maturity, and Responsibility

7. Re Responsibility
8. So Socialization
9. Sc Self-control
10. To Tolerance
11. Gi Good impression
12. Cm Communability

Class III. Measures of Achievement Potential and Intellectual Efficiency

13. Ac Achievement via conformance

---

6. In choosing a test of this sort as our example of an attempt at a more scientific assessment of human character in contrast to the humanistic sort of assessment followed by a historian like Clarendon, we are fully aware that psychologists would be the last to claim a high degree of scientific reliability for such tests. All the same, these tests are interesting for the very reason that they do represent a sincere, even if still somewhat imperfect, effort at employing scientific techniques to understand the character and capabilities of human beings. Accordingly, even though not too much is claimed for such tests in a scientific way, they are very revealing as indicating the sort of thing that it is assumed must be done if a properly scientific understanding of human personality is ever to be achieved.

7. Harrison G. Gough, *Manual for the California Psychological Inventory* (CPI), (Palo Alto, Calif.: Consulting Psychologists Press, 1957), p. 7.

14. Ai Achievement via independence
15. Ie Intellectual efficiency

Class IV. Measures of Intellectual and Interest Modes

16. Py Psychological-mindedness
17. Fx Flexibility
18. Fe Femininity

And so back to the Earl bent over the questions, of which the following would be a sample:

1. I enjoy social gatherings just to be with people.
2. I looked up to my father as an ideal.
3. Our thinking would be a lot better off if we would just forget about words like "probably," "approximately," and "perhaps."
4. I have a strong desire to be a success in the world.
5. When in a group of people I usually do what the others want rather than make suggestions.
6. I usually go to the movies more than once a week.
7. It's a good thing to know people in the right places so you can get traffic tags, and such things, taken care of.
8. I doubt whether I would make a good leader.
9. I get very tense and anxious when I think other people are disapproving of me.
10. I like to boast of my achievements every now and then.
11. I am afraid of deep water.
12. I like large, noisy parties.
13. Only a fool would try to change our American way of life.
14. I often think of how I look and what impression I am making upon others.
15. I am bothered by acid stomach several times a week.

Of course, such a test as we are imagining the Earl to be taking is so devised as to be capable of being scored. Fortunately, however, we perhaps can largely pass over the technical details of the devices used to this end. Suffice it to say that there will be scores for the individual scales, e.g., Dominance, Sociability, etc. But in addition the interaction between the scales will need to be computed. For example, with respect to the Dominance scale a high-scorer tends to be seen as "aggressive, confident, persistent and planful; as being persuasive and verbally fluent; or self-reliant and independent; and as having leadership potential and initiative. In contrast, a low-scorer will be seen as retiring, inhibited, commonplace, indifferent, silent and unassuming; as being slow in thought and action; as avoiding of situations of tension and decision; and as lacking in self-confidence." [8] With respect to the Sociability scale, a high-scorer will tend to be seen as "outgoing, enterprising and ingenious; as being competitive and forward; and as original and fluent in thought." In contrast, a low-scorer will tend to be seen as "awkward, conventional, quiet, submissive and unassuming; as being detached and passive in attitude; and as being suggestible and overly influenced by others' reactions and opinions." [9] Accordingly, when it comes to the matter of interaction between the scales, one will have to be alert to the correlation between high or low scores on the Dominance scale and high or low scores on the Sociability scale. For instance, the typical correlation between these two scales is $+.65$.

Next, given such various correlations between the scales, the examiner will also want to move on to consider the complete profile of the inventory considered as a whole, for it is by such means that he can perhaps achieve something like "a total over-all picture of the person being tested." For example, in the Manual for the *California Psychological Inventory*, a brief account is given of the profile of a 38-year-old man who took the *CPI* as part of an extensive battery of tests used in selection procedures for an executive position. It seems that he had generally high scores on Do, Cs, Sc, Gi, Ac, and Ie, and low scores on Fx and Ai. Considering all of these data,

a picture of the applicant begins to emerge. We see him as a very ambitious, hard-working, systematic, and persistent man with an excellent mind. He is probably fluent and persuasive and skillful enough socially, but he is a bit too earnest and serious to make a delightful golf partner or, indeed, to relax and enjoy social activity for its own sake. His intellectual abilities should probably be utilized on problems which yield to systematic and persistent analysis, not those requiring creative improvisations. Finally, his needs to succeed, to make a good impression, to do the proper and accepted thing are such that he may tend to be quite deferential to authority and pretty conservative generally.[10]

Now why might not a comparable profile for the Earl of Strafford emerge, once he had finished the test and his answers had been scored? True, we would hardly expect his "total over-all picture" to be quite like that of the 38-year-old would-be executive. No doubt, like the executive, the Earl probably wouldn't be too "delightful a golf partner." Yet one would hardly expect his test to show him to so need "to make a good im-

8. *Ibid.*, p. 12.   9. *Ibid.*   10. *Ibid.*, p. 16.

pression, and to do the proper and accepted thing, as to be quite deferential to authority." But surely this is only as it should be, for the Earl's profile must necessarily be the Earl's, just as the executive's is the executive's. Moreover, is it really so improbable that the total picture which one might get from the Earl's profile would turn out to be quite strikingly consonant with Clarendon's character of him? And if so, then would not our entire case appear to have simply collapsed — the case, that is, that we have been trying to make out for the radically different ways of understanding people and things that are typified by scientific procedures on the one hand and by humanistic procedures on the other?

Not at all. For on closer inspection it should become clear that in using the *CPI* as a means of understanding the Earl we would be operating with a relating-logic, whereas Clarendon was clearly using a what-logic. To substantiate this contention let us compare and contrast certain of the key logical moves that are made in the construction of the inventory, as contrasted with those made in the determination of the character. In the first place, consider exactly what the nature of the correlation is between the answers to the questions on the test and the eventual determination of the scores for the individual scales such as Dominance, Sociability, etc. For example, let us suppose that a negative answer to a question such as, "I am afraid of deep water," were taken to be indicative of the character trait of dominance. On what grounds would it be so taken?

The explanation which the *CPI* gives of how true or false answers to certain types of questions came to be correlated with certain types of character traits is as follows:

The basic method of scale construction was what has come to be called the "empirical technique." In this method a criterion dimension which one seeks to measure is first defined. An example is personal dominance. Second, inventory statements which seem to bear a psychological relevance to the criterion dimension are assembled in a preliminary scale. These questions are then administered to persons who can be shown by some procedure entirely independent of the test to be strongly characterized by this trait or dimension. In the case of dominance, subjects were selected for testing by having persons rate their acquaintances on dominance, and analyses were then made of the item responses of individuals with very high, and very low ratings.

The goal of these item analyses is to discover those questions which are answered in a differential way (either "true" more often, or "false" more often) by the nominated subjects. Items which empirically reveal such discriminations are selected for further study and refinement. The "correct" response to an item is the one given more often by subjects with the "high" ratings.

The result of a series of such steps for any one of the criteria used is the identification of 30 to 40 items each possessing a demonstrable relationship to the behavior being measured. For the Do (Dominance) scale, one of the items chosen was "I have strong political opinions." "Dominant" people very often answer "true" to this item; "submissive" people very seldom say "true." Therefore, the "true" response is scored + 1 on the dominance scale." [11]

By this account one can see that it is a reliance upon a so-called empirical technique that is decisive for determining which questions are to be correlated with which character traits. Indeed, it is just this technique that provides the requisite "demonstrable relationship" of a given item or question "to the behavior being measured." Moreover what this means is that this so-called demonstration of the relationship does not turn upon a consideration of the peculiar nature and character of the question, on the one hand, and the nature and character of a certain trait on the other, as if the one might be seen to be relevant to the other by its very nature, or simply by virtue of what it is. Rather the demonstration turns on nothing more than an observed conjunction or correlation between a true or false answer to a given question and the sort of behavior that has been defined as being characteristic of the trait in question. For example, in the illustration of the correlation between "true" answers to "I have strong political opinions" and the possession of the trait of Dominance, while commonsensically we might suppose that it "simply stands to reason," that dominant people would tend to answer such a question by "true," it is not this standing to reason that is here being relied upon. Instead, what is being relied upon is the mere observed correlation between a person's answering the question with "true" and his manifesting the kind of behavior that has been given the label of "Dominance."

Indeed, one might even say that to the extent to which such a test approximates to the ideal, the correlation between a certain type of question and a certain type of behavior would become progressively less and less of the sort which just stands to reason and would become progressively more and more of the kind that is based merely on an observed connection. Thus to use a rather more fanciful example, suppose that it were to be found simply as a matter of empirical observation that the answer "false" to the item "I am afraid of deep water" was almost invariably correlated with an exhibition of "dominant" behavior. Or, better still, suppose that people who answered "true" to "I usually go to the movies more than

11. *Ibid.*, p. 21.

once a week" turned out almost invariably to be people who exhibited a "dominant" behavior. Such questions — for which there would appear to be almost no reason for suspecting any correlations between the answers given to them and certain types of character or behavior, but rather only an observed correlation between the two — would be precisely those that would be ideal for such a test. The reason they would be ideal is that they would enforce an exclusive reliance upon a purely "empirical technique" for gauging a person's behavior rather than a reliance upon what would seem to stand to reason in regard to a person's behavior and character.

But what would such a reliance upon an "empirical technique" involve, if not precisely the invocation of a relating-logic in place of a what-logic? For it would seem evident in Clarendon's case that what he was doing in seeking to explain the Earl of Strafford's behavior was to rely simply upon a consideration of the peculiar nature of Strafford's pride, of how in his earlier career it had not been checked by failure or adversity, with the result that it would simply stand to reason that such pride would tend to make Strafford "more transported with disdain of other men, and more contemning the forms of business," etc. In other words, Strafford's conduct and behavior are here being rendered intelligible in the light of an understanding of what he was, of the kind of man he was, and more specifically of the distinctive sort of pride and arrogance that were characteristic of him. In contrast, were one to attempt to arrive at a personality inventory of the Earl through relying upon something like the so-called empirical technique of the *CPI* test, then the entire procedure would in principle turn on little more than a correlating of certain answers to questions with certain specified types of behavior. And what is there about the questions that would lead one to expect that answering them in a certain way would be indicative of a certain trait of character? Or what is there about that trait of character that would lead one to expect that it would go with a particular way of answering certain types of questions on a personality inventory? The answer is, "In principle, nothing." For the entire point of relying upon an "empirical technique" is that it serves to establish a purely factual correlation between certain answers to questions and certain traits of character. And the point of such a purely factual correlation is that it rests only upon, to use Hume's terms, an observed "constant conjunction," and not at all upon any supposedly "necessary connections" — i.e., in the latter case, upon a connection of which it might be said that it stands to reason that the one thing would be connected with the other simply by virtue of what the things in question are.

Accordingly, harking back to Lewis' earlier suggestion that "logical analysis is not dissection, but relation," we can now see how the eventual aim of an empirical technique such as that employed in the *California Psychological Inventory* would presumably be to eliminate entirely any analysis of a character trait such as that of dominance or pride or what not in terms of what its essential constituents are. Instead, the ideal analysis of dominance would in principle amount to a simple relating of certain types of action and modes of behavior labeled dominant behavior to the further modes of behavior involved in answering certain types of questions in certain particular ways. And, vice versa, rather than to ask just what it is or what it means for a person to answer certain questions in certain ways, or what kind of a person it stands to reason would answer these questions in this particular way, it is much more sensible simply to ask what further actions and types of behavior the action of answering questions in that particular way is related to or correlated with. Or again, paraphrasing the passage from Toulmin, just as in geometrical optics it isn't to the point to ask "What is it that travels?", but rather only "Where from? Where to? And by what path?", so likewise in the context of modern psychological inventories of personality, it would scarcely be to the point to try to determine what Strafford's peculiar nature and character were, in terms of which his conduct and behavior could thus be made intelligible. Rather, the aim and scheme of the investigation would appear to be such that, by virtue of certain statistical laws that correlate various observable human responses with various observable traits and qualities, the actions and behavior of a particular man, Strafford, would be rendered more or less predictable and/or retrodictable.

Accordingly, we might sum up this entire discussion by simply saying that in the respective approaches to an understanding of human beings — the humanistic and the behavioristic — the interest shifts, as it were, from a concern with the intelligibility of human behavior to its predictability. Or, alternatively, one might say that in the scientific approach the concern is not so much one of understanding things in terms of what they are, as in terms of the relations they enter into. Indeed, the logic of modern science, one might suggest, is one in which things are understood not in their own natures and "whats," but in their relations. For example, to take a case from outside the behavioral sciences altogether — consider Snell's Law:

Whenever any ray of light is incident at the surface which separates two media, it is bent in such a way that the ratio of the sine of the angle of incidence to the sine of the angle of refraction is always a constant quality for those two media.

Such a law might properly be said to be a law of the behavior of light. But note that in this law the behavior of a ray of light in refraction is not made intelligible in terms of the nature of light or of what light is. Rather, if anything, what light is is to be identified simply with its behavior under varying circumstances and conditions, among them that of refraction. Nor can there be said to be any effort made in such a context to render the behavior of light rays intelligible — at least not in the sense in which, as we have already used that term, Clarendon in his character of the Earl of Strafford might be said to have sought to make the Earl's behavior intelligible. Instead of any reason or explanation being given as to why a ray of light should be refracted in just that way, it is merely asserted that it is so refracted, and in ways that are accurately and specifically predictable. In other words, intelligibility gives way to predictability the minute one passes from a humanistic to a scientific account of things.

Finally, that in the actual statement of Snell's Law the logical formulation is not that of what we might call a what-statement at all. Just as a statement, it is not in the form of an answer to any question "What?" (What is light? or What is anything else?). Rather, it is simply a statement of a ratio or a correlation between two measurable quantities, viz., the sine of the angle of incidence and the sine of the angle of refraction. Thus again, we see how the very logic of scientific statements is ordered to an understanding of things in terms of their correlations with other things, and not in terms of what they are or of those things' own natures and essences.

Humanistic Knowledge vs. Scientific Knowledge

But perhaps we digress somewhat. For our primary purpose is not merely to contrast a logic of the humanities with a logic of the sciences, a bee-logic with a spider-logic, but rather to point up the far more basic contrast between a what-logic and a relating-logic, of which the division between the humanities and the sciences may serve as but a single, even if somewhat contentious, example. Nevertheless, it might be well to consider rather more carefully some of the respective by-products that may be expected from the use of the one kind of logic as over against the other. And since the palmary examples of such fruits as may be derived from the use of a relating-logic are to be found in modern science and technology — its use in philosophy being little more than tandem and imitative — our discussion must turn pretty much on instances drawn from the sciences.

First, what about the admittedly rather invidious contrast that was drawn in the preceding paragraphs between the fruits of intelligibility that were held to be associated with the use of a what-logic, as over against those of mere predictability that were associated with a relating-logic?

In drawing this contrast we did little more than, as it were, let the examples speak for themselves. For is it not immediately obvious that in the light of Clarendon's character of the Earl we are sensitive of having been brought to an understanding of the man and of his behavior and even of his fate, but without our having so much as an iota of the sort of knowledge that makes for scientific prediction? To be sure, if we had been contemporaries of Clarendon, reading his character of the Earl, or even if we had been Clarendon himself, reflecting on the character of the Earl before his fall, we might on the basis of our understanding of the Earl's character venture a prediction as to what would be likely to happen to him, or even as to the likelihood of his coming to a tragic end. But this would in no wise be on the order of a scientific prediction. In fact, it could not even be compared with a prediction as to the angle of refraction of a light ray, given the angle of incidence. For that matter, it could not be compared with such predictions as a physician or psychiatrist or clinical psychologist might make, given a diagnosis of the Earl's physical ills or psychic complexes. Nor is it merely a case of such scientific predictions of the Earl's behavior being considerably more accurate and reliable than those that a historian might make. For must we not all acknowledge that such understanding as we might have of the Earl's character, from Clarendon's account of it, would really not be enhanced by our being able to predict his behavior in the manner of a physician or a psychiatrist? And, vice versa, a psychologist's or sociologist's predictions as to a person's behavior are not and do not have to be based on an understanding of the man's character of the sort that we are assuming to be mediated by Clarendon's character. Indeed, it is precisely the virtue of properly scientific predictions that they can be made, and even ought to be made, in the absence of any knowledge of the "whats" of the things in question.

Perhaps, though, this point might be made clearer through still another example — this time one drawn from the history of science. As we understand it, it has become almost a truism for historians of the great scientific revolution of the seventeenth century to consider that Copernicus' proposal of the heliocentric theory was not nearly so disturbing and up-setting to the Aristotelian traditionalists as was Kepler's proposal that the planets be conceived as moving in elliptical orbits. For Aristotle had de-creed that circular motion was the most perfect motion, and therefore the only motion appropriate to heavenly bodies. Accordingly, since Copernicus' heliocentric theory had not challenged this most fundamental tenet of Aris-totelian astronomy, it proved to be rather less shocking than what Kepler proposed.

All well and good. Yet the question that seems often not to be asked in this reading of the history of science is just why the Aristotelians should have clung so tenaciously to this theory of the circular motion of the heavens: why should they have been so much more reluctant to sacrifice this principle of their astronomy than the principle of geocentricism? Could it be that they were influenced by the comparative intellectual satisfaction — or at least the different intellectual satisfaction — that is vouchsafed by a what-logic, as over against that which comes from a context-logic?

Suppose that one glances at the first four chapters of Book I of the *De Caelo*. What is almost certain to strike one is the pains which Aristotle takes to show, first, just why and how circular motion must be the most perfect motion, and then just why there must be a simple body, at once prior to and more perfect than earth, fire, air, and water, a body to which circular motion as the perfect motion is peculiarly appropriate. In other words, Aristotle undertakes to infer both the existence of the *aether*, as well as the characteristics which such a body must have, from the fact of circular motion and the perfection of such motion as compared with all other motions. Hence the *aether* was, as it were, tailor-made in Aristotelian astronomy for the express purpose of supporting circular motion. Little wonder, then, that once it had become established and generally recognized that heavenly bodies were of this nature, it would seem impossible that such bodies could move in other than circular orbits. On the contrary, one had but to understand what such bodies were and what their nature was, and one could see that their circular motion was thereby rendered completely intelligible.

Now contrast the sort of alternative that was offered by Kepler's theory. Suppose that the planets did move in ellipses and not in circles, there was then literally nothing about the nature of such planetary bodies — nothing in their "whats" — that rendered such motion on their part intelligible.

Indeed, it seems that Kepler was sufficiently exercised by the unintelligibility of his own proposal of an elliptical motion of the planet to venture to explain such motion, not, to be sure, through the nature of the heavenly bodies that displayed this motion, but rather through the agency of an outside or external cause, the cause being in the case of each planet a sort of guardian angel who conveniently and accommodatingly kept the planet moving on its elliptical course [12] — a sort of *angelus ex machina*.

It is true that in resorting to such an explanation Kepler made a move that has subsequently afforded us the sort of amusement that only we lesser lights can enjoy at the exposure of the foibles and mistakes of our betters. But though in fact Kepler's move was desperate to the point of being laughable, in principle it was shrewd enough. For the movement of the planets being no longer intelligible in terms of what the planets themselves were, the sensible thing to do was to try to make it intelligible in terms of outside causes; or, to describe Kepler's move in the language of Aristotelian causes, what he tried to do was to account for planetary motion not in terms of the formal causes of the planets' own natures, but rather in terms of external efficient causes. And, indeed, eventually the Newtonian theory did account for planetary motion precisely in terms of external causes, viz., gravitational forces.[13]

But this last is another story. For the present, we are not even concerned with the question of whether by resorting to efficient causes one can ultimately find a surrogate for the sort of intelligibility that springs simply from an understanding of the conduct and behavior of things in terms of what those things are. Suffice it to say that when Kepler did propose to conceive of the planets as moving in ellipses rather than in circles, he was in effect, and against the background of the Aristotelian science of his day, simply sacrificing an account of the motion and behavior of planets that was quite intelligible in terms of the what-logic of Aristotelian science, and was substituting for it an account of planetary motion that was radically and disquietingly unintelligible. Little wonder that under the circumstances he should have invoked the agency of angels to extricate him from his predicament, and that the Aristotelian scientists for their part

12. See the passing reference to this in H. W. B. Joseph, *An Introduction to Logic*, 2d ed. (Oxford: Clarendon Press, 1916), p. 535.

13. This is not necessarily to imply that such forces were efficient causes in any properly Aristotelian sense. But, then, this is indeed a most complicated question in the history of science as well as of philosophy.

should have felt that the very principles of intelligibility were being flaunted by Kepler's theory.

Of course, it is easy enough for us nowadays, from the standpoint of the subsequent development of modern science and with all the wisdom of hindsight, to dismiss this sort of intelligibility as irrelevant for scientific purposes. And perhaps it is. After all, given Kepler's theory of planetary motion, was it not possible to account beautifully for the then hitherto observed positions of the planets at various times, and also to predict accurately all possible future positions of the planets at future times? And in doing all this, did not Kepler's laws provide the means of saving all of the appearances, and saving them most elegantly? To which the answer can only be an emphatic and ungrudging "Yes."

Yet the point is that however irrelevant the intelligibility of a what-logic may be for scientific purposes, it is not therefore necessarily irrelevant for all purposes. On the contrary, the very example of the contrast between the Aristotelian theory of the motion of the planets and Kepler's theory, just like our earlier example of the contrast between a logic of the humanities and a logic of the sciences, serves to show that there are certain kinds of questions which a context-logic is in principle incapable of providing answers to, and a kind of intelligibility in respect to which only a what-logic can give satisfaction.

Why could we not put it this way? Let us readily concede that when it comes to things like the movements of the planets, and indeed when it comes to scientific matters generally, it may well be that the sort of intelligibility that can be provided only by a what-logic is unattainable, and in this respect irrelevant. Yet it should not be thought that, merely because in the sphere of the modern natural sciences we cannot seem to achieve proper answers to our what-questions at all, such questions are therefore not proper questions and the intelligibility which they seek to attain is not a legitimate intelligibility. After all, the very logic of Kepler's theory does not make, and is not capable of making, the movements of the planets intelligible in the way in which the Aristotelian theory did; and albeit the Aristotelian theory was false, and no other theory using a similar what-logic has since been devised to do the trick, that still does not mean that the sorts of question which the Aristotelian theory sought to answer have been answered. Nor does it mean that the modern sciences, using as they do for the most part a context-logic, have succeeded, with all their triumphs, in making nature intelligible in the same way in which it would have been made intelligible had a what-logic proved to be applicable, or had a scientific program using such a logic been capable of success.

With this we find ourselves once more back with the question of the humanities and of the distinctive kind of knowledge which they may be thought to convey in contrast to the sciences. As we have already intimated, a common view nowadays is that greater knowledge and understanding are not at all the sorts of things which one seeks to derive from a study of the humanities, it being rather with the values of taste and of artistic appreciation and aesthetic enjoyment that students of literature and of the arts tend to concern themselves. As for the humanistic disciplines being able to offer a kind of knowledge of man and of nature that would amount to no less than an alternative knowledge to that of the sciences — this is a claim which many of our more timid professionals in the various fields of the humanities would be the last even to entertain, must less to push. Yet might not the reason for such a timidity on the part of the professionals concerned be due to their widespread assumption, as curious as it is uncritical, that all knowledge of matters of fact and of nature cannot possibly be other than a knowledge of the type that is proper only to science? And might not this assumption in turn be due very largely to a failure to recognize that there may well be logics other than the logic of modern science, and that given such a different logic the knowledge that will thereby be mediated cannot be other than radically different from scientific knowledge in the usual sense? In any case, the thesis that we should like to put forward, albeit quite gingerly and tentatively, is that the sort of logic that we have been calling a what-logic or a bee-logic is peculiarly proper and congenial to the humanities, and that no sooner does the nature and functioning of such a logic come to be understood than it will at the same time be recognized that through the use of this type of logic a characteristically humanistic knowledge may perhaps be brought about — a knowledge that may readily be seen as an alternative to the so-called scientific knowledge that is so dominant, and in its very dominance so distressing, a feature of our modern culture.[14]

14. For an illuminating, not to say moving, account of how in the literary criticism of the nineteenth century there were repeated desperate efforts to secure for literature and particularly for poetry a kind of knowledge that would be independent of, and could not be displaced by, the regnant scientific knowledge, see M. H. Abrams, *The Mirror and the Lamp* (New York: The Norton Library, 1958), Chap. 11, "Science and Poetry in Romantic Criticism."

Chapter III

The What-Statements *of a* What-Logic:

Why They Are Not Analytic Truths

HAVING THUS SET FORTH in a rough and ready way the contrast between the two logics — a what-logic and a relating-logic, a bee-logic and a spider-logic, a logic of the humanities and a logic of the sciences — we now need to render this contrast more precise, as well as to justify it more scrupulously. To this end, we propose to follow the somewhat complicated and tortuous course of first trying to exhibit one by one various of the characteristic logical powers of a what-logic; then, shifting to the context of a relating-logic, of trying to see why and on what grounds such powers have been either decried or repudiated; and, finally, recurring to the standpoint of a what-logic, trying to show how it in turn may perhaps defend itself against the strictures that modern analytic philosophers have so confidently leveled against it.

We may well begin with a consideration of the logical proposition,[1]

---

1. Be it noted that we are not using the term "proposition" in so sophisticated a sense as

to see how very differently this is conceived in the two types of logic. In the first chapter we made something of a beginning in this direction. Taking the logic of *Principia Mathematica* as an example, we sought to point out that the structure of atomic propositions being conceived as it is, the consequence would appear to be that certain sorts of things quite literally cannot be said or thought in such a logic; more specifically, one cannot say or think what anything is. Accordingly, by way of contrast, one might rightly suppose that in a what-logic the objective will be precisely that of making possible just such an understanding of things in terms of what they are. Still, it needs to be asked what the specific instruments will be that are presumably adapted to such a purpose. For example, if the function-argument schema of *PM* logic is an instrument that is totally incapable of serving such an end, then what sort of an instrument will a what-logic avail itself of to this same end?

Hardly, though, is such a question raised than everyone will immediately anticipate the answer and just as immediately find it wanting. For what else can the characteristic instrument of a what-logic be than something on the order of the ancient and honorable, but thoroughly hackneyed and berated, device of the subject-predicate proposition of Aristotelian logic? Yet this woefully shopworn tool has in recent years been made the scapegoat for just about all the logical sins of the past. And what could be more embarrassing for the progress of our present argument than having to carry in our baggage the sheer dead weight of the S-P proposition? For this is indeed the twentieth century in philosophy, in which everyone is desperately engaged in trying to outdo both himself and his neighbor in doing the done thing and casting the first stone. What chance, then, does the hapless old S-P proposition have in a philosophical world such as ours today?

All the same, enlightened as we are in our contemporary philosophy, we would certainly be ashamed if we were to be found guilty of perpetuating an old-world, not to say Old Testament, superstition like that of the scapegoat. And so, if not our sense of justice, then at least our anxiety to avoid being thought superstitious, will perhaps serve to persuade us to have at least another look at the old subject-predicate device of Aristotelian logic.

Even if we may be thus reluctantly persuaded, still, to act on such a per-

would distinguish it from "judgment," "statement," or even "sentence." Rather for our purposes all such terms may be used more or less synonymously.

suasion will be nothing if not difficult. For hardly shall we have started to make the initial effort in this direction than our ears will be filled with the steady droning of criticism to the effect that Aristotle's partiality for the subject-predicate form of the proposition was the result of nothing more than a historical accident, viz., that the basic sentence form of Indo-European languages just happened to be of a structure not unlike that of subject-predicate. And such a supposed truism usually begets still another to the effect that had Aristotle's native language been Swahili rather than Greek, we should probably never have had such a thing as Aristotelian logic as we know it today. But to any and all such speculations-become-truisms, we are inclined to make only the sour response, "So be it, but so what!"

After all, the pertinent philosophical issue is not whether the S-P form is the only possible logical form in which one can formulate a proposition as to what a thing is. Quite the contrary; human language forms being various, and human imagination being exceedingly fertile, there is no reason to suppose that there might not be any number of alternative ways of symbolizing the form or structure of the logical tool that comes into play whenever we attempt to understand things for what they are. In this respect there is nothing sacrosanct about the S-P form. Indeed, if anyone should be able to produce some other logical form that might better serve to exhibit the logical character of what-statements, especially as these manifest themselves in non–Indo-European languages, then more power to him! For ourselves and for our immediate purposes, however, we would merely remark that whether the S-P form is the only conceivable form that might be adapted to this task or not, it at least is a form that is so adapted. And being the only form that we happen to know of that functions in this way, we shall simply use it for purposes of illustration. Besides, should someone continue to have a lingering anxiety lest our use of the S-P form might make it almost impossible for our Swahili-speaking readers to understand what we are about to say, we feel that that is a risk which we can perhaps afford to run. After all, it has not infrequently been pointed out that the only way in which the major part of Aristotle's own writings came to be transmitted to the Latin west was through the Arabs. Yet ironically enough, Arabic is not an Indo-European language, nor — at least so we have been told — do its grammar and syntax permit of a subject-predicate form of sentence structure. Somehow, though, this supposed linguistic disability seems not to have deterred the Arabs in their understanding of Aristotle.

So why worry about the Swahilis? What the Arabs could do, surely the Swahilis could do as well.

That subject-predicate propositions are adapted primarily to the business of stating what things are, we have asserted more or less dogmatically. But, as to just how these propositions bring off such an intention of things in terms of what they are, we have so far not specified. Nor do we purpose to undertake this explanation in detail just at present. Suffice it to say that the subject-predicate relation is not to be construed after the pattern of a function-argument relation, or that of a substance-accident or thing-property relation, or that of a concept-object relation, or that of a particular-universal relation, and so on. For we have already had occasion to remark on the fact that not one of these latter relations is capable of showing forth the precise sort of relation that holds between a thing and what it is. In contrast, the subject-predicate relation we should simply declare to be one in which the subject term in the statement stands for what we are talking about,[2] or are concerned to know about, and the predicate signifies what we take such a subject to be, or what in our judgment it is.

Nor ought we to stop there. For there would also seem to be, within the context of the same general subject-predicate type of relation, a number of different ways in which the predicate may relate to its subject as expressing its "what." Thus, speaking rather loosely, we should surely say that we recognize a difference between saying what a thing is essentially and saying what it is only accidentally. For example, one might say of the distinguished American Philosopher, Professor Quine, that (1) "Quine is a modern logician," or (2) "Quine is human." Considering the matter objectively and quite without prejudice, there would seem to be no necessary incompatibility between those two predicates. One might say, (3) "Quine is

---

2. No doubt we shall be taken to task for our apparent blithe disregard of the cavils which Strawson has leveled at Geach on the score of the latter's use of terms like "about" and "stand for" in an effort to point up the difference between subject and predicate in propositions (Cf. P. F. Strawson, *Individuals* [London: Methuen, 1959], pp. 143 ff.). In reply, we would merely observe that we are not at all sure that in our use of "about" and "stand for" we are vesting these words with quite the same function that Strawson thinks Geach would ascribe to them and that he, Strawson, would begrudge them. Besides, the subtle force of Strawson's objections rather escapes us. Thus Strawson takes as an example the sentence "Raleigh smokes" and suggests that such a sentence could well be so used that one could say that it was about Raleigh, but it could perhaps equally well be said to be about smoking. Unfortunately, this very telling objection would appear to lose something of its effectiveness, largely because Strawson has not bothered to consider that if such a sentence could be said to be about smoking, it surely could not be said to be about smoking in quite the same sense in which it was about Raleigh.

famous." Considering the matter commonsensically, and forgetting for the moment the somewhat sophisticated flights of fancy of the more extreme advocates of the doctrine of internal relations, it would seem that certainly in (3), if not in (1), one is asserting what Quine is only accidentally, or to borrow Quine's own turn of phrase, one is purporting to assert merely "what is true of" him.

To put this same point in rather more abstract language, we might say that within one and the same genus of what we are choosing to call what-statements, there are various kinds and species of is-relationships. Indeed, it will be recalled that the traditional doctrine of the so-called predicables specified at least five such relationships — five different ways, that is, in which a predicate might express what its subject is. Thus to use the trite and true examples:

"Socrates is an animal" — genus
"Socrates is rational" — differentia
"Socrates is a man" — species
"Socrates is a language-user" — property
"Socrates is snub-nosed" — accident

It is not to our present purpose to speak as to the adequacy of this fivefold classification of predicable relationships. At least on the face of it, there would seem to be no very serious reason why certain further such relationships might not be added, or certain of the original five reduced to the others. Be this as it may, we have doubtless said enough by way of illustrating how so-called what-statements of the subject-predicate type can exhibit quite different sorts of predicable relationships.

A Specific Disability of PM Logic

Now let us turn our attention to a different, yet closely related, feature of these predicable relationships in what-statements. This is a feature which involves not so much the recognition of still other predicable or is-relationships as, instead, a certain shift in what might be called the incidence of all the predicable relationships.[3] For example, having said that Quine is

3. Members of the McKeon school have made much of this shift of incidence in the doctrine of the predicables, insisting that to conceive of the predicable relationships as having an incidence with respect to individuals as subjects of predication, and not merely with respect to universals, represents a major Platonic distortion of Aristotelian logic, effected largely through the agency of Porphyry. Indeed, such a shift of incidence is said to have profoundly affected the entire course of Western philosophy,

a modern logician, we recognized that this is what Quine is, or at least what we take him to be. But then, just what is it to be a modern logician? After all, having declared our subject to be a horse of this strange color, few of us would want to stop there. For what is a modern logician anyway? Surely, those of us who didn't know could scarcely contain ourselves for curiosity, and those who did know could scarcely contain ourselves for wishing to divulge the mystery.

This time, however, the kind of what-statement that is called for will be of a different character. For it will not be a statement in answer to a question of the type, "What is Quine?" Rather it will be in answer to a question of the type, "What is a modern logician?"[4] And suppose one answers:

(4) "A modern logician is a formalist."

(5) "A modern logician is a man who doesn't read Aristotle and doesn't care."

(6) "A modern logician is a rigorist."

And, last but not least, one might even concede that in spite of all temptation to be born of other, not nations perhaps, but species:

(7) "A modern logician is a human being."

From all this, then, it would appear that what-statements of the type of (1) to (3) quite naturally give rise to, and even in a sense might be said to demand, what-statements of the type of (4) to (7). What, though, is the nature of the difference between these two types of what-statements, both of them being equally answers to what-questions? At this point, it might be interesting and illuminating to shift our attention to a relating-logic and to see how these two different types of what-statements would be dealt with in such a logic.

---

not just in respect to logic but to metaphysics as well (Cf. E. A. Moody, *The Logic of William of Ockham* [London: Sheed and Ward, 1935], esp. Chap. 3; see also the article by Manley Thompson, "On the Distinction between Thing and Property," in *The Return to Reason*, ed. John Wild [Chicago: Henry Regnery, 1953], pp. 125–51).

Unhappily, we must confess to having remained insensitive and uncomprehending as to this supposed import of the shift of incidence in the doctrine of the predicables.

4. Perhaps it should be noted in passing that a similar shift of incidence in predicable relationships is noticeable in the examples which we employed in Chapter II, as over against those used in Chapter I. The latter examples were designed to illustrate the incapacity of a *PM* logic to make what-statements of the one kind, whereas the examples used in Chapter II were illustrations of the incapacity of a *PM* logic in regard to what-statements of the second type.

This difference will assume considerable importance later on, when we try to determine rather more precisely the connotation of our term "relating-logic."

We have seen how statements of the type of (1) to (3), in a relating-logic such as that of *PM*, cannot be handled as what-statements at all. That is to say, their logical structure is construed in terms of a function-argument schema — ϕ (*a*); and as we sought to point out earlier, the relation of an argument to its function is not that of an is-relationship: a function is never to be regarded as being what its argument is.

What, though, of statements of the type of (4) to (7)? How are they dealt with in *PM* logic? Surely all of us are familiar with the usual ploy whereby, in such a logic, a statement like (7) would be rendered:

(7a) "(*x*) . *x* is a modern logician . $\supset$. *x* is human."

Now does such a rendering of (7) in *PM*-ese succeed in preserving the character of the original what-statement, as the earlier considered rendering of (1) to (3) in *PM*-ese certainly did not do? A little reflection should convince us that in the one case no more than in the other does *PM* logic provide us with a means for asserting what things are.

For consider how the "$\supset$" is to be understood in such a proposition. As we all know, in *PM* logic "$\supset$" is taken as a truth-functional connective, and the meaning of such a connective may be rigorously specified in terms of the truth tables.

p	q	p $\supset$ q
T	T	T
T	F	F
F	T	T
F	F	T

Accordingly, the whole point and purpose of such a truth-functional interpretation of "$\supset$" or of "if-then" is that it allows the truth of the proposition as a whole to be determined, as it were, formally and without one's having to consider the content of either the *p* or the *q* at all. Thus it makes no difference what *p* says specifically, or what *q* says specifically; all that is required for the truth of *p* $\supset$ *q* is that either *p* be false or *q* true.

Moreover, the *PM* formulation for a proposition such as (7a) — i.e., a formulation in terms of (*x*). $\phi x . \supset . \chi x$ — is said to be an instance of formal implication, as over against the sort of material implication that is involved in *p* $\supset$ *q*. And yet the term "formal implication" signifies no more than a summation of a number of material implications. Thus suppose one has a series of propositions of the form:

69

$$\phi a \cdot \supset \cdot \chi a$$
$$\phi b \cdot \supset \cdot \chi b$$
$$\phi c \cdot \supset \cdot \chi c$$

etc.

These may be simply summed up as

$$(x) \cdot \phi x \cdot \supset \cdot \chi x$$

Clearly, though, no sooner does one interpret the sign "$\supset$" of the standard *PM* notation as signifying either material or formal implication, in the senses of these terms just indicated, than it becomes apparent that to construe our original what-statement (7) in the manner of (7a) is thereby to deprive it precisely of its peculiar and distinctive character as a what-statement. For in (7a) the connection between being a modern logician and being human can only be understood truth-functionally. That is to say, the specific content of the protasis, viz., that a particular person is a modern logician, has nothing whatever to do with determining whether the apodosis, viz., that this same person is human, is consequent upon it or not.

Contrast, though, the situation in (7). For there it is precisely a regard for the specific, even if odd, nature of the particular subject matter under consideration, viz., modern logicians, that leads one to concede in spite of everything that such a thing is after all human. For that matter, in all of our examples (4) to (7), it was our own understanding of the subject matter of our proposition that led us, rightly or wrongly, to make our various judgments to the effect that this same strange specimen could be none other than a formalist, a rigorist, a non-reader of Aristotle, yes, even a human being.

To sum up, it should now be clear that a what-statement of our second type is one whose truth or falsity can only be determined by a consideration of the subject matter, or of the content of the statement, or of what in the statement we are talking about. In contrast, in the standard form in which such a statement is rendered in *PM* logic — viz., $(x) \cdot \phi x \cdot \supset \cdot \chi x$ — the truth or falsity of the proposition is supposed to be determined not by the content of the proposition, but by the purely formal (in the sense of truth-functional) relation between the "if" and the "then" clauses. But this means that to render a statement like (7) in the manner of (7a) is not simply to set it forth in a different but alternative logical form, but rather to change its logical character altogether. Thus (7), as we saw, was an answer to a certain type of what-question; but a statement of the type of (7a) does not answer any sort of question "What?", nor as a statement is it competent to give information as to what anything is at all. Accordingly, those various forms and types of what-questions, which as we saw earlier the traditional subject-predicate type of proposition is peculiarly adapted to answering, must remain both unasked and unanswered in a logic of the type of *Principia Mathematica*. Thus: "What is that?" "That is a square?" "And what is a square?" "A square is a rectilinear figure of four equal sides." Just such a series of questions and answers, then, would appear to be completely outside the competence of a logic such as *PM* to deal with.

What-Statements as Analytic Truths

To all of this, however, the obvious rejoinder that must immediately occur to a modern logician, and even to a modern philosopher, and perhaps still more generally (since there would appear to be an unhappy if tenuous connection between them) to a modern man, is simply "So what?" If all that we intended to show is that *PM* logic is incapable of expressing what-statements, or of marking in any unequivocal way the difference between essential and accidental predicable relationships, then it would seem that the foregoing discussion had succeeded in doing no more than to point up the trivial and the obvious. For who would deny that what-statements, as we have described them, are quite outside the scope of the new logic and simply cannot be formulated within it? For that matter, it is not just that the new logic is unable to formulate what-statements; it does not want to!

Even so, supposing that we have done no more than call attention to what every right-thinking modern logician would admit, our purpose nonetheless was the ulterior one of showing that instead of there being only one logic, there might well be more than one — i.e., more than one instrument or device for understanding and expressing the way the world is. More specifically, we wanted to argue that the world as seen through the eyes of a relating-logic is bound to be very different from the world as seen through the eyes of a what-logic. Now to this larger and more ambitious claim, the rejoinder is likely to be not so much "So what?" as simple bafflement. For it is not the wont of modern logicians, or even of modern philosophers, to say nothing of modern men, to address themselves to

philosophical issues of this sort, for might not such an issue come dangerously close to being metaphysical? Still, if they could be got to face the
issue, it is not hard to imagine what they would say. In all likelihood,
they would maintain that although a superficial case might be made out
for a what-logic's being a different sort of logic from a relating-logic, still
when the claims of such a what-logic are subjected to careful analysis
it will turn out that these claims cannot properly be maintained. And what
these modern critics would particularly wish to single out for attack in
such a what-logic would no doubt be those same what-statements which
by our account are the peculiar stock in trade of this very kind of logic.
"For what-statements," these critics would insist, "can surely be no more
than mere analytic truths."

Just what is the import of such a reduction of what-statements to analytic truths? [5] To see this, we have no choice but to tread again the dreary,
well-beaten path that leads to that still more dreary, well-worn notion
of analytic truth. And such a path leads directly back to the forbidding
figure of Kant himself, the originator of what some might take to be the
great red herring of modern philosophy, the notion of analytic truth. As
Kant characterized it, an analytic judgment is one in which "the predicate
B belongs to the subject A, as something which is covertly contained in
this concept."

5. There will be a certain ambiguity in our use of the term "what-statement."
From our use of the term so far, it should be clear that any subject-predicate proposition that is interpreted as involving an is-relationship must be a what-statement, because in any such proposition the predicate is used to express what the subject is.
Nevertheless, although all propositions involving is-relationships will at the same
time be what-statements, it must not be forgotten that there are various specific kinds of
is-relationships, and also of what-statements. Thus according to the Aristotelian doctrine of the predicables, there are no less than five different kinds of predicables or is-
relationships. Accordingly, simplifying this doctrine somewhat with respect to what-
statements, we might say that what-statements will differ from one another according
to whether their predicates express what their subjects are essentially or what they are
accidentally.

However, as we begin to turn our attention to the question of how what-statements
are to be compared and contrasted with analytic truths, or with synthetic a priori
truths, or more generally with necessary truths in the modern sense, it is obvious
that only those what-statements will be in question whose predicates express what
their subjects are essentially. Accordingly, we shall frequently use the term "what-
statement" as if such statements were simply equivalent to necessary truths. Strictly
speaking, however, only one or more species of what-statements are so equivalent, not
what-statements generally. Nevertheless, it should always be clear from the context just
which sense of what-statement is the relevant one.

If I say, for instance, "All bodies are extended," this is an analytic judgment. For I do not require to go beyond the concept which I connect with "body" in order to find extension as bound up with it. To meet with this predicate, I have merely to analyze the concept, that is to become conscious to myself of the manifold which I always think in that concept.[6]

So characterized, analytic judgments may be seen at once to have a number of still further properties or notes. For one, analytic judgments cannot be other than necessary truths, in the sense that to deny them could only be self-contradictory. That is to say, to deny a judgment such as "All bodies are extended" would, on Kant's analysis, be quite literally a case of taking back in the predicate what one had already given or conceded in the subject. For the concept of the subject term "body" already contains the concept "extended," so that to deny that any body was extended would be tantamount to denying that a body which was extended was extended.

Moreover, this necessity which pertains to analytic truths is of a rather distinctive kind, and one that is not always clearly noted and understood. For again, consider what is the precise incidence of the necessity in the case of such analytic truths. It is quite misleading to say that where the necessity in such judgments is to be found is in the connection between *A* and *B* (to use Kant's symbols); rather, what is necessary is not any connection between *A* and *B*, but the connection between *AB* and *B*. To see this more clearly, it might be well to take an altogether different example from the one of bodies being extended. For, naturally, in bringing forward this example Kant had been careful to condition his readers beforehand, so that they would consider the concept of "body" as already containing "extended" within itself. That is to say, the concept "body" was already supposed to mean "extended body." Hence an incautious reader might suppose that in the statement "All bodies are extended" the necessity might be taken to lie in a connection between *A* and *B*, whereas more properly it lies only in the connection between *AB* and *B*.

In any case, to bring this out more clearly, let us take an example of two concepts which presumably no one would consider to be necessarily connected at all — say, the concept of being a modern logician and that of being filled with the milk of human kindness. Surely, no one would want to assert, "All modern logicians are filled with the milk of human kindness," as if that were an analytic truth in the manner of Kant's example,

---

6. Immanuel Kant, *Critique of Pure Reason*, trans. Norman Kemp Smith (London: Macmillan, 1929), Introduction, § IV, B 11.

"All bodies are extended." Suppose, though, we simply take the notions of being a logician and of being filled with the milk of human kindness, and arbitrarily combine them to form a new concept, one of a truly remarkable new manner of man which we shall henceforth designate as a "logimilk." Accordingly, given this notion of a logimilk, it now becomes possible to assert as an analytic truth, "All logimilks are filled with the milk of human kindness." This assertion will be comparable to Kant's example, "All bodies are extended."

In other words, an analytic truth is quite unmistakably a necessary truth. But the necessity involved is never a necessity that holds between anything on the order of distinguishable features or notes or characteristics of things; rather it is always and only such necessity as holds between *AB* and *B*.

There is a second feature of the notion of analytic judgments as conceived by Kant. Not only will such judgments be necessary truths, in the sense just indicated, but they will also be judgments which are completely nonfactual, in the sense that they cannot and do not give us any information about any facts in the real world. As Kant observes in another passage: "The understanding in its analytic employment is concerned only to know what lies in the concept; it is indifferent as to the object to which the concept may apply." [7] Or putting the same point a little differently, he says, "An analytic proposition . . . is concerned only with what is already thought in the concept, it leaves undecided whether this concept has in itself any relation to objects." [8] In other words, a judgment such as "All bodies are extended" not only tells us nothing about physical bodies in the real world — they may not be extended at all in spite of what such an analytic judgment might seem to say to the contrary — but also such an analytic judgment does not even profess to be a judgment about real physical bodies; instead, it is a judgment only about our concept of "body," and what is contained in it.

A third or last feature would seem to pertain to analytic judgments as conceived and defined by Kant, although this feature is not one which, as far as we know, Kant himself ever recognized in so many words. For that matter, it is not a feature which at first glance seems altogether compatible with the second feature. Be this as it may, what this third feature amounts to is that analytic judgments not only give no factual information

7. *Ibid.*, B 314.   8. *Ibid.*

about the world, they give no information about anything — not even about what is contained in our own concepts. Or, put a little differently, not only are analytic judgments not about the world, they aren't really about anything of any specific nature at all.

Consider, what is the source of that necessity that attaches to analytic truths; what is it that makes them necessary truths, in the sense that they cannot be denied without self-contradiction? To such a question Kant's answer would presumably be that an analytic judgment merely analyzes or spells out in the predicate what is already contained in the subject: an analytic judgment, "as adding nothing through the predicate to the concept of the subject, but merely breaking it up into those constituent concepts that have all along been thought in it, although confusedly, can also be entitled explicative." [9] In other words, as we have already seen, "All bodies are extended" owes its character as a necessary truth simply to the fact that it says again in the predicate the very same thing that has already been said in the subject: "All bodies, being extended, are extended." Still, even supposing that in a given proposition "'the connection of the predicate with the subject" is, to use Kant's cumbersome expression, "thought through identity," just why should such an identity connection be a necessary one? Presumably the answer must be that "All extended bodies are extended" is a necessary truth by virtue of the more general principle that "All *A* is *A*." But from this a curious consequence would seem to follow: if "All extended bodies are extended" is true simply by virtue of the general principle "All *A* is *A*" (or "All *AB* is *B*"), then its truth would not seem to depend on anything having to do specifically either with the nature of extended bodies or even with the specific meaning of the concept "extended body"; however, if such a necessary truth, supposedly about extended bodies, is not dependent upon our knowing anything at all about such bodies, then surely it cannot be a truth about extended bodies. "I know, e.g., nothing about the weather when I know that it rains or does not rain" — so spake the late great voice from out of the whirlwind! Or was it the burning bush? [10]

In any case, in the light of this third feature, one can see how the notion of analytic truth can be extended and interpreted so as to be made equivalent to such currently fashionable notions as "formal truth" or "logical

9. *Ibid.*, B 11.

10. The quotation, of course, is from Wittgenstein's *Tractatus Logico-Philosophicus* (London: Kegan Paul, Trench, Trubner & Co., 1922), 4.461.

truth," a formal truth, for example, being defined as a proposition which is true not in virtue of its content or of what the proposition is about, but solely in virtue of its form — e.g., "Any *A* that is *B* is *B*" or "No non-*A* is *A*," and so on.

What-Statements: Necessary Truths about the World

So much then for the notion of analytic truth. Nor would it appear to require much in the way of either imagination or argument to understand how any proposal to construe what-statements as analytic truths would have the effect of eviscerating what-statements entirely. Yet such is just the proposal that contemporary analytic philosophers would tend by and large to accept almost without question.

To bring the issue directly to a head, suppose that we take Kant's example of "All bodies are extended," and that instead of taking this as an analytic truth we simply regard it as a what-statement. Placing this construction upon it, we should in effect be presupposing — and indeed it is a presupposition which ought not to put too great, even if it be a somewhat unfashionable, strain upon our imaginations — that we found ourselves to be living in a world of physical objects and that we simply wanted to know what such physical bodies really are. Our resulting judgment would be, somewhat in the manner of Descartes — or of Aristotle, too, for that matter — "Physical bodies are extended." This, in other words, is what we would take it pertained to the very nature of such bodies; it's just the kind of thing they are. Moreover, supposing further, just for the sake of argument, that we were right in our conjectures, and that there actually are such things as physical bodies and that what these bodies are is extended, then our what-statement turns out to be no less than what in modern parlance would be called a necessary truth about the world.

But now, presto chango! One has but to take precisely the same statement, "All bodies are extended," and construe it this time as being analytic, and immediately it ceases to be a necessary truth about the world. Indeed, it doesn't just cease to be such a truth, it becomes impossible for it to be such a truth. For putting together the first and second criteria of analytic truths, it turns out that any truth that is a necessary truth, in the sense that to deny it would involve one in self-contradiction, could not possibly be a truth about the world; and vice versa, any truth that is a truth about the world could not possibly be a necessary truth — unless, of course, having relaxed the first criterion of analyticity, one were then to admit the possibility of there being what Kant called synthetic a priori truths.[11]

However, so far as what-statements are concerned, this latter possibility is not an open one. For a what-statement is such that when it is true, it is necessarily true, precisely in the sense that the predicate term merely explicates or exfoliates what is already contained in the subject. That is to say, it is a necessary truth in the sense that it cannot be denied without self-contradiction. Indeed, in this one respect at least, what-statements are no different from analytic truths.[12]

In all other respects, however, a what-statement must surely differ, *toto caelo*, from an analytic truth. Consider once more our two examples, or rather our single example construed now as a what-statement and now as

11. The alternative of supposing that what-statements are to be understood not as being analytic truths, but rather as synthetic a priori truths, is one that we shall consider in the following chapter.

12. This point may occasion some surprise. For it is usual nowadays, among the few philosophers who are still inclined to challenge the current fashion of simply equating necessary truth with analytic truth, to insist that the only way to weaken such an equation is to acknowledge that there are truths which are necessary but which are not analytic, for the reason that they are synthetic a priori. Expressed in terms of the illustrations and formulas that we have thus far been using, the contention of these philosophers would be that the necessity of the connection of predicate with subject in a necessary truth is not to be understood as any mere formal connection of B with $A B$, but rather as a material connection of B with A. In other words, if "All A is B" is to be a necessary truth, but not in the sense in which "all $A B$ is B" is necessary, then the only alternative, it is usually supposed, is to regard it as being a synthetic judgment a priori.

One philosopher who chooses to follow this particular course, and does so with extraordinary skill and persuasiveness, is Professor Brand Blanshard in his Carus Lectures, *Reason and Analysis* (La Salle, Ill.: Open Court, 1962), especially Chap. 6, "Analysis and A Priori Knowledge." Indeed, the very telling critique which he mounts of the various flaccid discussions of necessity and necessary truth which recent analytic philosophers have been wont to put off on our largely uncritical present-day philosophical world is one that we would heartily subscribe to. Nevertheless, we cannot go along with the moral which Professor Blanshard would apparently want to draw from his lively tale of current analytic philosophy. For he supposes that the only way to salvage necessary truths that are other than trivial and vacuous is to plump for truths that are synthetic a priori. However, as we shall try to show later, synthetic a priori truths, no less than analytic truths, are a resource of a relating-logic, and hence improper to and incompatible with a what-logic.

Our task in the current chapter, however, is to show that even if one accepts the first criterion of analyticity, viz., that the predicate is analytically contained in the subject, it is still possible to develop an account of necessary truth that will be free from the usual disabilities that are associated with the notion of analytic truth.

analytic. Thus "All bodies are extended" construed as a what-statement is a truth about bodies. But construed as analytic, this same statement will no longer be about bodies, but rather, applying the second of the two criteria of analyticity, it would presumably only be about "bodies." That is to say, an analytic truth merely explicates what the term or concept "bodies" means, whereas a what-statement purports to state what bodies themselves are. Likewise, if we should choose to apply the third criterion of analyticity, we should need to say that "All bodies are extended" is really not about either bodies or "bodies." In order to know that such a statement is true, one does not need to know — or at least such is the contention — anything about the nature of bodies or the meaning of "bodies"; rather, all that one needs to know is the purely formal truth that AB is B. In sharp contrast, though, if "All bodies are extended" is taken as a what-statement, then one does need to know specifically what physical bodies themselves are, in order to put it forward as a necessary truth that all bodies are extended: this is no mere formal truth, but a material truth, precisely about physical bodies.

Conceding then that there is a radical difference between what-statements and analytic truths, let us imagine ourselves as simply going along with the great majority of modern logicians and analytic philosophers in repudiating what-statements altogether and in recognizing only analytic truths. Must not the consequence be that we should thereby commit ourselves to the use of a markedly different sort of logic from that which all of us may be presumed to employ in our ordinary everyday thought and discourse about ourselves and our world? For in a logic that will acknowledge no necessary truths other than analytic truths, not only will one not be able to say or to think what anything is, but even the very whats or characters (that in our more naive moments we might suppose the things of our everyday world to have) must turn out to be not anything at all, or at least not anything real. Thus, for instance, a thing's being an apple rather than an oasis in the desert, a middle c sound rather than a logician, a stroke of the oars rather than a line of English poetry, we should normally suppose must necessarily involve certain real, determinate features and characteristics, much as being a physical body might be supposed really and necessarily to involve being extended. Yet if the only logical instrument that one recognizes as the proper means for expressing such necessary features of things is an analytic truth, then the inevitable consequence will be that the very notion of what an apple is or what a middle c sound is or what a physical body is must simply be ruled out as meaningless. For what a given thing is and is necessarily cannot even be expressed in a logic of analytic truths; all that admits of being necessarily true is what a given word or concept means.

Moreover, the upshot of one's thus eliminating what-statements from one's logic in favor of analytic truths may now be seen to amount to nothing but the elimination of all real necessity from nature and from the world, and the relegating of such necessity exclusively to the sphere of the mere meanings of our words and concepts. Also, the minute the necessity of a body's being extended — to recur again to our prime example — is transmogrified into a mere necessity that is consequent upon just which notes we may happen to have packed into the meaning of our concept "body" and which ones we have chosen to leave out, then it is not the nature or essence itself of a physical body that determines whether it is extended or not,[13] but rather it is we ourselves and our own conventions

13. The point made here will be readily recognized as one that is associated with a certain classical metaphysical or ontological doctrine which obviously lies quite beyond the scope of this book. Suffice it to say that the issue as it here emerges, in the context of our total effort to draw a contrast between two logics, is what the source is of the unity that enables us to think of something as being one kind of thing rather than another. It was this question which Aristotle wrestled with in Book VII of the *Metaphysics* (see especially Chaps. 4 and 12), where he asks why it is that *man,* for example, even though composite, is one kind of thing, one essence, whereas *white man* ("cloak") is not one kind of thing, not a single essence at all — nor is the *Iliad* one kind of thing either, in that it may be said to be a single definable essence. (Cf. Aquinas' effort to deal with this same question as to the unity of so-called composite essences. See *On Being and Essence,* trans. A. Maurer [Toronto: Pontifical Institute of Mediaeval Studies, 1949], Chap. 2.)

So far as modern analytic philosophers are concerned, with their doctrine of analytic truth, there simply is no metaphysical or ontological problem as to how the various component elements in a composite essence are united together to form one essence; for these philosophers it is we human beings who do the uniting, and we do it, as it were, arbitrarily and simply to suit our own needs and interests. It is in this sense that the notion of "logimilk" might be taken as a paradigm of how our concepts of the *whats* of things are constituted and put together.

On the other hand, in the context of a what-logic, where through the device of what-statements we seek to know what things are (as contrasted with our mere names and notions of things), it is impossible not to recognize that the unity which pertains to one kind of thing as over against another kind, or to one nature or essence as over against another, has a real or metaphysical source and not a mere source in human decision and convention.

At the same time, this question — whether the unity that attaches to the so-called natures or essences of things is a properly essential unity or only a conventional one — is but indirectly connected with that of the logical necessity that attaches to so-called necessary truths. For whether such necessary truths are construed as being analytic or as what-statements, in

and stipulations as to the meanings of our words and concepts that determine whether "being extended" is included in the notion of "body" or not. It is in this sense that our earlier example of "logimilk" might be regarded as almost a paradigm of how it comes to be determined just which notes enter into the composition of a given concept and which do not: it is *we* who determine this.

Perhaps it is possible now to begin to see how analytic truths, as we have been describing them, cannot fail to be a favorite resource of what we have chosen to call a relating-logic. For a relating-logic, as we have seen, is one which seeks to understand things not in terms of what they are, but rather in terms of their relations to other things. And, in turn, these relations, in terms of which things are thus supposed to come to be understood and rendered intelligible, are not real relations in the world so much as they are logical devices and arrangements which we human beings have set up in the interests of such intelligibility. Accordingly, the logical or linguistic relations that are involved in our concepts and propositions are in nowise relations that are determined by the way the world is; rather it is we ourselves who determine these relations, in the sense that we actually do the relating. Little wonder, then, that a concern such as that of seeking to know what physical bodies are, viz., extended, should not be a concern appropriate to a relating-logic. Rather, in the case of the latter, the concern shifts from one of seeking to know what physical bodies are to one of determining which notes we wish to relate to which others in fleshing out the meaning of a given term or concept, "physical body," for example.

Nevertheless, we cannot leave the issue of analytic truths vs. what-statements simply at that. Granted that analytic truths are not propositions of the same kind as what-statements, and that a logic that admits only of analytic truths to the exclusion of what-statements must be an entirely different sort of logic, still the challenge which the notion of analytic truth poses for a what-logic is not simply that of an alternative logic. Rather, the decisive challenge lies in the fact that the proponents of analytic truths invariably assume that what-statements are nothing but analytic, that they are directly and properly reducible to analytic truths,

---

either case the purely logical necessity of the proposition is derived from the formal connections of the predicate B with the subject A B. Accordingly, it is not in respect to this logical necessity of necessary truths that the champions of what-statements take issue with the proponents of analytic truths. Instead, their differences turn rather on the question of whether the unity of A B is a real essential unity or only an arbitrary and fabricated one.

indeed, that there are no proper what-statements at all, and hence no such things as a what-logic of any kind.

Just what is the basis of such an assumption? Surely on the face of it the assumption does seem a bit incredible. For to put it crudely, a statement about bodies is decidedly not a statement about "bodies." Indeed, to suppose that it is would be a bald confusion of what modern logicians would call "use" with "mention." If we again recur to one of Kant's ways of characterizing analytic truths, viz., that "in its analytic employment, the understanding is concerned only to know what lies in the concept [and] is indifferent as to the object to which the concept may apply," then it scarcely needs pointing out that in its employment of what-statements the understanding is not at all concerned with what lies in the concept, but is concerned with the very object to which the concept is taken to apply. In other words, all the evidence seems to point to the fact that what-statements have a logical character that makes them radically different from analytic truths. How then, could the curious assumption have ever gained currency that what-statements are nothing but analytic truths?

Presumably, the basis of the assumption lies in the first of the above-mentioned criteria of analytic truths, viz., that "the predicate *B* belongs to the subject *A*, as something which is covertly contained in that concept," with the result that for anyone to deny such a predicate of such a subject would involve one in an express contradiction. Now it is just this first criterion of analyticity — a criterion which we have suggested is equally pertinent to what-statements — that is generally supposed to lead to and even to entail the second criterion, viz., that analytic truths cannot be truths about the world, that they are entirely non-factual, being in effect no more than assertions as to what is contained in our own ideas or concepts and not at all assertions as to the objects to which such ideas and concepts are taken to apply. Thus to quote again one of Kant's ways of characterizing the situation, in affirming that all bodies are extended, "I do not require to go beyond the concept which I connect with 'body' in order to find extension as bound up with it. To meet with this predicate I have merely to analyze the concept." Kant might have added, I do not need to consider the object to which that concept applies at all. To put the contention even more succinctly: in order to know that all bodies are extended, I do not need to consider bodies, I need only consider "bodies." [14]

14. Professor D. P. Dryer in his recent excellent book (*Kant's Solution for Verification in Metaphysics* [Toronto: University of Toronto Press, 1966], esp. pp. 85–98)

Why Analytic Truths at All?

Such, as we would suggest, are the grounds for the assumption that the first criterion of analytic truth somehow entails the second, and that in consequence any what-statement, in claiming to be a necessary truth, cannot be other than analytic. To be sure, the assumption still appears somewhat fantastic. For how can I possibly claim to be able to know about bodies by taking account of nothing more than "bodies," i.e., of nothing more than the meaning of the word or concept "bodies"? If my evidence is confined only to a knowledge of "bodies," then the necessary truth which I assert on the basis of such evidence would presumably have to be a truth only about "bodies" and not about bodies. Yet even the great Kant seems to have supposed that the statement that is analytic is precisely the statement "All bodies are extended," and hence not any mere statement as to the meaning of the word "bodies."

Moreover, unless we are very mistaken, Kant and all other partisans of the notion of analytic truth would appear to have fallen afoul of a rather simple *non sequitur* in their supposition that the second criterion of analytic truth is somehow necessitated by the first. Thus we all know that the word "concept," for example, is ambiguous: it can mean either (1) that idea or concept in the mind which means or signifies something other than itself; or (2) that which is thus conceived or meant or signified, i.e., the object that is so meant or conceived. Accordingly, when Kant insists that in order to know that all bodies are extended "I do not require to go beyond the concept which I connect with 'body' in order to find extension as bound up with it," he is entirely correct, if by "concept" he means that which is conceived, or the object to which the concept or the word "body" applies. For, "All bodies are extended" being a necessary truth, and one the opposite of which would be self-contradictory, one is required to consider only the nature of bodies and what pertains to them essentially — what they are, in other words — in order to recognize that essentially and necessarily they are extended. Yet merely because we need

---

emphatically denies that for Kant an analytic truth is never any more than a judgment "about the meaning of terms" — i.e., to recur to our own example, that an analytic judgment about bodies is never about bodies, but about "bodies." No doubt, as regards the historical question as to what Kant actually meant, Professor Dryer may be correct. But as to the more properly philosophical question of how, supposing that in Kant's eyes an analytic judgment about bodies is about bodies and not about "bodies," Kant could then suppose that analytic judgments could not possibly yield truths about the world, Professor Dryer unhappily does not speak.

consider only bodies in order to know that bodies are necessarily extended, why should Kant have supposed that this means that we need consider only "bodies"? Surely, this is a case of having confused the meaning of "concept" in sense (2) with its meaning in sense (1). Although it is undeniable that for the assertion of a necessary truth no more is required than an examination of the subject concept in sense (2), it certainly is not the case that all that is required is an examination of the concept in sense (1). Accordingly, the supposed entailment of the second criterion of analytic truth by the first is not an entailment at all, but a plain *non sequitur*. What is more, it is a *non sequitur* that seems to implicate one in an exceedingly dubious, not to say dangerous, confusion of use with mention: it inveigles one into talk about bodies, when presumably by the admission of the very defenders of analytic truth the sole evidence for such talk amounts to no more than a knowledge of "bodies." [15]

Indeed, the more one reflects upon the matter, the more incredible this entire notion of so-called analytic truth becomes. For what could ever have possessed Kant, not to mention almost the entire company of contemporary analytic philosophers, to have supposed that because a truth was a necessary truth, in the sense that its denial would be self-contradictory, it could not therefore possibly be a truth about the world? Might it be that so odd a doctrine was perhaps more the product of epistemological, than of properly logical, considerations? Considered merely logically, it would certainly seem that any number of the statements that we use in our everyday talk and thought about the world are clearly on the order of what-statements. They are, like "All bodies are extended," considered as being at once necessary truths and truths about the world. Moreover, such truths will be recognized as necessary precisely in the sense that, to use an old-fashioned term, they are self-evident.[16] In the above example, for instance,

15. It will be noted that in the present chapter our critical remarks are directed almost exclusively against the second criterion of analytic truth, and that we appear to say almost nothing about the third criterion. For this our excuse in part is that the third criterion of analyticity will reemerge later on as a somewhat analogous principle that is thought to govern deductive explanation and demonstration, at least as these latter are construed in a relating-logic. Accordingly, we shall have more to say on this score when we come to Chapter X.

16. We are also taking this term in what is presumably its old-fashioned sense, namely, of something *per se notum*. For an attempt to show in rather more detail just how this sense has a very direct bearing on current issues, see our article, "St. Thomas and the Question: 'How are Synthetic Judgments a priori Possible?'", *The Modern Schoolman*, XLII, No. 3 (March, 1965), 239–63.

it is recognized as pertaining to the very nature of a physical body to be extended, that this is simply what a physical body is, and that to suppose anything else would be tantamount to supposing that a physical body was not a physical body.

Could it be that just at this point the proponents of the doctrine of analytic truth suddenly find themselves beginning to get epistemological cold feet? "How can anyone claim," we can imagine them as asking, "that he knows all bodies to be extended necessarily and in fact? For to do so is to claim to have a universal and necessary knowledge of physical bodies in the real world. And what is this if not the height of presumption? Worse still, is it not actually a return to pre-Kantian dogmatism in philosophy? Surely, therefore, something must be amiss somewhere. What is it? Perhaps the trouble arises from one's thinking that the relevant necessary truth was a statement about bodies, whereas the evidence for the truth of the statement was entirely confined to one's concept of 'physical body.' Perhaps, therefore, we ought to revise our account of the logic of a statement like that of 'All bodies are extended': it isn't a statement about physical bodies at all, but only about our concept, 'bodies.' "

Very well, suppose that epistemological considerations of just this sort originally gave rise to the analysis of necessary truths as being no more than analytic: that is to say, since we cannot pretend to have a universal and necessary knowledge of bodies, it must be that our universal and necessary truth is not about bodies, but only about the meaning of the concept, "bodies." Suppose that all this is conceded, it still would not speak very well for the resultant logical analysis of "All bodies are extended." For, logically considered, that statement is patently about bodies; and regardless of the epistemological difficulties that may be connected with supposing such a statement to be a necessary truth about the world, they would hardly seem to justify the curious hocus-pocus whereby advocates of analytic truth would pretend that "All bodies are extended" is after all not about bodies but about "bodies." Epistemology aside, as a piece of straight logical analysis this surely commits the fallacy of confusing use with mention.

Further, the more one pursues the matter, the less likely it would appear that one can ever give a properly logical justification for construing any proposition as being analytic. To do so would, by the second criterion of analyticity, mean that the statement under consideration was not about the real world or the things in it at all. Yet just what would such a statement be like? And more specifically, would there be any properly formal logical criterion whereby such an analytic truth might be distinguished from a what-statement? Suppose we again consider two of our somewhat overworked examples of necessary truths: (1) "All logimilks are filled with the milk of human kindness"; and (2) "All bodies are extended." Now in view of our earlier explication of (1), it would seem clear that it certainly is not a statement about anything in the real world at all: logimilks, for better or for worse, just aren't a natural species; they are no more than a kind of fiction, an entity that we ourselves have deliberately fabricated. In contrast, (2) quite patently professes to be a statement about real objects in the world, viz., physical bodies. On the basis of such differences, then, are we to say that (1) is only an analytic truth, whereas (2) is a what-statement? If we answer "Yes," then indeed we should be conceding that the distinction between analytic truths and what-statements is based solely on material considerations. For in point of formal structure, both of these necessary truths would appear capable of being represented as having roughly the same form, "All *A*'s that are *B*'s are *B*'s."

Nevertheless, it must not be forgotten that in our foregoing discussions of the second feature of analytic truths, we have pretty much assumed, albeit without much explanation or justification, that one consequence of this feature might well be that since analytic truths are not able to be about things in the real world they must be restricted to our concepts of such things or the words used to describe them. For example, if (2) were to be construed as an analytic truth, then the proposition could not be taken to be about bodies at all, but rather about "bodies." But this clearly would involve a difference on the order of what modern logicians are wont to call a difference between the use and mention of terms, or of what the Scholastics called a difference in the *suppositio* of terms.[17] And might not such a difference provide a basis for a rather more properly formal distinction between analytic truths and what-statements? Let us put it to the test in terms of our examples. May we say, using scholastic terminology, that in (1) the *suppositio* of the subject term is of an entirely different type or kind from what it is in (2)? Or, to use more modern terminology, may we say that in (1) the subject term, viz., "logimilk," is not being used, so much as mentioned, whereas in (2) the subject, "bodies," is clearly being used and not mentioned? Supposing that we do answer such ques-

17. On this, see note 3 in Chapter IV.

tions in the affirmative, we would indeed appear to have got a properly formal criterion of the difference between analytic truths and what-statements, viz., that of the difference between mention and use.

Immediately, though, we can imagine a hostile critic saying that such questions cannot be answered in the affirmative at all, that in the case of (1), for example, it simply isn't true that the subject term is being mentioned but not used. If this were the case, then the subject "logimilks" would need to appear in quotes in the proposition. Instead, "All logimilks are filled with the milk of human kindness" is a perfectly straightforward assertion as it stands, without the subject term's having to be put in quotes at all.

Nevertheless, the upshot of such an objection may be rather different from what might at first be supposed. Far from having the effect of eliminating a possible formal logical difference between analytic truths and what-statements, it may actually serve to indicate that analytic truths turn out to have a somewhat different character from what has been traditionally supposed. Thus, recurring again to Kant's words, insofar as "the understanding in its analytic employment is concerned only to know what lies in the concept" and "is indifferent as to the object to which the concept may apply," it would seem that any properly analytic proposition that had to do with logimilks would have to be concerned only with the concept "logimilk" and not with such objects as the concepts may apply to — i.e., logimilks. After all, a concept such as "logimilk" may certainly be thought of as being applied to certain objects, viz., logimilks, just as the concept "gremlin" may be applied to gremlins, or that of "yahoos" to yahoos. True, in such instances these so-called objects to which the relevant concepts are applied will be no more than imaginary objects, or fictional entities. But whether they are purely imaginary objects or not, the distinction between such objects and our concepts of these objects is still a necessary and inescapable distinction.[18] Accordingly, if we follow Kant's

18. The considerations brought forward in this paragraph might be taken to have a direct bearing on those examples of purely analytic or linguistic truths which have become the stock-in-trade of so much of the English literature on the subject — viz., "A brother is a male sibling" or "A bachelor is an unmarried man." As soon as such sentences are uttered as statements, they quite obviously cannot be regarded as statements of fact. To say that a brother is a male sibling, for instance, is clearly not a statement of zoological import, but only a statement about how the word "brother" is used.

Now this point, just as it stands, may well be true: it is quite likely that a person who declares that a bachelor is an unmarried man may intend no more than a declaration about

own instructions for the analytic employment of the understanding, then any analytic judgment involving "logimilks" will be a judgment about "logimilks," not about logimilks, just as any analytic judgment having the term "physical bodies" as its subject will be a judgment about the concept "physical body," not about physical bodies.

To return to our examples, we can now see how (1) "All logimilks are filled with the milk of human kindness," just as it stands, is not, strictly speaking, an analytic truth at all, but rather a what-statement; it is a statement not about the concept "logimilk," but rather about the objects to which the concept applies. Similarly, with respect to (2), "All bodies are extended," just as it stands, this is not, and cannot be, an analytic truth, whatever Kant may have thought to the contrary; instead, it is quite patently a what-statement, inasmuch as it is a statement not about "bodies" but about bodies.

Analytic truths, then, in all strictness would appear able to be truths only about the concepts or the words that we use, and never about the things or objects which we use our words or concepts to signify. They would have to be truths on the order of " 'Physical body' is a notion that includes 'extension' as one of its notes," or "The term 'logimilk' is used to designate only fictional entities." Moreover the formal logical difference between analytic truths and what-statements thus turns out to be simply a difference between sentences or propositions in which certain terms are mentioned but not used, and sentences or propositions in which those same terms are used but not mentioned. And there we have it, surely! At long last, we seem to have got our desired distinction between analytic truths and what-statements, and a properly formal distinction at that, too.

Still, we wonder if we should or even can stop here. For having succeeded in establishing the integrity and independence of what-statements by restricting the domain of analytic truths to that narrow sphere of state-

English usage, in which case he would really be talking about "bachelors" and not about bachelors. Nevertheless, even if sometimes we do mean no more than this when we utter so-called necessary truths, it certainly does not follow that we never mean any more than this. Thus Blanshard (p. 255) is quite right to point out that whatever may be true as regards the use of a sentence like "All bachelors are unmarried," statements like "A straight line is the shortest line" or "A material thing cannot be in two places at once" would scarcely seem to be in a like case.

Quite apart from this, and even acknowledging that upon occasion in making statements we may appear to be using a certain subject term, whereas in fact we are only mentioning it, that still does not preclude the possibility that on other occasions we may use the very same sentence in such a way that the subject is really used and not mentioned.

ments and propositions that merely mention their subject terms and don't use them, why might it not be possible to go a step further and eliminate analytic truths altogether? For why should the mere fact that one makes a statement about a concept or word preclude the possibility of its being a what-statement? Why, in other words, may not one assert what a given word or concept is, and what it is necessarily and in fact? For instance, suppose I say, "The notion of 'physical body' cannot be conceived apart from the notion of 'extension,'" or "A concept such as that of 'physical body' is capable of functioning either as subject or as predicate in an S-P proposition." Could I not claim in such instances to have enunciated certain necessary truths that are informative and do give information, not about the world, to be sure, but still about a certain concept, viz., that of "physical body"? And if so, then are not my assertions what-statements and not analytic truths at all?

Just as we earlier found that the mere fact that a statement is about a purely fictional entity such as a logimilk does not suffice to make it analytic or preclude it from being a what-statement, so now we see that the mere shift from the use to the mention of a term — e.g., from talk about physical bodies to talk about "physical bodies" — does not suffice either to render a statement analytic or to preclude it from being a what-statement.

What, then, is the proper mark or criterion by which one may recognize that a certain statement is an analytic truth, rather than a what-statement? Alas, there just do not seem to be any. Recalling those criteria which we mentioned earlier as pertaining to analytic truths, it would appear that there is really no way in which one can succeed in applying the second of the three criteria so as to distinguish analytic truths from what-statements. For supposing that an analytic truth is not a truth about the world, but only about what is contained in the subject concept of the proposition in question, then does that mean that analytic truths are about mere fictional entities, or does it mean that they are truths in which the subject term of the proposition is mentioned but not used? Apparently, it does not mean either one. Or if it does, then as we have just seen, neither alternative suffices to enable one to distinguish an analytic truth from a what-statement.

Perhaps, though, there is a third alternative. And perhaps we have still not managed to put our finger directly on the sort of proposition which Kant had in mind when he insisted that analytic truths must not be construed as being about the object to which the subject concept of the proposition applies, but rather about that which lies in the subject concept itself. Presumably, in the light of what we have just seen, Kant may well not have meant that such an analytic statement was to be construed as being about the subject concept, in the sense that such a concept having been used in one proposition it now comes to be mentioned in another proposition and so is made the object of still another subject concept. No, for that would mean that such a subject concept was now no longer functioning precisely as a subject concept, but rather as the object of another such concept; and this would violate Kant's stipulation that in an analytic truth one is concerned not with the object of the subject concept, but rather with the concept itself and with its functioning as subject. If such is the sort of thing which Kant had in mind, then his stipulation as to the character of analytic truth may now be seen as a sheer logical impossibility; and with it, the very criterion of analytic truth which he laid down becomes an impossibility as well. For it is as if Kant were requiring that in an analytic truth the subject concept should be regarded not as being used but as being mentioned, and yet not as being mentioned either. Rather it is as if the subject concept were somehow to be caught or seized in its very use, and yet without its being thereby made into an object of still another concept. That is to say, in an analytic truth the subject concept will not be used, so much as considered in its use, and yet still in such a way as not actually to be mentioned.

Put a little differently, one might say that Kant seems to have envisaged analytic truths as being not about any objects meant, but only about meanings, and yet in such a way that these meanings will not in turn be meant at all. "But how can this be?" you will ask. The answer is, "It can't be. An analytic truth is a sheer logical impossibility." What is one to say then of the entire conception and account of analytic truth as first propounded by Kant, and then subsequently and uncritically repeated by countless neo-analytic philosophers? Surely there would appear to be little else to say than "Bah, humbug!" [19]

19. It might seem that nothing would be easier than simply to read the quite literally unintelligible notion of analytic truth right out of the philosophical vocabulary. But we cannot do this, for, be it sheer humbug or not, the notion of analytic truth has become so much a part of the very substance of what we have chosen to call a relating-logic that we cannot very well go on talking about the latter without drawing in the former. Accordingly, we shall continue to make references to analytic truth, even though we must confess ourselves quite unable to say just what such a truth is.

Chapter IV

The What-Statements of a What-Logic:

Why They Are Not Synthetic Truths

THE PRECEDING CHAPTER attempted to give the very notion of analytic truth an out-damned-spot treatment. But, unhappily, the tradition of such a treatment has long been that it doesn't work, that, in fact, "all the perfumes of Arabia," etc., etc. We can readily imagine how many partisans of a neo-analytic philosophy will make but a facile and fatuous response to our strictures on analytic truth: "Suppose that your precious what-statements are not to be shuffled off as mere analytic truths; then they must be synthetic truths. And if synthetic, they will find themselves to be no less at home within the confines of a spider-logic than if they were analytic."

But this won't do either. Indeed, to treat what-statements as synthetic, whether synthetic a priori or synthetic a posteriori, would be no less a violation of their integrity than to treat them as analytic. Nevertheless, before we speak directly to this issue, it might be well if once again we tried to make somewhat clearer the nature and basis of the claim that what-statements are capable of mediating necessary truths, which at the same time are truths about the world. The very philosophical charter and title deed of any logic on the order of a what-logic is the simple, and presumably self-evident, principle that things are what they are, and that our knowledge and understanding of things can ultimately come only through a recognition of this. Challenge it, and a what-logic does not even have the necessary standing in court to plead its own cause. On the other hand, if it is true that things are what they are, then the propositions in which we assert what they are must be necessary truths. Moreover, it would seem that the necessity of such necessary truths can only proceed from the very natures of the things that the propositions are about, or that make up their content. All such considerations may be fairly obvious, yet they have so frequently been either neglected or misconstrued that perhaps it would be well to examine them more closely.

Suppose that the principle mentioned above is taken as a basic ontological principle, or principle of First Philosophy, viz., that each thing is what it is. Or it might simply be said that nothing can be or exist without being something. From this, then, it can readily be seen that what a thing is in this sense, it is necessarily, and not just contingently.

Of course, in particular concrete cases it may be far from easy to determine unequivocally just what is of the essence of the thing in question and what is only accidental to it. Inasmuch as we have already taken Professor Quine's distinguished name in vain, perhaps he will not mind if we borrow it again, this time to fabricate around it a curiously fanciful difficulty in regard to the determination of just what he, Quine, is essentially. Suppose, on the one hand, that we bring forward a peculiarly bluff, down-to-earth, matter-of-fact sort of individual who exclaims, "Quine, you say? Well, of course, if Quine — or, for that matter, if anything or anybody else whom you care to mention — is anything at all rather than just nothing, then of course there is something that he is necessarily or essentially. Otherwise, he would not be identifiable even as being himself. Thus take the fact of Quine's being a logician. This must surely be something that he is only contingently, in the sense that were he not a logician, or should he cease to be one, or should he never have become one in the first place, still he, Quine, would nevertheless be what he is, i.e., he would still be the person, thing, being, or entity that he is. The latter, in other words, would thus be

91

what Quine is essentially or necessarily, as contrasted with his being a logician, which is something that he is only accidentally or contingently."

But now, on the other hand, suppose we imagine some peculiarly cranky and captious character, perhaps even a logician, or at least someone who is very sensitive about the honor of logicians. Let us suppose that such a person feels that to deny that Quine is essentially a logician would be an insult to the dignity and integrity of all logicians, to say nothing of being a grave injustice to Quine himself. Thus we might imagine such a person's making this rejoinder: "But come now, if it is the great logician Quine whom you are talking about, in his case being a logician is by no means something that he is only contingently. Far from it, for Quine just wouldn't be Quine if he were not a logician. In fact, he is nothing but a logician, that being no less than the be-all and end-all of his existence. Though the comparison is in many ways far from apt, one might nonetheless call to mind those creatures of Swift's fantasy in whom curiosity had become so identified with their very being as to render each of them nothing but one great, enormous ear. Now of course this is not to say that Quine as a logician is quite like that. Yet much as in the case of one of those all-eared beings, of whom it would scarcely be correct to say that they were even human beings at all, but simply ears, so analogously in the case of Quine, his being human might be a matter of really no essential import, as compared with his being a logician!"

Suppose such a fancied interchange does show how difficult it may be to determine with respect to any particular thing or entity just what it is essentially, still is not the principle of the distinction between essential and accidental, or between necessary and contingent, traits thereby confirmed and reinforced? That which a person, thing, or entity is, in the sense that he would not be the thing that he is without it, is what he is essentially; and that which he is, but without which he would still be the person, thing, or entity that he is, is what he is only contingently. It is not hard to see what the general sense is of the necessity on the one hand, or the contingency on the other, that is said to attach to propositions which assert what a given thing is essentially, as over against those which assert what it is accidentally. Thus when a proposition in such a case is said to be necessary, this but points to the fact that were one to deny rather than to affirm of the subject in question that which it is essentially, then one's proposition would be self-contradictory. For instance, if a given figure drawn on the board were that of a triangle, then to assert that it was not a triangle would be not merely false, but self-contradictory. On the other hand, to say that it is now

lighted up by the rays of the sun streaming through the window of the classroom would be to assert of that same figure something that was surely
no more than contingent.[1]

Moreover, just as the principle applies, to any and every concrete particular thing or entity in the world, that such a thing is what it is, essentially and not just contingently, so the same principle applies, though as
it were on a different level, with respect to the very *whats* or natures or
essences themselves of these same individual things or entities. Thus, just
as Quine is something or other and is so necessarily, so likewise that very
character or nature which is Quine's is specifiable in a certain determinate
way and not otherwise, and it is so necessarily. Indeed, as we have already
had occasion to note in the preceding chapter, just as we can ask what
Quine is, and answer that he is a logician, or is human, or what not, so
also we can ask what a logician is or what a human being is. Nor can the
answers to such questions be put forward as other than necessary truths.
After all, just as a triangle simply is the kind of figure that it is, so also a
logician is a certain kind of being too, however odd; nor is a human being
any less the kind of being that it is, than a logician is the kind he is; and
similarly, for any and all of the other types and kinds of things there are.
Moreover, when one undertakes to say what any particular kind of thing
is — say, that a triangle is a three-sided rectilinear figure, or that a human
being is a rational animal — then one cannot put forward such assertions
as being other than necessary truths. For they are no more than specifications of the principle that any one kind of thing is the kind of thing that it
is; and to suppose that it were not would be patently self-contradictory.

The Analytic-Synthetic Distinction as Irrelevant to What-Statements

With these explanations behind us, it should now be possible to see just
how and why what-statements cannot properly be construed as being synthetic, any more than they can rightly be construed as analytic. For to

---

1. Needless to say, any such distinction between essential and accidental would be
sharply contested by latter-day advocates of the doctrine of internal relations. For that
matter, we might as well plead guilty to the still more general charge that we have
failed to give any sort of account of how it is that the essence or nature of a thing
exists in that thing and so causes it to be the very thing that it is. These, however, are
all metaphysical or ontological questions, and as such lie beyond the scope of our present inquiry. We are concerned here only with the logical character of statements or
propositions that assert what a thing is essentially (or accidentally), and not at all with
the ontological character of that real state or condition of things which such statements
or propositions assert or may be said to be about.

construe them as synthetic would be to take them as either synthetic a posteriori or as synthetic a priori. But synthetic a posteriori they cannot be, for that would go counter to their character as necessary truths.

Why, though, might they not be synthetic a priori? After all, if the account of what-statements which we gave in the preceding chapter is correct, then such statements are materially true; they are not true simply in virtue of their formal logical or linguistic structure. Or put a little differently, what-statements, since they do not represent mere verbal explications or exfoliations of what is already contained in their subject terms or concepts, quite unequivocally purport to be truths about the world. But are not these just the marks that are characteristic of synthetic judgments?

To meet this issue, let us begin by again having recourse to the description which Kant gave of synthetic judgments:

Either the predicate B belongs to the subject A, as something which is (covertly) contained in this concept A; or B lies outside the concept A, although it does indeed stand in connection with it. In the one case I entitle the judgment analytic, and in the other synthetic. . . . The former, as adding nothing through the predicate to the concept of the subject . . . can also be entitled explicative. The latter [i.e. synthetic judgments], on the other hand, add to the concept of the subject a predicate which has not been in any wise thought in it, and which no analysis could extract from it; and they may therefore be entitled ampliative.[2]

Surely, though, if we go by this characterization, what-statements as we have described them could no more be synthetic than analytic. For one thing, what-statements are indeed explicative rather than ampliative. And so far from its being the case that no analysis could extract the predicate from the subject of a what-statement, it is precisely by an analysis of the subject that we come to pronounce on what the subject in a what-statement is. To be sure, in the case of what-statements it may not be exactly the subject "concept" that is submitted to such a process of analysis and extraction; instead, what-statements being assertions about the world rather than simply about words or concepts, it is clear that what gets analyzed in such a statement is no mere concept, but rather the thing or entity which that concept is a concept of, or to which it "refers," to use Kant's term.

Again taking Kant's example of "All bodies are extended," and construing it as a what-statement rather than as analytic, being extended is

---

2. *Critique of Pure Reason*, trans. Norman Kemp Smith (London: Macmillan, 1929), A6 = B10–A7 =B11.

asserted to pertain to the very nature of physical bodies — not merely to our concept, "physical bodies," but to physical bodies themselves. Or, we have only to remind ourselves once more of the context of search and inquiry to which what-questions are appropriate and in which they naturally arise: confronted with things and happenings in the world about us, we want to know what they are — "What is this?" "What is that?" Suppose in answer to such a what-question, we recognize that the thing or object before us is a physical body. "And what is a physical body?" we may then ask. Quite patently, we here want to know what such a thing really is, and not merely what the word "body" means, or what is contained in our concept "physical body." Just as patently, we are not asking after something "additional to" or "outside of" that which is involved in being a physical body; on the contrary, we are asking precisely what it itself, viz., a physical body and considered just in itself and as such, is. But this must mean that a what-statement of the sort we are considering — and that is offered by way of answer to a what-question, arising in a context such as we have described — is neither analytic, it being a statement about things in the world and not merely about our concept of such things, nor synthetic, it being a statement that merely analyzes what such a thing as a physical body is, neither going outside it nor adding anything to it. In other words, Kant's dichotomy of analytic and synthetic sets forth alternatives that are neither exclusive nor exhaustive, and one can only marvel that Kant, or for that matter anyone else, should ever have thought them to be so.

Surely, though, in thus summarily dismissing the analytic-synthetic distinction, we are going much too far too fast. After all, it will hardly do to dismiss Kant as if he had been but a philosophical hippie who was concerned with nothing more than tossing off the analytic-synthetic distinction in a kind of defiant gesture of would-be self-commitment. While one might be inclined to be somewhat less charitable toward the numberless fashionable gentlemen-philosophers of the present day who so uncritically accept the Kantian distinction between analytic and synthetic, without ever stopping to ask whether it is justified or not, still there must be some reason other than blind post-Kantian traditionalism for the strange intellectual mortmain which this distinction has so long exercised in philosophy.

Superficially, of course, what makes the distinction so incredible from the point of view of a what-logic is that it tends to involve a patent confounding of two very different distinctions in logic. One is the distinction between propositions that are purely verbal, on the one hand, and propositions that are of substance, or, as the common expression is nowadays, are about the world, on the other — for example, the distinction between " 'Brother' is an expression for male sibling" and "An accident cannot exist save as an accident of a substance." [3] The other is the distinction in predicable relationships between propositions in which the relation of predicate to subject is an essential one and propositions in which the relation is only accidental — for example, the distinction between "Men are animals" and "Men are miserable." [4] In other words, the confusion that is involved here is the one which we have so persistently been trying to point up with our question, "Why, just because a proposition is a necessary truth, must one suppose that it is purely verbal and hence not a truth about the world?"

The Problem of Truth-Conditions in What-Statements

So much, then, for the seeming enormity of the analytic-synthetic distinction. In defense of the distinction, however, one might consider a serious difficulty which any theory of what-statements such as we have been expounding can scarcely avoid, and yet which a theory of propositions as classifiable into either synthetic or analytic would seem quite effectively to obviate. The difficulty we are referring to might properly be called a logical one, or perhaps still more precisely a semantic one: it concerns the question of what might be called the criterion for the truth of what-statements. Thus it is fashionable now always to ask, with respect to any given type of statement or assertion, just what the truth-conditions are for a statement of that type. For example, Waismann remarks:

3. In Scholastic logic, such a distinction would be in the so-called *suppositio* of terms, as in the case of the difference between " 'Man' is a three-letter word" and "Man is mortal." For an attempt to resurrect this distinction in a modern context, see H. Veatch, *Intentional Logic* (New Haven: Yale University Press, 1952), pp. 193–213.

4. One might, of course, object that this second distinction is not involved in the analytic-synthetic distinction at all. For while it might be said that a proposition in which the relation of predicate to subject is analytic bears some likeness to a proposition in which the predicate is essential to the subject, it could hardly be said that in a synthetic a priori proposition the predicate is only accidental to the subject. But why isn't the latter relation one of accident? For insofar as such propositions are synthetic, the predicate cannot be thought of as pertaining to the very essence of the subject. At the same time, such propositions being a priori, they must be universal and necessary. Accordingly, it would seem that this universality and necessity would be of a sort that would characterize only those features of a given subject which, though pertaining to the subject universally and necessarily, would nevertheless not be of the essence of the subject, and hence would be accidental.

Previous philosophers have almost always directed their attention to the *answers* given in reply to philosophical questions. Their disputes were all concerned with the answers, their truth or falsity, their proof or refutation. The new point of view differs from all the others in that, from the start, it ignores the answers and directs all its attention towards the questions. . . . If we want to understand the meaning of a question, we must know under what circumstances it should be answered by "yes," and under what circumstances it should be answered by "no." [5]

Surely, all this is reasonable enough. Very well, then, with respect to the original what-questions to which our what-statements were supposed to be proper answers, we need to ask, "Under what circumstances are questions of this sort to be answered 'Yes' and under what circumstances are they to be answered 'No'?" Suppose we take what-questions and answers of the sort we have already considered: "What is a human being?" — "A human being is a rational animal." "What is motion?" — "Motion is a transition of something from something to something else." "What is hydrogen?" — "Hydrogen is an element." Then suppose that we recast such questions and answers into the relevant question-form recommended by Waismann: "Is a human being a rational animal?" "Is motion a transition of something from something to something else?" "Is hydrogen an element?"

Once these questions are recast, it would seem that there could scarcely be any doubt, in view of our entire argument thus far, of just what the circumstances are under which such questions are to be answered "Yes" or "No." For we have been consistently emphasizing that what are involved here are necessary truths. Accordingly, the questions are to be answered "Yes," insofar as it is recognized that any other answer would be impossible, in the sense of being self-contradictory.

Yet no sooner do we thus set up something like self-evidence, or the opposite's being self-contradictory, as the criterion of the truth of what-statements than a most embarrassing consequence would seem to result. For how, then, will what-statements differ from mere analytic truths? Will not the truth-conditions of the one sort of statement be exactly the same as the truth-conditions of the other? More specifically, has not our argument tended to show that in what-statements, quite as much as in analytic statements, the predicate is supposed to be related to the subject by a certain distinctive sort of logical relation, which for want of a better

5. F. Waismann, *The Principles of Linguistic Philosophy*, ed. R. Harré (New York: St. Martin's Press, 1965), pp. 3–4, 20.

term may be called "containment"? Have we not also insisted that in what-statements, no less than in analytic truths, the test or criterion for the truth of the statement is that its opposite is self-contradictory? But must not this mean that there just are no distinguishable truth-conditions for what-statements, as over against those for analytic truths? And if there is no criterion whereby what-statements may be distinguished from analytic truths, will not the whole argument for their distinction in Chapter III simply collapse? [6]

Happily, however, our situation may not be quite so desperate as it might seem. For recurring briefly to the preceding chapter, it may be noted that in at least one place a suggestion was made that could well be taken to indicate how the truth-conditions of what-statements are after all different from those of analytic truths. In discussing how the second criterion of analyticity was nowise applicable to what-statements, we sought to make the point that what-statements are statements about the world — i.e., about what physical bodies really are in "All bodies are extended," or about what change or motion in fact is in "All change is necessarily of something from something to something else," or about what hydrogen is by its very nature, and yet at the same time really so and in fact, in "Hydrogen is an element." But in addition we implied that such professed what-statements might conceivably turn out to be false. After all, to take just the one example, is it not at least conceivable that what chemists today call hydrogen might turn out not to be an element after all? If it is a question of what hydrogen really is, there is at least a possibility that we might have got it wrong, that what we were once so certain must pertain to the very nature or essence of hydrogen — i.e., must simply be what hydrogen in fact is — might well not be so after all. True, such a possibility may well appear as simply incredible. Yet we need only remind ourselves that there once was a time when men were thoroughly convinced that it was of the very nature of the sun to be stationary, or of the planets to move in circular orbits. But the latter sort of what-statement about planets would now be thought to be clearly false. In other words, when it comes to knowing

6. This precise issue has been raised and aimed directly at the present writer in a very telling article entitled "Realism and Necessity Reconsidered," by Moltke S. Gram, in *The Review of Metaphysics*, XIX, No. 30 (March, 1966), 565–77. Professor Gram's article is in reply to still another article critical of our notion of what-statements as being necessary truths about the world. The latter article, by Ronald Jager, was entitled, "Realism and Necessity," and appeared in *The Review of Metaphysics*, XVIII, No. 4 (June, 1965), 711–38.

what things really are, then both a general humility and the repeated specific lessons of history counsel us to adopt a principle of falliblism, as C. S. Peirce called it.

Having once adopted this principle, then the truth-conditions of what-statements become quite different from those of analytic truths. It is more than a case of the former having the capacity of being false, whereas the latter do not. It would seem that in the case of analytic propositions truth criteria are at once necessary and sufficient conditions of the truth of such propositions as the predicate being contained in the subject, while in the case of what-statements, these criteria, although they are certainly necessary conditions, are by no means *sufficient* conditions, of the truth of such statements.

Put a little differently and somewhat more concretely, what this difference in truth-conditions comes down to is something like this. Supposing that hydrogen is an element, or that motion necessarily is of something from something to something else, then clearly the opposites of such what-statements would be self-contradictory. To say that hydrogen is not an element or that motion is not motion of something from something to something else would be tantamount to saying that hydrogen is not hydrogen or that motion is not motion — i.e., that neither of them is the thing that it is. In other words, if a what-statement is true, then it cannot be other than a necessary truth: that its denial would be self-contradictory is thus a necessary condition of any true what-statement.

On the other hand, it does not work the other way around. Given that a statement appears to be such that its opposite is self-contradictory, it does not necessarily follow that what we have is a true what-statement. To see this, we need do no more than call to mind once more the case of the seeming necessity of planets moving in circular orbits. Prior to Kepler, it seemed to men to be self-evident that planets should move in circular orbits; this was just the sort of thing that a planet was, and to suppose that the motion of planets might be other than circular would certainly have struck most men of the time as being tantamount to supposing that planets might not be planets. Yet as it turned out, the circular motion of planets proved not to be a necessary truth after all, and assertions to the effect that such motion pertained to the very essence of planets were eventually dismissed as false. So the fact that a statement appears to be such that its opposite is self-contradictory is by no means a sufficient condition of its actually being a true what-statement.

But this does seem to result in a curious situation, for it amounts to a proposal to regard propositions or statements of a certain type as having, at one and the same time, truth-conditions that presumably are mutually exclusive. Thus we were suggesting that a proposition such as "The planets can only move in circular orbits," considered as a statement about the natural world, is subject to the usual empirical procedures of verification and falsification. Yet if such empirical observation confirms the truth of this proposition, then it will also have to be recognized as a necessary truth, i.e., a truth that is self-evident, or evident in the light of the very nature of those entities that are called "planets." But how can a proposition on the order of a what-statement be considered, at one and the same time, evident in the light of experience and also self-evident?

The Devil Returns

With this question, it begins to look as if the analytic-synthetic distinction is like the devil: drive it out with a pitchfork, and it returns through the window! For no sooner do we acknowledge that it must be either through empirical evidence or through self-evidence, and not both, that the truth of a proposition must be made evident, than what we have is simply the analytic-synthetic distinction all over again. For if a proposition is evident just in and through itself — i.e., simply through the meanings of the terms involved [7] — then it is analytic, and as such cannot be false. On the other hand, if a proposition is falsifiable, in the sense that further

---

7. A word such as "meanings" in this context is dangerously ambiguous. Yet its ambiguous usage is so established as to make its use in such a connection practically unavoidable. Suffice it to say that if by "the meaning" of a term or concept one understands that which is meant by that same term or concept, then what necessarily pertains to "the meaning" in this sense will have to be determined not by a regard for the mere logical or linguistic or even psychological character of the term or concept, but rather by a regard for the objective nature or essence of that which is signified by the term or concept. Meaning in this sense would then provide the basis for necessary truth in precisely that sense of necessary truth that we are ascribing to what-statements. On the other hand, if by "the meaning" of a term or concept one understands simply those notes or features which happen to be either conventionally or arbitrarily associated with a particular word or concept, then such meaning would be sufficient to provide the basis for necessary truth in the sense of analytic truths. In this latter sense of meaning, the truth of an analytic proposition may be determined simply in the light of the meanings of the terms involved and quite irrespective of those features of the real world which those terms or that proposition happened to be about. Cf. our earlier discussion of "concept" in Chapter III.

experience might upset it, then by this very criterion it can be no more than empirically evident, and as such synthetic.[8]

Moreover, this very dichotomy between analytic and synthetic, as well as the dichotomy between the truth-conditions of self-evidence and of empirical evidence, has come to be, as it were, fixed and frozen as a result of the standard analysis of propositions that has been given in the context of modern logic. Thus we are all familiar with how a what-statement like "All planets move in circular orbits" — supposing it to be interpreted as a necessary truth about the world — is not really in proper logical form at all, but rather is exponible as two propositions rather than one:

(1) "If anything is a planet, then it can only move in a circular orbit."

(2) "There are such things as planets," or "Planets do exist."

Accordingly, taking (1) as analytic,[9] then (1) will be true necessarily and in virtue of the meanings of its terms alone. Also, the truth of (1) will be completely unaffected by the truth or falsity of (2). If (2) is true, then such planets as there are will, of course, move in circular orbits, simply by definition and in virtue of the truth of (1). On the other hand, if (2) is false, then (1), being purely hypothetical, will not be in the least affected as to its truth by the falsity of (2).

Indeed, on the particular analysis of what we have been calling what-statements that was developed so effectively by C. I. Lewis, any such statement must be exponible first as a proposition on the order of (1),

---

8. It will be noted that these alternatives of analytic and synthetic leave quite out of account the possibility of the still further alternative of synthetic a priori propositions. For these latter propositions are held to be of such a kind as to be neither true in the sense that their truth is determined simply on the basis of the meanings of the terms contained in them, nor falsifiable in the sense that further experience might upset them. On the contrary, their truth can be assured only through the operation of a transcendental apparatus of a Kantian sort: "Synthetic *a priori* judgments are thus possible when we relate the formal conditions of *a priori* intuition, the synthesis of imagination and the necessary unity of this synthesis in a transcendental apperception, to a possible empirical knowledge in general. We then assert that the conditions of the *possibility of experience* in general are likewise conditions of the *possibility of the objects of experience*, and that for this reason they have objective validity in a synthetic *a priori* judgment" (*Critique of Pure Reason*, A158 = B197).

9. Since (1) is a hypothetical and not a categorical proposition, to call it "analytic" is surely to stretch the meaning of analytic. Yet even though (1) can scarcely be said to be analytic in the sense that the concept of the predicate is already contained in that of the subject, it is analytic in the broader sense of being supposed true not on the basis of the way the world is, but simply on the basis of the meanings of the terms involved. Thus see Brand Blanshard, *Reason and Analysis* (La Salle, Ill.: Open Court, 1962), pp. 257–86.

which will be true simply in virtue of the meaning of its terms, and second as a proposition on the order of (2), which of course will be subject to the test of experience. Moreover, in regard to a statement like (2), the issue of its truth or falsity is simply an issue as to whether any things exist in the world that might be subsumed under the concepts defined in statements on the order of (1). Thus, so far as (1) specifically is concerned, one cannot say that this Aristotelian or Ptolemaic principle was ever upset by modern scientific evidence. Instead, all this sort of evidence may be taken to have shown is that bodies on the order of planets in Ptolemy's sense just don't exist in the world. In other words, whereas in the context of ancient science (2) was held to be true, in the context of modern science empirical evidence has led us to believe that it is false.

So by the simple device of the exponentiation of what-statements into two propositions rather than one, the embarrassing situation of two apparently quite diverse criteria for the truth of what-statements is neatly avoided. For such statements are to be taken as involving on the one hand an assertion which is simply analytic and for which the truth condition is that of self-evidence, and on the other hand an assertion which is synthetic and of existential import, and the condition of whose truth is its verifiability or falsifiability in experience.

Faced, then, with this challenge to the validity and logical practicability of what-statements, is there anything further to be said in their defense? For taking what-statements at face value and in the way we have been urging that they be taken, it would seem that the criterion for the truth or falsity of such propositions is an impossible one: self-evidence and empirical evidence are equally necessary as truth-conditions of such statements, and neither is a sufficient condition; yet in the very nature of the case it would seem that these truth-conditions are mutually exclusive and so cannot be jointly operative.

The Devil Exorcized

To all this, however, we would make the direct rejoinder that appearances to the contrary notwithstanding, there isn't really any necessary incompatibility between these two truth-conditions at all; that, instead, there are very good reasons for recognizing the utility and even the indispensability of propositions which require both empirical evidence and self-evidence as criteria of their truth; and that if these truth-conditions are judged to be mutually exclusive, the result will be an impoverishment of our logical tools and instruments such as will make it impossible to say or to think certain things which, on more general philosophical grounds, it is quite important that we be able to say and to think.

Indeed, we believe that the case here is analogous to what emerged from our discussions in the first chapter. There we found that while it might be possible arbitrarily to decree that a function-argument schema for atomic propositions be used to replace the is-relationship of traditional S-P propositions, and while an entire logic could then be constructed on the basis of such a decree, still the logical costs of such a convention would be that we could no longer say or think what anything is. Analogously, in this present context, we would suggest that while it is possible simply by decree to rule out the possibility of a proposition's being subject at once to the truth-conditions of self-evidence and of empirical evidence, and thus to construct a logic which observes a rigid dichotomy between analytic and synthetic truths, once more the logical cost of such a convention will be to deprive us of the possibility of being able to say or to think, not merely what any given individual thing is, but rather what any kind or type or species of thing is.

Accordingly, in justification of this contention, let us once more consider carefully and in terms of specific examples just why and how the exigencies of the everyday knowledge that we have of our human world compel us, as it were, to recognize our what-statements as being both self-evident and empirically evident.

Doubtless we have already said enough to show that, just as a simple matter of fact, our everyday knowledge of our everyday world certainly does express itself in what-statements. Yet surely no one would consider that such knowledge as is embedded in these what-statements is innate, in such a manner as it was fashionable to suppose among the seventeenth-century rationalists. We do not come into the world knowing that hydrogen is an element, or that motion is always of something from something to something else, or that each thing is what it is, or that what is composite must be made up of simples, or even that men are animals. No, these are all truths that we come to learn, as we should certainly think, from experience.

At the same time, learning such principles from experience cannot be altogether like learning various empirical generalizations from experience — e.g., that a black cat's crossing one's path always brings bad luck, or that the melting point of silver is 960.5° C., or that a railroad tie that is hewn will last longer than one that is sawed. In the latter cases we are clearly conscious of our knowing only that the thing is so, without being able to understand why. But in the examples of the foregoing paragraph, the knowledge that we have of such principles seems to lack nothing in the way of evidence: we would not, for example, say that we knew only that whatever is composite is made up of simples, but didn't know why; on the contrary, the fact which is being asserted in the proposition strikes us as being perfectly evident just in itself.

Accordingly, from the common-sense view that we are currently adopting, while experience would certainly seem to be a necessary condition of our knowing the *whats* and basic principles of things in the world about us, at the same time it would appear to be by no means a sufficient condition. Experience alone, as Kant might say, does not suffice to yield the universality and necessity — or, as we would say, the self-evidence — that is so patently characteristic of what-statements of the kind cited above. And so, over and above the testimony of experience and of sensory perception, what-statements would also seem to be attested to by what may loosely be called the testimony of the intellect: they are principles that seem to be true by the light of reason, to use an old-fashioned phrase.

No sooner, however, does one thus describe the manner in which what-statements become evident to us than it would seem that the appeal to experience as a necessary condition for a knowledge of what-statements had thereby been tacitly abandoned altogether. One might continue to insist that experience was a necessary condition of such knowledge in the sense of a mere psychological necessity, much as Plato recognized that sensory presentations were necessary for our acquiring a knowledge of the Forms, inasmuch as such presentations provided a needed psychological stimulus, or prompting, to the properly intellectual act of anamnesis, or recollection. But that sensory experience should be in any logical sense a necessary condition of a knowledge of what things are would seem to be excluded by our very use of the expression "self-evidence" with respect to what-statements: such statements are seen to be true just in and of themselves, and not through any appeal to experience.

This last conclusion may still be an overhasty one. For if we are to continue to remain faithful to what we have called the common-sense point of view, or what Husserl would call the natural attitude, we must reckon with a curious but quite distinctive feature of what-statements. For the fact is that in seeking to know what things are, we are not seeking a knowledge of *whats* and essences as such, but rather a knowledge of what things *are*.[10] To put it another way, it is the *whats* of things, of real things in the real world, that we are seeking to know about. And for such knowledge, the senses are indispensable, it being through the senses, and only through the senses, that we are ever brought into any sort of actual cognitive contact with the concrete, particular existing things of the world. True, our senses and perceptual faculties as such do not suffice to inform us of what these things are, or even, in so many words, of the fact that they are; and yet it is only insofar as our intellectual faculties can be brought to bear on things that are thus presented in sensory perception that we can ever become informed of what these things are, or of the fact that they are.

In other words, in our ordinary, everyday, natural human attitude, what-statements unmistakably present themselves to us as necessary truths; and yet just as unmistakably they present themselves as truths about the world. Accordingly, this can only mean that, logically considered, such statements must be subject to a dual criterion, so far as the conditions of their truth are concerned. It is only through their being verified in experience that we can claim them to be truths as to what things in fact really are, and it is only through their own self-evidence that we can recognize them to be truths as to what these things are necessarily; each condition therefore is necessary for the truth of such a statement, and neither condition is sufficient.

What, then, of the difficulty as to how one and the same statement can be at once self-evident and empirically evident? The answer is that the difficulty should by now have simply evaporated, or rather that it should now be clear that there never was a difficulty in the first place, but only a superstition which we have been beguiled into accepting presumably because of the academic hold which the analytic-synthetic distinction has upon us. Yet we have only to step outside the philosophy classroom and into the open air of everyday human existence to realize that the things and events of the world are what they are necessarily and self-evidently; but for us to know what motion is, or what hydrogen is, or what the color red is, or what we ourselves as human beings are, we can do no other than accept the tutelage of experience, both in its initial promptings and in its continuing corrections.

10. Incidentally, should this point prove to be well taken, it would reflect seriously upon the propriety of that common dogma of modern logic according to which universal categorical propositions are to be interpreted hypothetically.

Chapter V

The Disabilities of a

Relating-Logic: The Fallacy

of Inverted Intentionality

SURELY IT IS HIGH TIME that we had some relief, preferably even comic relief. Let us, then, give over, for the time being, all talk of what-statements and a what-logic, and turn our attention to a consideration of a relating logic, particularly to its exigencies and disabilities. To this end, suppose we simply put to ourselves this question: What must the enterprise of human knowledge and understanding be like, so long as one restricts oneself simply to the instruments and devices of a relating-logic and solemnly forswears the use of what-statements altogether? For example, just consider the case of the late C. I. Lewis and his peculiar brand of so-called conceptualistic pragmatism. Here one finds an unusually lucid account of how it is thought possible to achieve a kind of knowledge of nature and of the natural order, armed chiefly with concepts which have quite arbitrarily determined meanings, the explication and exfoliation of which is simply a matter of purely verbal or conceptual analysis. To recur to our own well-worn illustration, suppose that our concept "planet" involved among its various notes that of moving in a circular orbit. As Lewis would see it, that this particular note should be contained in our concept of planet would be entirely of our doing, it being up to us to define our concepts in any way we might choose, packing into them only those notes that we ourselves might decide we wanted them to contain, and leaving out those that we did not want.

But our freedom ends there. Having once determined quite freely and by our own conventions just what notes shall pertain to a given concept, say that of "planet," then *that* concept has thereby become determined in that particular way and we are no longer free to say just which notes *that* concept contains. On the contrary, to explicate and exfoliate just what that concept involves is a matter of enunciating a series of analytic truths, each one of which simply unpacks from the subject concept "planet" what has already been put into it, and each one of which will therefore be a necessary truth in just the way that *AB* is *B* is necessary. In other words, our freedom nowise extends to the point of our being able either to accept or to reject such analytic truths simply at will.

It must also be acknowledged that while we are entirely free to legislate just what will go into our concepts and what will not, this freedom of legislation must nowise be thought to extend to the data of experience or to what is in the world. Thus, given our concept "planet," the proposition "A planet moves in a circular orbit" is necessarily entailed thereby, and is itself an analytic truth, hence necessary. Nevertheless, when we undertake to apply such a concept to the world and thus to characterize certain of the bodies which we observe in the heavens as being "planets" (in the sense defined, of course), it remains to be seen — i.e., it remains for empirical observation to determine — whether the things to which we have applied our concept "planet" are properly so-called or not. Indeed, so far as the present example goes, we have all been instructed *ad nauseam* by the scientists that the concept "planet," as we are supposing it to be defined, does not apply, nor do the so-called planets move in circular orbits at all. Does that mean, then, that the supposed analytic truth, "A planet moves in a circular orbit," is thereby rendered false? Not at all. It is just that, given the particular definition of "planet" that we have been supposing, the analytic truth, "A planet moves in a circular orbit," is shown not to be false, on the basis of experience, but simply irrelevant; and the concept "planet," instead of proving to be a useful and fruitful one so far as ordering our experience and describing the empirical world is concerned, might just as well be discarded.

Suppose that one does not fancy Lewis' particular way of showing how an understanding of the world can be effected through the use of logical instruments such as analytic judgments on the one hand and synthetic judgments on the other. One can receive a somewhat similar instruction, not to say illumination, by placing onself in Wittgensteinian hands and submitting to the leading strings of expressions like "rules of use," "language games," "the logical grammar" of expressions, etc. More specifically, instead of the notion of "analytic truths" one might prefer the more up-to-the-minute notion of "grammatical rule." Thus, as Waismann remarks:

> We spoke, in the examples, of *the analysis of the meaning*. In what does this consist? In nothing more than giving the rules for the use of a certain sign, whether a word or a mathematical symbol — for example, the rules for manipulating infinite series, the definition of simultaneity for events at different places, the logical rules for the use of the term "all." Now these rules of calculations, definitions, conventions etc., form only a small part of the body of rules governing the usage of our language. These rules are called the *grammar* of the language. . . .
>
> By grammar we mean everything about language which can be fixed before language is applied. We contrast grammar with the actual application of language. The relation between grammar and language is similar to that between deciding upon the metre as the unit of length and carrying out a measurement, or indeed between the adjustment of a telescope and an observation made through it. Grammar is, as it were, the installation and adjustment of signs, in preparation for their use.[1]

In other words, the distinction which Waismann here draws between "grammar," as that in language "which can be fixed before language is applied" and "the actual application of language" (or between "the installation and adjustment of signs" and the "use" of signs) is, it would seem, quite analogous to Lewis' distinction between analytic truths,[2] which turn on the arbitrary or conventional fixing of the meanings before they are applied, and synthetic truths, which involve the application of those meanings to experience.

Moreover, just as Lewis insists that we are completely free in determin-

1. F. Waismann, *The Principles of Linguistic Philosophy*, ed. R. Harré (New York: St. Martin's Press, 1965), pp. 13-14.

2. This is not to say, of course, that there are not also marked differences between rules of use and analytic truths. For one thing, the latter are truths, whereas the former are rules. Such differences, however, are irrelevant in the context of the present argument.

ing what the meaning of our concepts will be, i.e., what notes are to be packed into them and what notes left out, so also Waismann declares, "Grammar is autonomous and not dictated by reality." [3] By way of example, he takes the much debated example of "Nothing can be red and green simultaneously." Is this a fact of experience in the sense of being a necessary truth about the world? Waismann suggests that it is not, but rather that it is "a veiled grammatical rule which forbids the formation of the word-sequence 'something is red and green simultaneously.'" [4] Moreover, it is a rule which we might very well change if we so desired,[5] just as Lewis might say that we could perfectly well discard or put aside our particular concept "planet" as a body that moves in a circular orbit, and replace it with another concept, say that of a body which moves in an elliptical orbit.

If one feels somewhat discomfited by the suggestion that it is simply a matter of convention what our grammatical rules are (or, in Lewis' terms, what is packed into our concepts), and that they can be changed at will, Waismann is ready with soothing reassurances:

We are, as has been pointed out, inclined to say that we cannot choose which word combinations shall be permitted; as if these were in some way determined by the nature of reality. So we say it is due to the nature of color and of surface that one surface cannot have two colors at the same time. This is sometimes put in the form, "We cannot conceive a surface being red and green simultaneously." But we fail to recognize that there are here two cases: (i) we have already a language whose grammar forbids such a combination of words; (ii) we abolish the rule and thus leave the beaten track behind. In the first case, this sequence of words is meaningless (against the rules). In the second it has *as yet no meaning* and it is for us to give it one. In so combining words we are stepping outside the confines of existing languages and have yet to lay down the use of the new word-sequence.[6]

Here again in this passage, we see a striking analogy between what Waismann is saying and one of the features of Lewis' account of analytic truth. For it will be remembered that although for Lewis it is entirely a matter of convention and of free decision what meanings shall be given to our concepts, still, once that meaning is given, then the analytic statements which explicate it are necessary truths and it is no longer a matter of our free decision whether we accept them or not. So likewise, even though Waismann in the above passage is more directly concerned with

3. *Ibid.*, p. 40.   4. *Ibid.*, p. 58.
5. *Ibid.*, pp. 60–65.   6. *Ibid.*, pp. 63–64.

making it clear how grammatical rules are alterable at will, still he recognizes at least by implication that once a set of such rules has become established and accepted, then we cannot continue *both* to accept the rules and at the same time try to deny them. We do so on pain of meaninglessness, he would say, much as Lewis would say that we deny an analytic truth on pain of self-contradiction. In other words, the Wittgensteinian account of necessary truths would seem to be sufficiently similar to the Lewisean account that we shall feel free henceforth to appeal to either of them indifferently, when we find ourselves in need of illustrations for some of the more characteristic features of a relating-logic.

Real Necessities Displaced by Mere Logical or Linguistic Necessities

Let us pause for a moment to merely suggest the moral of the contrast between a relating-logic such as we have just been describing, with its reliance upon devices like analytic truths and language rules, and a what-logic with its reliance upon what-statements which purport to be necessary truths about the world. Clearly, all this should serve to bring home to us the absolute inadmissibility of anything on the order of what-statements into the corpus of a relating-logic. Admit what-statements into one's logic, and the consequence will be that one is committed to a recognition of something in the nature of real necessity or necessity in fact, as over against a mere logical or linguistic necessity. And that would never do!

Moreover, if still more is needed by way of evidence to prove that contemporary analytic philosophers do indeed have a radical and deep-seated suspicion of, not to say aversion for, anything on the order of what-questions and what-statements, just consider the following passage from Waismann:

What is a circle? . . . Normally we say something of the form "A circle is a plane curve which . . ." or "A circle is the geometrical locus of all points which . . ." Here it seems as if we had given the *genus* of the concept under discussion. . . .

[But] we obviously proceeded in the wrong direction when we looked for an explicit definition of the concept *circle*. The solution of the problem emerges when we alter our attitude. We must first realize that all geometrical propositions involving circles can be reduced to a common form, i.e., "A point lies on (or inside or outside) a circle." For example, the proposition "A straight line cannot cut a circle in more than two points" can be put, "There are not more than two points which lie both on one straight line and on one circle"; "These two circles do not intersect" means the same as "There is no point which lies on both

110

these circles." If only we succeed in giving the meaning of these combinations of words our problem will be solved; we shall be able to understand all statements in which the word "circle" occurs. Now a circle C is determined by its center M and the radius A B. Any point X will lie on the circle if, and only if, M X = A B; if M X $\gtrless$ A B, X will lie outside or inside the circle respectively. Accordingly we define

X lies outside C means M X > A B.

X lies on C means M X = A B.

X lies inside C means M X < A B.

It is important to be quite clear what is achieved by such a definition. First of all, we have shifted the goal of our questions. We are no longer bent on saying what a circle is; we simply explain the meaning of the sentence "A point lies on a circle." We give another expression whose meaning is exactly the same, but in which only known signs (that is to say, primitive signs and signs derived from them) are used. We might also say, "We do not explain what the word 'circle' means in isolation, but only what it means in a given context." With Russell we will call such a definition a "definition in use." [7]

Note that in this passage there is a conscious and explicit repudiation of what-statements as proper instruments of knowledge. We are even told that such a repudiation amounts to no insignificant detail; it requires that we do no less than "shift the goal of our questions" and "alter our attitude." Nor does "alter our attitude" mean any less than alter our "logic," in the sense in which we have been using that term in this book. Moreover, once we do thus alter our attitude, which is to say our logic, then we are committed, Waismann seems to be suggesting, to a program in investigation in which we seek to learn not what a thing is in itself, [8] but rather in context, and more specifically "in a given context."

Now such a project of a contextual logic is just the sort of thing that we should wish to designate by the term "relating-logic." Still, just what is the force of this recommendation that things are to be understood in context and in relation? To speak to this question, we propose once more to direct attention to the notion of an analytic truth. More specifically still, let us recall just what is involved in the business of packing various notes into a concept so as to make possible a subsequent unpacking of these notes in a series of analytic propositions or truths. We have already stressed the fact that we are entirely free as regards the original packing, just as we cease to be free when it comes to the subsequent unpacking. In other words, how our concepts are defined, or what it is that our grammatical

7. *Ibid.*, pp. 169–70.
8. Waismann's expression is "in isolation."

rules prescribe, is entirely a matter of convention, "grammar" being "autonomous" and nowise "dictated by reality."

What this implies, however, so far as a relating or a contextual logic goes, is that the formation of our concepts or the laying down of grammatical rules is not just a matter of rela*tions*, but of a rela*ting* that we ourselves carry out and that is thus entirely within our human disposition. Thus, for example, with respect to the earlier illustration of red and green, I do not — once my "attitude" has been "altered" and "the goal of my questions" has been "shifted" — ask what red is; rather I set "red" in a certain context, a context that excludes its conjunction with "green" at the same place at the same time. This particular way of relating "red" to "green," Waismann would say, is no more than a matter of convention. I might, or human society as a whole might, or a particular association of men, say, the scientists, might come to relate "red" to "green" in an entirely different way, or perhaps not at all. Grammatical rules, in other words — or, better, the contexts for the use of terms which such rules specify — are ultimately a matter simply of human determination.

Moreover, in a relating-logic, as an alternative to a what-logic, it is not merely the relations of things to other things that is the means of their being known and understood, but rather our human conventions whereby things are related to other things that are the resource of knowledge. In our earlier discussion in Chapter III we were at pains to point out that the necessity of a supposed analytic truth such as "All bodies are extended" was not traceable to any sort of material connection between being a body and being extended, but only to a purely formal or logical connection between being an extended body and being extended. But such formal or logical connections are scarcely thought of as being "dictated by reality." This must mean, then, that such necessity as there is in the association of extension with corporeality can only be determined by us and by the conventional rules that we lay down as to what shall be associated with what. It is for this reason, accordingly, that we have chosen the term "relating-logic" (as over against terms like "relational logic" or "contextual logic") to designate both the characteristic logical implement and the characteristic logical activity that are currently fashionable as offering an alternative to that of the more common, everyday what-logic.[9]

9. Kant's celebrated pronouncements in regard to "combination" (*Verbindung*) in the second edition of the first *Critique* are certainly not irrelevant in this connection. Cf. *Critique of Pure Reason*, trans. Norman Kemp Smith (London: Macmillan, 1933),

The Face of Nature as Seen through the Eyes of a Relating-Logic

Taking all of our description and discussion thus far of the characteristics of a relating-logic, is it really clear as to just what the face of nature will look like once it is seen through the eyes of such a logic? We have already insisted at some length upon one paradoxical feature of such a view of things — that nothing in the real world will present itself to us as being anything at all, this being the necessary consequence of the exclusion of what-statements from a relating-logic. However, we should now be able to appreciate still another paradoxical feature of this new look which things will have once the medium through which they come to be known is that of a relating-logic: there will be nothing in the entire face of nature that will be seen or understood as being in any way bound up with or necessarily associated or connected with anything else. Paradoxical as this second feature may seem, it is nonetheless an inevitable consequence of that rigid dichotomy between analytic and synthetic, or between language rules and statements of fact, in terms of which a relating-logic must operate. For as we have already suggested, what this dichotomy means is that all necessary connections are confined exclusively to the sphere of the linguistic and the logical: they represent only our human devices for relating and connecting things, and not any real connections or relations in things themselves. Necessity, in other words, can never be a matter of fact even in principle, for the very reason that necessity itself is nothing but the purely logical or formal necessity which we described earlier in connection with our explication of the notion of analytic truths. Nor would there seem to be any way even of talking about or conceiving a factual necessity or a necessity of things without invoking what-statements. These, in turn, would require by way of truth-conditions that they be both self-evident and empirically evident — which, of course, to any respectable modern thinker would be downright scandalous.

Really, though, for all one's efforts to be modern and up-to-date in philosophy, this does seem somewhat incredible. After all, consider how in this new look of things which the new logic has provided, the very thing that for poor old Kant was almost like a quest for the Holy Grail — namely, as to how synthetic judgments a priori might be possible — has

---

B134–35: "Combination does not, however, lie in the objects. . . . On the contrary, it is an affair of the understanding alone, which itself is nothing but the faculty of combining *a priori*, and of bringing the manifold of given representations under the unity of apperception."

nowadays been cavalierly brushed aside by our latter-day analytic philosophers as an affair of utterly no consequence. Even Hume was at least concerned about necessities in fact. One might even say that to the extent to which he had serious reservations as to the status of his own skeptical doubts, he may be regarded as having readily accepted the fact of necessary connection and as having doubted only the possibility of that fact's ever being known — at least on any of the criteria of knowledge that he could see his way clear to accepting. Be this as it may, it would seem that modern analysts, equipped with their relating-logic, don't even bother to sweep under the carpet what is perhaps the central problem of modern philosophy. They just blandly deny that the problem exists.

Nevertheless, what presently concerns us is not so much the sheer incredibility of the face of the world as seen through the eyes of a relating-logic, but rather the question of whether the actual moves that have to be made in such a logic, in order to bring off this sort of account or picture of the world, may not be moves of doubtful logical propriety. More specifically, we want to examine just what it is that takes place, within the context of such a logic, when one makes the transition from the setting up of various logical or linguistic rules to their use and application in the formulation of statements about the world. Or to express it in a little different terminology, what contribution do purely analytic or logical truths make to our actual knowledge of the world as formulated in synthetic judgments?

Can Rules Governing Words also Govern Things?

To bring the issue directly to a head, let us recur to Waismann's illustration about the impossibility of red and green being in the same place at the same time. This, we are told, involves no more than a "veiled grammatical rule." Very well, suppose we try to formulate the rule: "The word 'red' is never to be used along with the word 'green' as a predicate jointly qualifying a single subject that in turn is used to designate a single stretch of space-time." Clearly such a rule, so formulated, governs only the use of certain words. It is, we might say, a rule only about words and nothing else.

What about the use or application of the rule? On Waismann's account, the statement "Red and green cannot be in the same place at the same time" would presumably be an example of the rule in use or as applied. Yet surely there is something odd about this. For the rule, as we saw, was about words, specifically the words "red" and "green." But in the supposed application of the rule the resulting statement turns out not to be a statement about words at all, but about certain things or entities in the world, namely red and green. How, though, can a rule which forbids only a certain use or combination of words in language be used or applied in such a manner as to exclude a certain combination of things or entities in the real world? Can it be that in passing from the rule to its supposed application, Waismann has been beguiled into committing an elementary confusion of use with mention? Hardly likely! But if not, then how could the rule, which is admittedly no more than a rule about words, possibly authorize its own application to a situation which does not concern words at all, but things? Or if the rule does not itself authorize such an application, on whose authority is the use or application being made? On Waismann's? Surely, that is a pretension which even a disciple of Wittgenstein might hesitate to arrogate to himself.

Still, one can never be too sure. We are all familiar with how Professor Gilbert Ryle, in a well-known passage in *The Concept of Mind*, proposed that so-called causal laws in nature be interpreted as "inference-tickets":

> At least part of the point of trying to establish laws is to find out how to infer from particular matters of fact by reference to other matters of fact, and how to bring about or prevent particular states of affairs. A law is used as, so to speak, an inference-ticket (a season ticket) which licenses its possessors to move from asserting factual statements to asserting other factual statements.[10]

Unhappily, for many of us the mere mention of tickets, not to say season tickets, may evoke unpleasant memories of grimy British railway cars. Even so, Professor Ryle's figure should do well enough by way of illustration. The only trouble is that when some naive, bumbling American who doesn't understand the ways, much less the tickets, of the English, and who certainly does not want to get in trouble with the established authorities, timidly asks, "But who issues such tickets?", he may find that it is difficult to get a straight answer.

No doubt, in the questioner's mind there may be some lingering, child-like feeling — a hang-over perhaps from our colonial past — that if such an inference-ticket is to be valid, it must be issued on the basis of some real causal connection in nature. To this Ryle at once responds with a great

10. (London: Hutchinson's University Library, 1949), p. 121.

show of matter-of-factness, appearing to say "Yes" straight off, but then, after wandering through a considerable verbiage of homespun illustrations and figures of speech, of both dubious authenticity and dubious relevance, appearing finally to say "No":

Now there is no objection to employing the familiar idiom "causal connection." Bacteriologists do discover causal connections between bacteria and diseases, since this is only another way of saying that they do establish laws and so provide themselves with inference-tickets which enable them to infer from diseases to bacteria, prevent and cure diseases by eliminating bacteria, and so forth. But to speak as if the discovery of a law were the finding of a third, unobservable existence is simply to. . . .[11]

Unhappily, prose of this kind in philosophy is difficult of interpretation, particularly when what Ryle pictures as being the horrible alternative to his own view is scarcely recognizable as an alternative that has played any sort of a role in Western philosophy. Still, if one may judge by appearances, Ryle seems to be saying that one may, if one likes, speak of inference-tickets being issued on the basis of causal connections in nature, simply because to say "causal connection" is practically to say the same thing as "inference-ticket." [12] But this is a funny business surely. If to say by whose authority I have a license to do something is but to say all over again that I do have the license, then presumably when I am challenged to state by whose authority I have the license, I need do no more than simply repeat that I have the license. Imagine such a thing! It amounts to claiming that one's tickets and licenses are literally self-validating. They aren't issued on the basis of any outside authority, but only on their own authority. Or still more generally, the supposed causal connections in the natural world, in virtue of which certain things or events might seem to be neces-

11. *Ibid.*, p. 122.

12. In fairness to Ryle, perhaps it should be noted that in the above-quoted passage he does not say this in so many words. Rather he states that to say that "bacteriologists do discover causal connections . . . is only another way of saying that they do establish laws and so provide themselves with inference-tickets. . . ." And yet just what is the sense and force of the expression "and so" in this connection? Is it a case of "and so inference-tickets," because there are real causal connections in nature? Or is it a case of "and so inference-tickets," because to say "causal connection" is really not to say anything more than "inference-ticket"? If the former is what Professor Ryle means, then his meaning would go directly counter to what he would appear to be arguing for in this entire section of his book. On the other hand, if the latter is what he means, then the interpretation which we have given of this highly dubious passage would appear to be the correct one — Q.E.D.

sarily dependent upon or bound up with [13] others, are really nothing more than our linguistic or grammatical rules, i.e., rules which "can be fixed before language is applied" and which therefore belong to the stage of "the installation and application of signs" before and "in preparation for their use." We can and do change such rules, of course, just as no less a rule than that for the use of the words "red" and "green" can be changed, Waismann assures us. And yet the point is that such a change of grammatical rules is never "dictated by reality." Indeed, it could not be. For this would imply that there were in the real world real necessities, real natures and essences of things, and real causal connections, in respect to which our judgments might be mistaken, and in virtue of which we might feel that we would need constantly to be revising our previous statements and judgments. And this would mean that what-statements would again need to be introduced into logic. Rather than tolerate that, any partisan of a relating-logic must insist that the essential and the necessary always be kept strictly confined to the sphere of language and logic, and never be allowed to trespass upon the domain of fact.

If we place this sort of construction upon Ryle's talk about inference-tickets, it poses the question of whether the very same difficulty will arise in connection with his examples that we earlier found in connection with Waismann's example of red and green. It all turns on the question of just what happens when one makes the transition from the formulation of a logical or linguistic rule to its application or use: as formulated, the rule seems to be a rule governing only the behavior of words; but in its use or application it somehow seems to become a rule governing the behavior of things. Thus it is one thing to talk about what one may or may not do with "red" and "green"; it is another thing to talk about red and green

13. By "necessarily dependent upon or bound up with," we mean simply that to affirm the cause and to deny the effect would be self-contradictory. To this, however, many might retort that if such be our criterion of "necessarily dependent upon," then we cannot be speaking of causal connections in nature, since, as both Hume and Kant recognized, causal connections in that sense simply do not exist in nature at all.

Such a retort, however, simply begs the entire question which we sought to raise in the preceding chapters about the possibility of necessary truths being about the world. Besides, in the specific context of the passage quoted from Ryle, he would appear to want to treat causal connections as mere inference-tickets, and hence presumably as being founded on no more than certain rules of language. Now whether, when causal connections are thus equated with mere grammatical rules, it is any longer proper to refer to them as "causal connections" is surely a matter of linguistic convention which might be appropriately left to Professor Ryle to determine.

themselves. Or to move on to Ryle, it is one thing to talk about inference-tickets, which license us to employ certain linguistic or logical moves of a specified kind; it is another thing to talk about such things or entities as we may mean or intend when we use such a ticket and make one of the licensed moves in our actual linguistic or logical practice.

The Fallacy: A Confusion of Use with Mention, or a Case of Inverted Intentionality

Granted that there does seem to be some sort of confusion at work here, just what is it? Can we specify it? And can we specify it in such a way as to show it to be a logical and not a mere psychological difficulty? For that there will be psychological difficulties involved in cases of the sort, no one would doubt, least of all linguistic philosophers like Waismann. On the contrary, the latter would be the first to sympathize with how hard it is for the poor in spirit to accustom themselves to the "altered attitude" that is the prescribed cure for all of the horrible nightmares that must surely result from believing in such things as real necessity. "But that is part of the price one has to pay if one is going to take the cure of linguistic therapy," these philosophers would say. On the other hand, they would surely not want to say that there was any logical difficulty, not to say an actual logical fallacy, involved in these therapeutic reconstructions of supposed necessities in things into mere disguised grammatical rules. That would be a very different story indeed!

Heretofore in our discussion of the issue we have done little more than hint that perhaps the logical confusion involved is that of use with mention. Thus a statement about red and green was held to be but a grammatical rule about "red" and "green." Yet to talk about men is certainly not to talk about "men." How then can one possibly construe a statement about what cannot be the case as a mere rule stipulating what cannot be said?

To pursue this line further, we will simply take our stand on the fact that men are not "men." Of the word "men," we may say that it is a three- and not a four-letter word, that it can be used as a subject of a sentence, that it is a universal term, etc. On the other hand, of men themselves, i.e., of what the word "men" is used to signify, we can say that they are fools, that they never are "but always to be blest," and that some of them at least are English. Clearly, then, is it not impossible — in this case, logically impossible — to suppose that whatever is truly predicable of "men" may be simply transferred to another subject and so be made predicable of men? Surely this possibility is excluded by the recognition that men are inescapably different from "men."

Immediately, though, we shall be told that this is not the issue. For no modern analyst or linguistic philosopher would ever claim that there was no difference between men and "men," and that whatever was predicable of the one was also and equally predicable of the other. Rather the claim is that in some cases, when we think we may be talking about real things — e.g., real necessity or necessary connections in the world — we are deceived; and we are deceived not merely because there are no such things, but also because expressions like "real necessity" or "necessary connections in fact" simply can't have any assignable meaning, or at least the meaning which we might ordinarily and naively suppose them to have. Accordingly, modern analytic philosophers have come up with the ingenious suggestion that people, in thinking they are talking about real necessities or real impossibilities in things, may in fact be talking only about rules for the use of certain words: thus in saying that red and green cannot be in the same place at the same time, we mean no more than that the words "red" and "green" cannot be used as joint predicates qualifying the same subject.

What is wrong with this? To revert to our earlier illustration, while it certainly would be a confusion of use with mention to say that to talk about men is to talk about "men," still could it not be the case that in supposing that we were talking about men, we really weren't talking about men at all, because the expression doesn't mean anything? Why not then suppose that maybe we were only talking about "men"? Here there is not strictly any confusion of use with mention: we are saying that sometimes in supposing we are using a term, we are not really doing so at all; instead, we may only be mentioning it.

However, this still does not obviate the confusion, or even the fallacy — although it may be a more subtle fallacy than that of a confusion of use and mention. Indeed, we propose to call it the *fallacy of inverted intentionality*, thus availing ourselves — though for our own purposes — of the Scholastic distinction between first and second intentions. For the interesting thing about this distinction is that it serves to point up what would seem to be an obvious and inescapable order of priority in regard to what we might call the various levels or orders of meaning or of intention.

Unfortunately, however, we cannot explain this save in terms of two successive steps. First, let us recur to the examples from Waismann and Ryle, making the obvious and perhaps even trivial point that presumably if red and green are such that no object can be both at once, then it is likely that human language-users will have some sort of logical or linguistic rule which restricts the use of the terms "red" and "green" accordingly. Or to get at the same thing a little differently, if a certain natural object or event is causally dependent upon another in fact — e.g., a certain disease upon the presence of certain bacteria — then this would surely be a sufficient justification for the issuance of an inference-ticket in language enabling us to pass from statements about the appearance of the disease to other statements about the presence of the bacteria. Moreover, so far as the distinction between first and second intentions is concerned, we may say that when we make statements about red and green, they are of first intention; and when we make statements about how the terms "red" and "green" are to be used, they are of second intention. And so likewise, *mutatis mutandis,* for statements of causal dependence in nature, as compared with statements that license inferences from certain statements to others.

Now for the second step. In the preceding paragraph we suggested that if red and green were necessarily ordered to one another in certain ways in fact and in reality, then it would be reasonable to suppose that there would be various linguistic rules which would govern the uses of the terms "red" and "green" accordingly. Now we will go further and say that there is clearly an order of priority involved here. It is only because of the sorts of things that words like "red" and "green," or logical devices like inference-tickets, etc., are used to mean or signify, that we are justified in laying down the various logical and linguistic rules for the use of such terms. Or put a little differently, logical and linguistic rules of use are determined by the use to which they are to be put; and the use to which the logical and linguistic items governed by such rules are often put is just that of meaning or signifying things other than themselves.

Clearly, though, if there is some such order of priority with respect to our logical and linguistic intentions — i.e., if our second-intentional logical and linguistic rules are determined in the light of what our words and sentences are used to mean or signify in first intention — then there would surely seem to be something quite wrongheaded about Waismann's suggestion that the impossibility of a thing's being red and green at the same time is but a veiled grammatical rule for the use of "red" and "green." Rather it is just the other way around, and Waismann would appear to have got the cart before the horse: it is not the impossibility of a thing's being red and green at the same time that is determined by the rule, but rather the rule about "red" and "green" that is determined with a view to the use of these expressions to signify just that very impossibility. Take away the impossibility, and what could be the point of the rule? [14] Ac-

14. Reference to P. F. Strawson is practically unavoidable at this point. For everyone is surely familiar with his discussion of "incompatible predicates" in the opening chapter of his *Introduction to Logical Theory* (New York: John Wiley, 1952), pp. 5–12. But does anyone understand it? He there raises the direct question, "And what makes predicates incompatible?" (p. 5). Yet a direct question does not necessarily mean a direct answer, and in Strawson's case the indirection of the answer is such as to seem almost perverse. Thus on the one hand, he seems to plump unmistakably for a position not unlike Waismann's; and in answer to his own question "What makes predicates incompatible?", he comes right out at times with the assertion, "We do." Thus: "Somewhere, then, a boundary must be drawn, limiting the applicability of a word used in describing things; and it is we who decide where the boundaries are to be drawn" (p. 5); "It is, then, our own activity of making language through using it, our own determination of the limits of the applications of words, that makes inconsistency possible. . . . We can create the possibility of inconsistency in statement, and hence of validity in argument. . . . We can deliberately fix the boundaries of some words in relation to those of other words. This is what we do when we *define* words or phrases. . . Accepting a definition is agreeing to be bound by a rule of language of this kind" (p. 9).

Then, as if to counter these seemingly straightforward declarations that incompatibilities between things are but the creations of our linguistic rules, Strawson blandly says, "[Not] that our boundary-drawing is a quite arbitrary matter; nor that the boundaries are fixed and definite; nor that the decisions we make when we make them are purely verbal decisions" (p. 5). And "What makes our decisions, for a word already in use, non-arbitrary is this: that our normal purpose will be defeated if the comparison implicit in the use of the word is too unnatural, if the similarity is too tenuous" (p. 6).

At this, one can hardly do other than throw up one's hands and cry, *Gott bewahre uns!* For one thing, the question as to nonarbitrariness, if it is to be anything more than utterly trivial, ought not just blithely to take for granted "words already in use," since the whole issue turns precisely on whether such a use is arbitrary or not. Moreover, having thus ruled out the one thing that should have been under consideration, Strawson then sententiously declares that the reason that it is not just an arbitrary matter whether we change an established use is that to do so would be too "unnatural." Clearly, though, what he must mean here is not "unnatural" but "unconventional" — which is a very different matter.

But surely it is pointless to pursue these Strawsonian ambiguities any further. (If the reader is interested, he might see if he can gain any more clarity from the discussions of § 8, pp. 9–12; § 12, pp. 17–18; and § 14, pp. 21–24.) Somehow one cannot avoid the suspicion that Strawson, like Ryle, may be trying to play a language game of having his cake and eating it too. On balance, though, it would seem that Strawson finally does come down on the side of those who would make all necessities and impossibilities a mere function of our language rules, rather than on the side of those who would insist that such rules must be determined out of a regard for real necessities and for what is really impossible in the world. Accordingly, Strawson may well be one who falls afoul of the fallacy of inverted intentionality.

cordingly, to say that a statement in first intention is not really in first intention at all, but is a veiled assertion about objects in second intention, may succeed in just barely skirting the confusion of use with mention; however, it still commits the fallacy of inverted intentionality: a statement of first intention is construed as being a statement of second intention; and yet the condition of the second intention is that the statement of first intention be taken at face value.[15]

Two Possible Rejoinders

So much, then, for the fallacy, which we feel cannot fail to touch any sort of a relating-logic in one of its most sensitive points. Nevertheless, any number of rejoinders to such an allegation of fallacy will doubtless promptly suggest themselves. Of these we shall consider only two, the one somewhat naive and irrelevant, the other somewhat more subtle, but equally irrelevant. The first sort of rejoinder we can put directly into the mouth of Professor Ryle himself. Indeed, we shall simply quote him verbatim:

It is sometimes urged that if we discover a law, which enables us to infer from diseases of certain sorts to the existence of bacteria of certain sorts, then we have discovered a new existence, namely a causal connection between such bacteria and such diseases; and that consequently we now know what we did not know before, that there exist not only diseased persons and bacteria, but also an invisible and intangible bond between them ["a third, unobservable existence," Ryle comments a little further down on the same page]. As trains cannot travel, unless there exist rails for them to travel on, so, it is alleged, bacteriologists cannot move from the clinical observation of patients to the prediction of microscopic observation of bacteria, unless there exists, though it can never be observed, an actual tie between the objects of these observations.[16]

But surely all we need do is to urge Professor Ryle not to get excited and not to be misled. Even if one were to say that expressions like "cannot"

15. This seems to be just the point that Professor Brand Blanshard wishes to make, and in our judgment succeeds in making quite tellingly, in § 19 of Chap. 6 of *Reason and Analysis* (La Salle, Ill.: Open Court, 1962), pp. 268–69. See also p. 277.

In view, however, of Professor Blanshard's sensitivity as regards various periods in the history of Western philosophy, we wish to make it quite clear that even though he may have wished to make the same point, he is certainly not to be accused of using the same terminology, as the Scholastics. Terms such as "first and second intentions" we feel sure, have never passed his lips, or perhaps even crossed his mind.

16. *The Concept of Mind*, p. 122.

or "must" or "is necessarily" are used to mean something, it does not follow that they must mean some sort of "new existence," some "invisible and intangible bond," some "third unobservable existence," some mysterious "rails of inference," etc. Clearly, there are other alternatives as to what "must" or "impossible" might mean or intend besides these obvious bogeymen which Professor Ryle has so gratuitously conjured up. Nor in the context of the present logical argument is it necessary for us to specify just what sorts of things or entities, or even whether there are any substantial things or entities, we may be supposed to commit ourselves to when we assert the impossibility of a thing's being both red and green in the same place at the same time. Instead, all that we are saying is that, in asserting such an impossibility, we do mean or intend something by it, and that what we mean or intend cannot possibly be a linguistic or logical rule. For to suppose the latter would be comparable to supposing that when we talk about men, we really mean "men" — a fallacy which, if it is not that of confusing use with mention, is certainly that of inverted intentionality.

Now let us look at the second, more subtle, line of rejoinder, which aims at questioning one of the presuppositions upon which the entire argument must rest if the case for an inverted intentionality is to be made out. The argument was that rules of use are only for the purpose of such use, and are consequently to be determined in the light of what the expressions thus subject to rule are to be used for. Further, what such linguistic and logical devices are used for, it was contended, is, in many instances, simply to intend or signify what exists in the real world. In other words, there is a clear priority of the first-intentional use of logico-linguistic devices over the second-intentional rules and regulations governing such use.

But why, the rejoinder runs, suppose that the use of such linguistic or logical expressions or devices is to intend what exists in the world? Perhaps they are not used to intend or mean or signify anything at all. Or put a little differently, there are all sorts of ways in which linguistic expressions may have meaning, but without the meaning having to be a meaning or a signifying of something other than and distinct from these expressions.

At this point of the rejoinder it goes almost without saying that the sacred metaphor of the language game will surely be invoked. For why not consider language to be a kind of game, and the various grammatical and logical rules governing the uses of expressions in the language to be simply analogous to rules of a game? Moreover, just as we earlier made much of the fact that linguistic and logical rules governing the behavior of expressions in a language are determined and set up entirely with a view to the use of these expressions, so also it may be said that in any game the rules governing the moves and the plays are certainly established with a view to the actual use of these moves and plays, i.e., with a view to the actual playing of the game. And right here, it will be said, is just where our earlier argument about the order of priority of intentions is certain to break down; for on the analogy of a game, any such order of priority may be seen to be altogether gratuitous and unnecessary. Thus recall how we sought to argue that since language rules are determined with a view to the use of linguistic expressions, and the use of linguistic expressions is for the purpose of signifying or intending the way things are in the world, it therefore follows that our language rules must ultimately be determined in the light of our first intentions as to the way the world is, rather than the other way around — i.e., as if our first-intentional statements might well be no more than veiled second-intentional rules.

Yet note that as regards ordinary games, this sort of order of priority and posteriority does not exist at all. To take a trivial example, in American football there is a rule to the effect that if a team on the offensive does not succeed in gaining at least ten yards in four plays, the ball goes over to the other side. Here clearly the rule may be said to be determined with a view to the playing of the game, much as language rules are determined with a view to the using of the language. But now suppose that in a game of football one team after four tries fails to make the necessary yardage and the ball goes over to the other side. Does this action in turn signify some further action or happening, outside the game of football altogether, which is normative with respect to the business of handing the ball over to the other team and which handing over the ball is supposed to intend or represent? The question is simply ridiculous. There is no action or event outside the game of football which this action in the game may be said to be of or about, in the sense of intending or signifying it, and which therefore must be presupposed as being the very basis and justification for the formulation of the fourth-down rule in the first place.

The point, then, of the entire rejoinder becomes apparent. For if language is a game like other games, then we need not suppose that the playing of the game is carried out for the sake of any cognitive end outside the game itself. Or put more accurately, we need not suppose that the moves in the game of language are for the sake of intending or coming to know things outside the game altogether, any more than are the moves or plays in any other game. But this means that the entire support for our contention that a relating-logic falls afoul of a fallacy of inverted intentionality would appear simply to collapse.

Not quite so fast though! For has the question been settled yet as to whether language is, after all, just like a game? Or better, the question is: supposing that language is a game, is it like those particular games the playing of which does not have, and is not supposed to have, any cognitive purpose? Indeed, we might even go a step further in our concessions and say that not only is language a game, but many of the moves in it are not made for the purpose of formulating or conveying a truth about the world. Thus it is not hard to imagine that an exasperated reader, at this point in the argument, might suddenly stop, throw down the book, and exclaim, "Well, I'll be damned!" Now such an utterance might inadvertently be a quite accurate description of the future state of the man's soul. Also it would certainly permit any bystander to infer that the man was indeed in a state, if not of condemnation, then certainly of exasperation. Yet clearly, taken just in itself, the utterance was not made with a view to enunciating any sort of truth about the world at all.

But so what? For granting that language is a game and that many of the moves in it are not made for the purpose of saying anything about the world, the relevant question has to do with linguistic utterances that do purport to say something about the world, and in terms of what must be the case, or of what cannot possibly be the case, etc. Why suppose that statements of this sort are never what they seem, that despite all prima-facie evidence to the contrary they are not really statements of first intention at all, but of second intention — and this despite the fact that such a shift from first to second intention seems clearly to invert the necessary order of priority and posteriority of so-called logical or linguistic intentions? Things do seem to have come to a curious state in philosophy, when after comparing language and logic to a game — which doubtless is reasonable enough — one then proceeds to insist that those very respects in which a language game might seem to differ from other games are precisely the respects in which it resembles these other games. However, we all know that these days it is fashionable not merely to talk about being, but actually to be, "logically odd."

Chapter VI

The World As Seen *through a* Relating-Logic

UNHAPPILY, the somewhat involuted character of the argument may have caused us to lose sight of at least one of the projected aims of the last chapter, which was to try to give some indication of what the face of nature and of the world must look like when seen through the eyes of a relating-logic. And yet can we not see clearly just what the consequences will be of relegating all real necessities to the sphere of analytic truths or mere language rules? It can only be as if the very forces of nature had been drained of their force. For consider how in our simplicity and naivete we should all suppose that we cannot hold back the tides, or cause the sun to stand still, or exert pressure on a gas without compressing its volume. Or even if we could do these things, at least we should suppose that it would take some doing — an undeniable counter-vailing of force with force. Even so honest and balanced a thinker as Lewis would have to admit that in asserting any such supposed necessities of nature, as for example that in a gas the pressure and volume vary inversely, we must be making either a linguistic pronouncement about the use of the word "gas," or a matter-of-fact assertion comparable to "Today is Tuesday" or "The guests are late for dinner."

Better still, suppose we call Andrew Marvell to witness, for he on at least one occasion manifested concern over the seemingly ineluctable flow of time: "And ever at my back I hear time's winged chariot hurrying near." Now, surely, this was an unnecessary concern on the part of the poet. What he needed was just a good, strong dose of linguistic therapy. For imagine how some latter-day linguistic analyst could have offered aid and comfort: "Come, come, Marvell, don't fuss and fret yourself over any supposed inevitability of the passage of time. Remember, it is only as a result of our grammatical rules that we have come to have almost a fixation on the matter of time's not being able to have a stop."

Think also of poor Macbeth. Not poor Yorick, but poor Macbeth! For did he not imagine that when everything looked desperate, there was at least one thing he could count on: "Come what, come may, time and the hour run through the roughest day"? But the murderer of Duncan was counting on too much, for he should have taken heed lest someone change the language rules on him, with the result that time and the hour would not run through the roughest day after all. Verily if the opponent of Macduff found himself appalled that Birnam Wood should move to Dunsinane, or that his avenger should suddenly prove to be no man of woman born, what would he have thought if he had had a linguistic analyst to deal with?

Science's Partiality for a Relating-Logic

However, even if the unalleviated use of a relating-logic would tend to make a mockery of our everyday world and render our human existence not so much absurd as simply unrecognizable, there is nonetheless a sense in which the use of such a logic may prove to be peculiarly congenial, not to say fruitful, to the sort of activity that we have come to associate with modern science. For instance, let us have a look at some of the late Professor Hanson's rather free-swinging but forceful and persuasive accounts of the matter of physical causation. In rare Don Quixote-like form he tilts magnificently against such windmills as the naive notion that the changes in nature involve actual causal chains binding events and happenings to one another. Says Hanson,

127

The elements of [the physicist's] research are less like the links of a chain and more like the legs of a table, or the hooks on a clothes pole. They are less like the successive generations of an old family and more like the administrative organization of an old university. . . .

Cause-words resemble game-jargon, as was noted earlier. "Revoke," "trump," "finesse" belong to the parlance system of bridge. The entire conceptual pattern of the name is implicit in each term: you cannot grasp one of these ideas properly while remaining in the dark about the rest. So too "bishop," "rook," "checkmate," "gambit" interlock with each other and with all other expressions involved in playing, scoring and writing about chess.

Likewise with "pressure," "temperature," "volume," "conductor," "insulator," "charge" and "discharge," "wave-length," "amplitude," "frequency," "elastic," "stretch," "stress" and "strain" in physics; "ingestion," "digestion," "assimilation," "excretion" and "respiration" in biology; "wound," "poison," "threshold" in medicine; "geartrain," "escapement," "pendulum" and "balancer" in horology. To understand one of these ideas thoroughly is to understand the concept pattern of the discipline in which it figures. This helps to show how cause-words are theory-loaded in relation to their effect-words.[1]

Here, doubtless, is an accurate and perceptive account of the theory-loaded words that appear in the languages of the various sciences. Also, in his examples Professor Hanson has carefully pressed the analogy between the language of science and the language of games. And then comes the climax:

Causes certainly are connected with effects; but this is because our theories connect them, not because the world is held together by cosmic glue. The world *may* be glued together by imponderables,[2] but that is irrelevant for understanding causal explanation. The notions behind "the cause X" and "the effect Y" are intelligible only against a pattern of theory, namely one which puts guarantees on inferences from X to Y. Such guarantees distinguish truly causal sequences from mere coincidence.[3]

Note how in this passage what Hanson says closely resembles the point which we found Ryle trying to make in regard to inference-tickets; it isn't the real causal connections in nature, as objects of first intentions, that are to be regarded as prior to, and as somehow guaranteeing, our second-intentional connections between the words and terms of our language game.

1. Norwood Russell Hanson, *Patterns of Discovery* (Cambridge: University Press, 1958), pp. 52, 61–62.
2. Why Professor Hanson should have introduced this curious "may be" pronouncement by way of qualification, or what he could possibly have meant by it, we have not the slightest idea.
3. Hanson, p. 64.

The linguistic connections are somehow autonomous and provide their own guarantee. Thus Professor Hanson observes a little farther on:

> The necessity sometimes associated with event-pairs construed as cause and effect is really that obtaining between premises and conclusions in theories which guarantee inferences from the one event to the other. . . .
> What philosophers sought as the objective necessity of causal sequences resides in the form of the theory which connects descriptions of these sequences.[4]

Here, then, we have a clear and unequivocal recognition of what we should like to label "the inverted intentionality" of modern scientific theories and principles: instead of supposing that real causal sequences in nature have somehow got to be logically prior to the second-intentional language rules and deductive interrelationships of our scientific theories, it is rather the case that the linguistic or logical form of such theories, providing as it does all sorts of inference-tickets and orderings of premises to conclusions, is somehow held to be ultimate, autonomous, and sufficient unto itself.

Nevertheless, the question that now arises is why such an inverted intentionality, which as we have seen can only make for utter incredibilities when applied to our everyday world, can nonetheless be made to seem reasonable and plausible when used as a principle of interpretation with respect to the language of science. At least one answer that would suggest itself is that, to the extent to which the sciences have come to use the language of mathematics, the language games of these sciences tend to approximate much more closely to ordinary games than does the rather special game of what we should want to call ordinary language. In the preceding chapter, we saw how playing an ordinary game like football according to its rules differs in one very marked respect from playing the peculiar game of ordinary language according to its rules. In the latter case, it would seem that the rules of use cannot be dictated solely by considerations intrinsic to the language game alone; instead, they are determined in large part by the fact that the linguistic expressions that are ordered by the rules have the further function of signifying and intending things in the world that are outside language altogether. In contrast, in a game like football, when a team on the offensive observes the fourth-down rule, its action in so doing does not, and is not supposed to, signify or intend anything outside the game at all.

Nevertheless, when the language game being played is that of mathe-

4. *Ibid.*, p. 90.

matics (assuming that mathematics is somehow a language game) rather than that of ordinary language, the need to consider the expressions of the language as intending or referring to things or entities outside the game is reduced to a minimum, if not eliminated entirely. The principal reason for this would seem to be the formal character of mathematics, by which we mean simply that feature of mathematical propositions and demonstrations according to which the content is irrelevant either to the truth of the propositions or the validity of the demonstrations. Thus to recall once more our earlier example of the truth tables in logic, suppose that we set the thing up purely formally as follows. First, without considering what the p's, q's, v's, and $\supset$'s stand for, or even what T and F stand for, we shall simply specify the following relationships:

p	~p
T	F
F	T

p	q	p·q
T	T	T
T	F	F
F	T	F
F	F	F

p	q	p∨q
T	T	T
T	F	T
F	T	T
F	F	F

p	q	p⊃q
T	T	T
T	F	F
F	T	T
F	F	T

Given these interrelationships, as thus specified, it then becomes possible to determine the proper T's and F's of a more complicated expression such as:

p	q	~p	~q	p⊃q	~q⊃~p	p⊃q·⊃·~q⊃~p
T	T	F	F	T	T	T
T	F	F	T	F	F	T
F	T	T	F	T	T	T
F	F	T	T	T	T	T

In other words, given these specifications, the propriety of associating T with $p \supset q \cdot \supset \cdot \sim q \supset \sim p$ in every possible case is demonstratively established. Nor, in order to establish the propriety of this association, is it in any way necessary to consider "what one is talking about" in such cases. For as we remarked before, it makes no difference what the p's and $\sim$'s

130

and *T*'s and *F*'s stand for; the propriety of the particular association of *T* with $p \supset q \cdot \supset \cdot \sim q \supset \sim p$ is rigorously established, no matter what these symbols mean.

Note, however, that when we say "no matter what these symbols mean," what this serves to exclude is the need to consider what the symbols signify or refer to outside of and beyond their interrelationships within the game. On the other hand, these same references and interrelationships which they have within the game are all-important. Indeed, in another sense of meaning, one might say that each of these symbols does have a specific and precise meaning within the game — namely, how it acts and behaves according to the rules of the game, or how it is used within the game. Here, surely, would seem to be a paradigm of Wittgenstein's principle that meaning simply is use.

Very well, then, if the language game of mathematics exemplifies the kind of meaning that we might call non-intentional — i.e., the rule-governed use of expressions in the game is not designed to intend or signify anything outside the game — and if the language of modern science, particularly modern physics, is largely a mathematical language, then it is not hard to understand how and why modern scientific theories might plausibly seem to be non-intentional, or of an inverted intentionality. Professor Hanson employs an unusually telling illustration to show how the scheme of supposedly physical interrelationships involved in accelerating bodies is indistinguishable from the linguistic scheme or notation in which these interrelationships are described:

Thus the logical structure of our conceptions of accelerating bodies is identical with the structure underlying 1–13 below:

1. $a = (v - v_0)/t$ definition
2. $v = v_0 + at$ from 1
3. $\bar{v} = s/t$ or $s = \bar{v}t$ from definition of average velocity
4. $\bar{v} = (v_0 + v)/2$ uniform change in velocity
5. $\bar{v} = \frac{1}{2}(v_0 + v_0 + at) = v_0 + \frac{1}{2}at$ via 2
6. $\therefore s = \bar{v}t = (v_0 + \frac{1}{2}at)t$ from 5
7. or $s = v_0t + \frac{1}{2}at^2$ from 2, 6
8. $t = (v - v_0/a$ from 2
9. $s = t(v_0 + \frac{1}{2}at)$ from 7
10. substituting $s = (v - v_0/a)\left\{v_0 + a(v - v_0)/2a\right\}$
11. $s = (v - v_0/a)(v_0 + v/2)$
      and
12. $2as = v^2 - v_0^2$
13. or $v^2 = v_0^2 + 2as$

These are our concepts of accelerating bodies; thus is their behaviour described. Any distinctions to be made in our mechanical ideas must be made in this notation. How could an essential change be made here which left our conceptions of acceleration unaltered? This "locking" of concept and language is fundamental in all physics.[5]

The Partiality for a What-Logic in Everyday Human Existence

When accounts such as this are given of the kind of enterprise which modern science may be taken to be, is it not clear that science is both the project and the product of a relating-logic? Data there are, but the concern is not with proving what we are thus being presented or made acquainted with in experience; rather it is with ordering these data one to another in ever more all-embracing schemes of organization. Moreover, as we have found Professor Hanson insisting, this ordering is not based on causal relationships, in the sense of efficient causes. Instead, the schemes of order are, one might say, mathematical rather than causal, being no more than purely formal patterns of relationships, when considered just as such and apart from their application. Even in their application, these formal patterns seem to function as inference-tickets or inference licenses — i.e., as ways that enable us to "go on" [6] from one point to another — and not as anything that might be considered as the actual order and framework of nature.

Moreover, the kinds of questions that we have thus far been pressing — what the warrant is for such inference-tickets; whether there must be

5. *Ibid.*, pp. 34–35.

6. In subsequent discussions we shall frequently avail ourselves of this Wittgensteinian expression of "going on" (see L. Wittgenstein, *Philosophical Investigations,* trans. G. E. M. Anscombe [New York: Macmillan, 1953], esp. § 151), though our use of the expression may not be in all ways consonant with Wittgenstein's use. Rather, what we wish to try to bring out by the use of the expression "go on" is that in science, in mathematics, and in many sorts of games the participants may very well know how to go on, but without their thereby being committed to acknowledging that there must therefore exist in the world, and quite independently of their thought and behavior, real guide lines or actual rails (to use Ryle's word) which govern and determine such an ability to go on. On the other hand, in activities other than those of mathematics or modern physics or the playing of ordinary games — notably in the cognitive activities of everyday life, where our concern is with trying to understand things in terms of what they are and why they are — a knowledge of how to go on in such contexts is one that does commit us, we would maintain, to the existence of real *whats* and *whys* in things, to real causes and necessary connections, which do provide a basis, and indeed the only possible basis, for the language rules and the prescribed logical moves in accordance with which we "go on" in such contexts.

necessary connections between things in the real world, and not just linguistic and logical connections between our words and concepts; whether first intentions must not be somehow prior to, and the reason for, our second intentions — are, in principle, rigorously excluded from science as not being the sorts of questions that it concerns itself with, or is in a position to answer. Indeed, it is just such questions that are proper in the context of a what-logic, and hence can only be ruled out of place and irrelevant in the context of a relating-logic.

But although the proper questions of a what-logic must be reckoned improper when asked in the context of modern physics, does this mean that they are improper altogether? For that matter, have we not already brought forward sufficient illustrations to indicate that however improper such questions may be in the domain of modern physics, they just cannot be ruled out where our everyday world is concerned — the world of Shakespeare, the world of Marvell, and the world of all of us — insofar as we have not become immured in the confines of modern physics and mathematics? Or put a little differently, the face or picture of the world as it appears through the medium of a relating-logic just isn't the world that we human beings live in, or perhaps even could live in. So to return to the concluding quotation from Professor Hanson, let us simply agree that a " 'locking' of concept and language is fundamental in all physics." But that still leaves open the question of whether what is fundamental in all physics is fundamental in all human life. Indeed, if our earlier illustration is at all valid, then it would seem that in the language of everyday life such a locking of concept and language — which is to say a blurring of the distinction between those things outside language which are intended through language and the language through which those things are intended — commits the fallacy of inverting intentionality and, besides, leads to quite untenable ways of regarding and talking about things. Accordingly, what may well be true of the mathematized and formalized language of physics need by no means be true, and in a measure cannot be true, of the language we use when playing backgammon with our friends.

However, the suggestion that there are perhaps different spheres of operation, one in which it is proper to use a relating-logic and another in which it is proper to use a what-logic, looks ahead to a theme which we are not yet in a position to treat at any length. Instead, let us move on to consider another illustration, drawn from a slightly different area, in which the use of a relating-logic in the context of everyday life would seem to lead only to incredibilities and absurdities, whereas in a scientific context it would seem defensible enough. This is the area of what today might be called factual truth or contingent truth, as contrasted with analytic truth or necessary truth. Thus far we have been concerned only with analytic truths and necessary truths, arguing that when these are excluded from being truths about the world, all sorts of unacceptable consequences follow, so far as the picture of our everyday world is concerned. But now suppose that, armed with a relating-logic, we attempt to make simple factual statements about the things and events in the world about us — e.g., "Falstaff was a lecherous, treacherous, bawdy villain"; "That's an apple"; "Addison was willing to wound and yet afraid to strike." Just what do statements of this sort, couched in the forms of a relating-logic, actually disclose to us about the world in which we find ourselves?

Embarrassment over Contingent Truths in a Relating-Logic

So far as a what-logic is concerned, we have already observed that assertions such as the above are of a kind to disclose not what the subject in question is essentially, but rather what it is accidentally.[7] Such assertions, being subject-predicate propositions, may thus be called what-statements, albeit in a somewhat extended sense.[8] But what now of a relating-logic? The question which we wish to examine is just what matter of fact it is that is being asserted when so-called matter-of-fact assertions are made in this sort of a logic.

At first one might be inclined to wonder why it should be supposed that there was any problem here. "Falstaff's a lecherous, treacherous, bawdy villain" — that is matter of fact enough, and why should anyone be in the least puzzled as to what sort of matter of fact is being asserted? Just the same, remember that in the context of a relating-logic there is the basic presupposition of an absolute dichotomy between mere analytic or linguistic statements as to the meanings of our terms and statements of fact, and there is no way in which an analysis of the meanings of our terms might be considered to yield any information about matters of fact. Yet note that in saying that someone is a lecherous, treacherous, bawdy villian, or that something is an apple, the meaning of "apple" or of "lecherous,

7. Strictly speaking, and going by our own account given in Chapter III above, insofar as "That's an apple" expresses the specific nature or *what* of the *that*, the predication is essential and not accidental.

8. On this, see above Chapter III, note 6.

treacherous, bawdy villain" is presumably determined by the sorts of things analysts like to call "verbal definitions," "the laying down of grammatical rules," or "the analysis of meanings." How, then, can such merely contrived verbal meanings ever give us the slightest information about either the real existing object before us which we describe as being an apple, or, for that matter, about Sir John Falstaff?

We might illustrate the same difficulty by taking a somewhat different tack. "What's in a name?" Shakespeare asks. "That which we call a rose by any other name would smell as sweet." Yet from the standpoint of a relating-logic, the poet couldn't really have meant what he appears to have said. For what he is apparently saying is that things are what they are, regardless of the names we give them: a rose will have its fragrance, regardless of whether we call it by the name "rose" or "weed," or whether we designate its scent as "fragrance" or as "stench." But how naive of Shakespeare! Did he not realize that in attributing fragrance to a rose, so far from the name's being nothing, the name is everything? For what else is there? If Shakespeare had read Wittgenstein, he would have realized that there is no fact, no being, no entity outside language that we may be supposed to mean when we say "fragrant" or "sweet-smelling," or "rose." Instead, the meaning of a name is but its use in language, and such use is determined by our grammatical rules. Change the rules, and roses no longer will smell sweet, nor will either "rose" or "sweet-smelling" mean what it once did.

But note the curious sort of difficulty which such considerations give rise to. For apparently, in describing our rose, what we say about it would seem to be something that is determined only by our grammatical rules, and "grammar," we are told, "is autonomous and not dictated by reality."[9] Besides, mere rules of use tell us nothing about the way the world is, or about any matter of fact. Accordingly, what is it that we are saying about the rose as a matter of fact, when we say that it smells sweet? Are we saying only that in the uses of our language "rose" and "sweet-smelling" are correlated in certain ways? But that, surely, tells us nothing about the rose in fact or as a matter of fact. Likewise, if by "sweet-smelling" we mean only a certain specific pattern of behavior or use which that word has in the language as contrasted with other words, then what does the use of "sweet-smelling" tell us about the rose?

9. F. Waismann, *The Principles of Linguistic Philosophy*, ed. R. Harré (New York: St. Martin's Press, 1965), p. 40.

In short, the problem which we are raising here in regard to what it is that factual statements in a relating-logic may be supposed to say or to disclose is derivative from the problem which we considered earlier in regard to necessary truths in such a logic. For while the statements which we are considering are all to be reckoned as contingent truths, synthetic truths, factual truths, or what you will, still all of them involve the use of predicates or function terms. And how is the meaning of such a predication or function term determined? The answer is, "simply by our grammatical rules." What possible relevance, then, can the meaning of such a term have with respect to so-called matters of fact?

We can readily imagine what the reply will be to this question. Yet it is a reply which we should prefer to formulate in Lewisean rather than in Wittgensteinian terms, clarity in a writer being at least sometimes preferable to mystification. Lewis would say that in a judgment such as "This is an edible apple," the predicate concept, "edible apple," is a concept, and as such its meaning may be exploited in a series of purely analytic propositions. Nor is the truth of any one of them either determined by or determinative of the world of fact. Thus, for example, the "edible apple" concept might be exfoliated in some such manner as this:

For all X's, if X is an edible apple,

then to look at it, it will be round and ruddy;

to smell it, it will be sweet-smelling;

to taste it, it will be tangy, etc.

Given such a series of analytic propositions,[10] Lewis argues that in effect this is a schema of verification, in terms of which a statement such as "This is an edible apple" can be put to the test of experience — i.e., if it is an edible apple, then it will be round and ruddy in appearance, sweet as to odor, tangy as to taste, etc. Accordingly, being thus verifiable, the statement is clearly a statement of fact. In other words, although the meaning of the predicate concept in such a proposition is determined quite independently of any matter of fact, this does not in the least militate against the proposition's being a statement of fact.

Plausible though this defense is, there are, nevertheless, two difficulties in regard to it. The first difficulty we might put this way: although Lewis

---

10. One might raise a question as to whether the above predicates are indeed essential to, or analytically contained within, the concept "edible apple." However, the example is Lewis' and we are simply borrowing it for our present purposes. See *Mind and the World Order* (New York: Dover Publications, n.d.), p. 119.

has seemingly provided a schema of verification for a proposition such as "This is an edible apple," still he has not made it too clear just what in the way of matter of fact is disclosed in the assertion. For one thing, since the concept "edible apple" is defined in terms of "tangy to the taste," "round and ruddy to the sight," and "sweet as to odor," each one of these notes, in turn, will be defined in terms of a similar series of possible verifying experiences. As a result, the actual data of experience — i.e., the matters of fact proper, as contrasted with our conceptual constructions whereby we order and relate these data with respect to each other — shrink, if not to the vanishing point, at least to the point of being literally "ineffable," and so, as it would seem, quite characterless.[11] As a result, the ordering of such data with respect to one another — indeed, the very characterization of them in any way — is entirely our work of conceptual construction, and in consequence is something that is neither determined by the facts (data), nor is as such a disclosure of any real relations or relations in fact between the facts. Indeed, putting the most charitable interpretation upon this theory, one might say that while there are matters of fact for Lewis they are presumably neither related nor ordered to one another in any way, nor even possessed of any characters or attributes, all such relations and characterizations being our work and hence not properly a part of the matters of fact at all. Accordingly, in the light of these considerations we find ourselves just as puzzled as we were before as to what in the way of

11. Lewis' embarrassment on this score is so well known as scarcely to require documentation. Thus on the one hand, the given is pronounced to be "ineffable," utterly characterless (cf. *ibid.*, pp. 53, 58). On the other hand, Lewis is equally insistent that the given data have so much of a brute-fact character about them that "the activity of thought can neither create nor alter" them (p. 47), and they are also said to have at least sufficiently determinate natures as to provide a "clue" (pp. 49, 157) to the classifications and meanings and interpretations given to them (see also pp. 59, 143–45). Now it is hard to see just how these two quite different ways of construing the given element in our experience are reconcilable with one another. It is true that in his later work, *The Analysis of Knowledge and Valuation* (La Salle, Ill.: Open Court, 1947), Lewis may have been rather more successful in such a reconciliation than he was in *Mind and the World Order*. (For an exceedingly interesting discussion of this issue, the reader might consult Moltke S. Gram, "Two Theories of the A Priori" [diss., Indiana University, 1965], Chap. 5, "The Paradox of the A Priori.") However, our concern here is not to give a full and rounded assessment of the work of C. I. Lewis, but only to illustrate the sort of embarrassment which one is likely to encounter in attempting to achieve an understanding of the things of the world through the use of a relating-logic rather than a what-logic. A comparable illustration might be given through citing and tracing out the vagaries of Wittgenstein's "seeing as" doctrine.

a matter of fact is actually being asserted in a statement such as "This is an edible apple," enunciated in the context of a relating-logic.

The second difficulty is one that recalls our earlier mentioned fallacy of inverted intentionality. From the standpoint of a what-logic — and it would seem to be the common sense of the matter as well — when one says that something is an edible apple, one means that the thing in question is really determined as to any number of other features and attributes as well. Thus to use Lewis' own list of such features, it must be round, ruddy, tangy, sweet-smelling, etc. Now surely, from the common-sense point of view, this can scarcely be supposed to mean only what Lewis says it means, viz., that our concept of "edible apple" has these further notes contained in it. No, commonsensically we should suppose that it is the real apple that involves these further features, and not just our concept "apple." It would be as if, parodying Shakespeare, we were to say, "An edible apple, by any other name, would still be something tangy, something round, something ruddy, something sweet-smelling, etc." Further, when commonsensically we thus suppose that it is the real apple that involves these further features, and not just our concept of apple, we don't for a minute imagine that such "involvement" is to be interpreted as merely something of our own doing and our own determination. There is something about the very nature of the apple itself that determines it to have these further features and attributes.

But contrast Lewis' account of the matter. How does it happen that our concept "edible apple" involves the further notes of "round," "ruddy," "tangy," etc.? It is simply because we have put them there: we packed these particular notes into our concept "edible apple," rather than certain others; we could, of course, have defined "apple" differently, but we didn't. In other words, there is nothing about either the nature of edible apples themselves, or even about our concept "edible apple," that requires such apples to be of a certain character rather than another; this is simply a matter of our own arbitrary decision.

Thus when commonsensically we suppose that a thing's being in fact an edible apple involves — also in fact — its being round, ruddy, tangy, etc., Lewis would have to say [12] that this is mistaken: we can't mean any

12. However, we are by no means sure that Lewis would have said it, simply because he never appreciated the embarrassing implications of the fallacy of inverted intentionality for his own position, particularly with respect to judgments that he would have considered to be straightforward synthetic judgments or judgments of fact.

real or factual involvement here; instead, we can only mean a conceptual involvement. But what is such an interpretation of the meaning of a factual statement if not an inversion of intentionality? It is similar to Waismann's attempted inversion of the intentions of red and green to "red" and "green."

This is not all there is to it. For suppose the statement "This is an edible apple" is true. As Lewis would construe it, this must mean that the statement has been put to the test of experience, and in consequence the further statements have been found to be true: "This is round"; "This is ruddy"; "This is tangy"; "This is sweet-smelling"; etc. Now so far as our concepts are concerned, there is a connection between "This is an edible apple" and the further statements that are supposed to constitute that statement's verification. Indeed, if there were not such a connection, then the latter statements could hardly constitute a verification of the former. On the other hand, what about the fact that is being asserted when "This is an edible apple" is true? Is the fact of something's being an edible apple nowise connected with the fact of its being round, or the fact of its being ruddy, or the fact of its being tangy, etc.? On Lewis' analysis all that one can mean by "connection" here is a conceptual connection, or a connection between the sentence "This is an edible apple" and the sentences "This is round," "This is ruddy," etc., and not at all a connection between the fact of something's being an edible apple and the fact of its being round and ruddy, etc.

Can Lewis really be serious about this? Does he honestly suppose that when "This is an edible apple" is true, one has no right to suppose that there is any single thing, or "this," or apple existing in fact, which in its own unity holds together and determines the further attributes of being round, ruddy, tangy, etc.? Instead, does he seriously believe that this statement asserts no more than a factual situation involving an utterly heterogeneous and disconnected congeries of data, or *qualia*, or possibly events, which, if there existed logically proper names for them, might be designated simply as "roundness$_2$," or "tanginess$_6$," or "ruddiness$_{11}$," etc.?

It is hard to believe that Lewis would seriously have entertained such a construction's being placed upon his notion of what is in fact the case when the assertion "This is an edible apple" is true. Yet should he repudiate such a construction, it would seem that Lewis was trying both to have his cake and eat it too — denying the common-sense understanding of what is in fact the case when "This is an edible apple" is true, and yet enjoying the fruits of just such an understanding in order to obviate the seeming utter paradox of his own understanding of that factual situation. One rather suspects that Lewis has gone in for inverting intentionality with his right hand and then setting it right again with his left, and of course without the right hand's ever knowing what the left was doing!

What Kind of Knowledge Is Scientific Knowledge?

Very well, suppose that a relating-logic must find itself in just such difficulties when it comes to explaining what is meant by "This is an edible apple"—or for that matter all other statements of a like contingency, e.g., "Falstaff was a lecherous, treacherous, bawdy villain"; "Fleance is 'scaped"; "Addison was one to damn with faint praise and assent with civil leer." Still, even though such difficulties might well be utterly insupportable in the properly human context of ordinary language, need they be in the least embarrassing where scientific language is concerned? Suppose a scientist makes a judgment to the effect that a given body in process of falling—call it body X—insofar as it is falling freely, is accelerating at the rate of 32 feet per second per second. If we further suppose such a judgment to be made in a properly scientific context, what then would be the point of asserting such a thing? It might be for some purpose such as calculating just when such a body would reach the ground, or, if X happened to be a projectile, the arc which X would have to describe if it were fired from a cannon or thrown from the hand of a baseball player. It is all-important that in a scientific context such predictions be verifiable in terms of comparatively unambiguous and communicable data like pointer-readings, flashes of light, etc.

Set in such a context, why might not the judgment "X, insofar as it is falling freely, is accelerating at the rate of 32 feet per second per second" be construed in just the way that a relating-logic would propose to construe it? In other words, the questions as to what such a body really is, independently of the language game in terms of which we describe it, is one which would simply be ruled out as belonging in principle to an entirely different logic. Likewise, the question as to what the "objective necessity" is in the "causal sequences" that maintain the body at this constant rate of acceleration—a necessity quite independent of "the form of the theory which connects descriptions of these sequences" [13]—would also be ex-

13. These are all Professor Hanson's terms which we are borrowing.

cluded as improper and irrelevant to the operative logical context. Indeed, all of the questions and difficulties which we sought to press with respect to Lewis' example of "This is an edible apple" would in one sense create just as much havoc if pressed with regard to "X is accelerating at the rate of 32 feet per second per second." That is to say, there would be questions as to what X is in itself, as contrasted with the mere data in terms of which it manifests itself to the investigating scientist, or questions as to just how in fact and in reality these data are held together in an actual pattern of organization that is more than a mere conceptual construction on our part.

Perhaps it begins to emerge rather more clearly just how a relating-logic functions, or should function, in a scientific context. Quite literally, it provides no description [14] either of things or of events in the natural world; it offers no sort of explanation either of how or of why things happen as they do in nature; it does not even set forth or exhibit the happenings and events in nature in their relations to one another.[15] Rather, all that it does is to provide the scientist with the means, so to speak, of "getting about," or of "going on" intellectually from one natural happening or occurrence to another.

Even the familiar metaphor of a map is not proper when we try to picture to ourselves just how a relating-logic provides the scientist with means for getting about and going on. For a map is perforce a map of something: it represents or sets forth, in a way proper to maps, the real geographical relationships that exist between various points and places in the real world. But a relating-logic does not function in a way that is in any respect a representing or a picturing of anything in the real world at all.

Perhaps, when all is said and done, Lewis' figure of the "conceptual go-cart" is the least inept and misleading in such a context. For a relating-logic does serve the scientist much as a go-cart: it enables him to get about and to go on in his investigations; but just as the use of a go-cart is not as such descriptive or explanatory of the countryside it traverses, so also the use of a relating-logic provides no descriptions, no pictures, no maps, no representations, no explanations, no anything — it just gets you there!

14. In one sense, of course, a logic as such is not supposed to provide a description of things; it is only the use of a logic which can do so.

15. In this connection it is important to note that it is one matter to relate things to one another; it is another matter to recognize things as being themselves related. It is the former that we are insisting is the characteristic work of a relating-logic, not the latter. Indeed, if a relating-logic were to function in the latter way, then it would not be a relating-logic at all, but a what-logic.

The question is how a logic which cannot serve as a means either of description or of explanation can possibly be considered as an organon or as an instrument of knowledge and understanding. However, insofar as the use of such a relating-logic does provide the scientist with what might be termed means of prediction and retrodiction, or with means of simply going on and getting about conceptually, and inasmuch as such forecasts and retrocasts are susceptible of verification and falsification, then the statements which he makes will still come under the heading "true-false," however much they may fall short of being either descriptive or explanatory of anything. Accordingly, while it would seem that what emerges from the scientist's use of a relating-logic is indeed a kind of knowledge, it is hardly a knowledge and understanding as one naturally thinks of them in the context of an ordinary, everyday what-logic.

It is at this point that Wittgenstein's metaphor of the language game, understood in the sense in which some of his disciples appear to have understood it, can perhaps be of some slight use and value. If we think of the language of physics as but a scheme or project for an unusually complicated and ingenious game with elaborate rules of use, and if we further suppose that scientific languages generally determine just so many games (not in the way in which ordinary language may be said to be a game, but rather in the way in which ordinary games are games), then we can begin to get a sense of how modern science, insofar as it involves the use of a relating-logic, does indeed yield knowledge of a sort, although not a knowledge that tells us what anything in fact is, either essentially or accidentally, or why it is, or how it is, or even anything about it at all. For just as in football the playing of the game is nowise significant of or representative of anything outside the game, so also in the language game of physics there are rules that determine when certain statements are to be pronounced "true" and when "false" — and yet such statements must not be supposed to intend or signify some physical reality or order of nature that is outside of and independent of the game altogether.

Such an account of scientific knowledge will no doubt strike many scientists and philosophers of science as utterly bizarre, not to say wrongheaded.[16] Indeed, there are any number of scientists who, when confronted

16. It should be clear by now that in putting forward a what-logic as one that is proper to the humanities and a relating-logic as one that is proper to the sciences, we are not so much describing what the present logic of the sciences and that of the humanities actually are, as recommending what they might be or ought to be. Particularly with respect to the humanities, it must have struck every informed reader that in most cur-

with questions of the sort we considered above, would take such questions at their face value and would attempt to give thoroughly realistic answers as to just what a given body, X, is in itself, or just what the real physical forces are in nature that are responsible for X's acceleration at a particular rate. In other words, just as commonsensically we all feel baffled when a statement like "This is an edible apple" is construed in the manner of a relating-logic, so many scientists would shy away from the consequences of what the face of nature would look like — or still more from the consequence that it wouldn't "look like" anything — if scientific judgments were to be construed in a similar fashion. Such a reaction would betoken a hesitancy, or even a downright unwillingness, to accept the all-out use of a relating-logic; rather, these scientists would appear to want to cling to a what-logic, even within the sphere of science itself.

Now far be it from us to make a judgment as to which logic ultimately is the proper one to use in scientific investigation. Yet considering the present dispensation in science, it would seem that the apparent paradoxes connected with the use of a relating-logic need cause no embarrassment so far as the realization of immediate ends are concerned: reliance upon publicly communicable and reproducible data, accurate prediction of events and happenings, precisely determined possibilities for verification and falsification of hypotheses and theories, etc., can be just as readily achieved if scientists rely exclusively upon the resources of a relating-logic.

For example, consider the following statement of Ernest Nagel's in regard to the question of the "physical reality" of the various theoretical entities that scientists talk about:

Even if some hypothetical scientific objects were physically real in this sense — for example, if the genes postulated by current biological theory of heredity could be made visible — the role of the theoretical notions in science, in terms of which such objects are specified, would not be altered. It is of course quite possible that if we could perceive molecules, many questions still outstanding about them would be answered, so that molecular theory would receive an im-

---

rently fashionable "theories of literature," for example, the relevance of a what-logic to the enterprise of poetry and of literature generally would be almost the last thing that contemporary critics and theorists would be inclined to concede. And similarly, with respect to science, not only many scientists but also a significant group of writers on the philosophy of science e.g., men of such different views as A. N. Whitehead, Teilhard de Chardin, Julian Huxley, E. L. Mascall, Errol Harris, to mention but a few — would insist upon an unequivocally realistic or at least on an empirically realistic account and interpretation of scientific knowledge, and hence would repudiate our suggestions as to the appropriateness of a relating-logic to serve as the logic of the sciences.

proved formulation. Nevertheless, molecular theory would still continue to formulate the traits of molecules in *relational* terms — in terms of relations of molecules to other molecules and to other things [17] — not in terms of any of their qualities that might be directly apprehended through our organs of sense. For the *raison d'être* of molecular theory is not simply to supply information about the sensory qualities of molecules but to enable us to understand (and predict) the occurrence of events and the relations of their interdependence in terms of pervasive structural patterns into which they enter. Accordingly, in this sense of the phrase the physical reality of theoretical entities is of little import for science.[18]

Suppose that Nagel is right and that the use of a what-logic, in place of a relating-logic, would not make the slightest difference so far as the achievement of the proper aims and objectives of science is concerned. The very scientists who suppose otherwise may simply be transposing to the domain of science a way of questioning and even an entire way of understanding which may be quite proper in the world of our everyday concerns as human beings, but may be out of place in the scientific realm.

At the same time, let us not lose sight of what could be the reverse case. Just as it may be inappropriate to foist a what-logic upon us in our role as scientists, it could presumably be just as inappropriate to foist a relating-logic upon us insofar as we are engaged in the business of trying to live our lives simply as intelligent human beings. Indeed, all of the paradoxes which result from the elaborate eschewing of what-statements and the deliberate inverting of intentionality, which perhaps need not bother us as scientists, could become and indeed in a measure have become, a downright scandal to us as men.

17. From the context it is not entirely clear whether Nagel means to imply that such relations are supplied as a result of the use of a relating-logic, or whether they are simply discovered in the realities themselves. Presumably, though, it is the former alternative that would be his choice. If so, then the quotation is an apt one for illustrating the sort of view of the world that is mediated by a relating-logic.

18. *The Structure of Science* (New York: Harcourt, Brace & World, 1961), p. 146.

144

Chapter VII

A What-Logic *and* Its

Supposed Commitment *to*

Essences *and* Substantial Forms

AT THE BEGINNING of Chapter IV we did a certain amount of trumpeting to the effect that each thing is what it is. The implication of this must be that each thing, in order to be what it is, must somehow have its own *what* or nature or essence. But has this not committed us to a metaphysics of completely discredited queer entities — essences, substantial forms, quiddities, *et al.*

To fend off such a charge, we might try invoking the authority of Leibniz:

I know that I am advancing a great paradox in pretending to resuscitate in some sort the ancient philosophy, and to recall *postliminio* the substantial forms almost banished from modern thought. But perhaps I will not be condemned lightly when it is known that I have long meditated over the modern philosophy and that I have devoted much time to experiments in physics and to demonstrations of geometry and that I, too, for a long time was persuaded of the baselessness of those "beings" *which, however, I was finally to take up again in spite of myself and as though by force* [italics added].[1]

Now what could have possessed Leibniz to make such a statement? What was it that forced him, as it were, and in spite of himself, to take up again such "beings" as substantial forms, essences, etc? Leibniz' own answer as it may be interpreted within the context of the *Discourse on Metaphysics,* was that with a view to doing metaphysics rather than just physics he found himself compelled to resuscitate substantial forms, as well as

to recognize that our moderns do not do sufficient justice to Saint Thomas and to the other great men of that period and that there is in the theories of the scholastic philosophers and theologians far more solidity than is imagined, provided that these theories are employed *a propos* and in their place." [2]

In other words, what Leibniz would appear to be contending for on the one hand and conceding on the other is that:

The consideration of these forms is of no service in the details of physics and ought not to be employed in the explanation of particular phenomena. In regard to this last point, the schoolmen were at fault, as were also the physicists of times past who followed their example, thinking that they had given the reason for the properties of a body in mentioning the forms and qualities without going to the trouble of examining the manner of operation; as if one should be content to say that a clock had a certain amount of clockness derived from its form, and should not inquire in what that clockness consisted. This is indeed enough for the man who buys it, provided he surrenders the care of it to someone else. The fact, however, that there was this misunderstanding and misuse of the substantial forms should not bring us to throw away something whose recognition is so necessary to metaphysics." [3]

It is not hard to imagine what our contemporary philosophical scoffers would say to all this: "It may be all very well for Leibniz to have resuscitated essences and substantial forms, since he wanted to do not just physics, but metaphysics. But who wants to do metaphysics nowadays? So what possible relevance can Leibniz' championing of substantial forms have for our present-day situation in philosophy?"

Yet might not Leibniz' plea for essences in the above-quoted passages be construed as having a logical point and not just a metaphysical one?

1. Sect. XI of the *Discourse on Metaphysics,* in *Leibniz: Selections,* ed. Philip Wiener (New York: Charles Scribner's Sons, 1951), pp. 303–4.

2. *Ibid.,* p. 304.

3. *Ibid.,* p. 302.

For is he not saying, in effect, that the use of a logic more or less on the order of what we have been calling a what-logic or a bee-logic will provide us with a quite different resource of intelligibility, to say nothing of an altogether different view of the world, from anything that can be vouchsafed to us through any mere use of the spider-logic of the physicists and mathematicians? True, Leibniz insists that it is not a case of one logic displacing the other; and, certainly, it is all-important that we avoid being misled into thinking that we can ever properly answer scientific questions through the use of a what-logic, any more than we can pretend to answer what-questions through a relating-logic. Rather, the point is that both of these logics must be "employed *a propos* and in their place." And what does this imply, if not just what we have been contending for all along?

However, it must be admitted that as a historical interpretation of Leibniz this is much too speculative. There is no evidence that he ever explicitly recognized that his attempted distinction of metaphysics from physics might have any implications for a duality of logics. Still, what a philosopher does not himself explicitly recognize may well be brought to light by an interpretive reading of those who come after. Even so awkward and trivial an example as the clockness of the clock would appear to be sug-gestive of something on the order of a complementarity of logics — at least in the sense of a material logic or a transcendental logic. For as Leib-niz acknowledges, to think of the clock as having "a certain amount of clockness derived from its form" is "indeed enough for the man who buys it." And, still more generally, is it not the case that in our everyday con-cerns as men, in contrast to our concerns as scientists and technicians, our knowledge is aimed at the *whats* of things — at what justice is, or what man is, or what time and eternity are, or what life is, or what the nature of things is, etc.? Accordingly, for knowledge and understanding of this sort, it must be a what-logic that we invoke, even though when it comes to the calculations and manipulations and predications pertaining to "the manner of operation" of things, it is the relating-logic of the spiders that we find we have to rely upon rather than the bee-logic of the humanists.

Essences as Philosophical Unmentionables

However, we are beginning to digress from what is really the main concern of this chapter. For regardless of whether we can read into or out of Leibniz any theory as to a complementarity of logics, the fact remains and

147

cannot be blinked away that a use of the sort of thing we have been calling a what-logic does indeed involve us in certain metaphysical or ontological commitments. Surely, if things are to be understood in terms of what they are, then such things must be what they are in order for them to be so understood. And for things to be what they are, each such thing must be of a certain nature or essence; it must have its own *what* or quiddity. And with that our metaphysical fat is indeed in the fire!

Nevertheless, in this book we are not going to do anything about trying to put out that fire. The line must be drawn somewhere, and we propose to draw it just short of becoming involved in discussions as to the precise ontological status and character of such "beings," as Leibniz called them, as essences, substantial forms, natural causes, etc.

What, though, of epistemological questions? For if one speaks of essenses or substantal forms, one's epistemological fat is in the fire as well. And this time, alas, we cannot allow discretion to be the better part of valor. For the very idea that a knowledge of essences is possible is enough to inflame all the right-thinking, right-minded philosophers of this world. As a matter both of history and of principle, one of the main reasons for the prevalence in the philosophical world today of the sort of thing we have called a relating-logic is just the desire on the part of modern thinkers to avoid any commitment to so seemingly hopeless an epistemological claim as that of having a knowledge of essences.

Let us attempt a little fire-fighting on behalf of this epistemological issue. To begin with, let us try to make clear just how the possibility of a knowledge of essences is to be compared with the defense of what-statements which we undertook in Chapter IV. There, it will be remembered, we sought to confine the question strictly within the bounds of logic. How was it possible, we asked, to have a proposition that was both a necessary truth and a truth about the world, that needed to be at one and the same time self-evident and empirically evident? Note that what we were inquiring about was a possibility understood simply in terms of logic: how was it possible to have a proposition that required seemingly incompatible truth-conditions? Suppose that in Chapter IV we succeeded in answering this logical question satisfactorily, thereby making what-statements logically respectable; that is still a far cry from making them epistemologically respectable. For is it possible for us ever to attain a knowledge of the *whats* or essences of things or of necessary connections in nature? Granted that if we could ever achieve such a knowledge we might be able to formulate it in logically respectable what-statements, still do we ever, and can we ever, achieve a knowledge of this sort?

With this we are brought face to face with both **Hume and Kant**. For if what-statements, as we have characterized them, are not merely logically feasible, but epistemologically possible, then Hume is thereby given the lie direct, and Kant's mammoth apparatus of the transcendental method to explain how synthetic judgments a priori are possible is made to appear not so much false as just much ado about nothing.

Not Essences but Family Resemblances

First, though, before we compound our indiscretion by taking on both Hume and Kant, let us pay at least passing notice to certain critics who are nearer to us in time. These are the neo-Wittgensteinians. Hard as it is ever to seize these Protean philosophers in definite and determinate philosophical doctrines of their own, they not infrequently leave us in less doubt as to which doctrines they wish to divest themselves of; and one of these that they seem unusually frank about repudiating is the doctrine of essences. The *locus classicus* of such a repudiation is of course the celebrated discussion in the *Investigations* of "games":

Consider for example the proceedings that we call "games." I mean board-games, card-games, ball-games, Olympic games, and so on. What is common to these all? Don't say: "There *must* be something common, or they would not be called 'games' " — but *look and see* whether there is anything common to *all*. — For if you look at them, you will not see something that is common to *all*, but similarities, relationships, and a whole series of them at that. To repeat: don't think but look![4]

While we are all thus straining hard not to think but to look, perhaps we might request a bit of philosophical discussion to be piped in from the background. It shouldn't distract us from our looking, mind you. Rather, it might just serve to relieve some of the tension of that thoughtless looking and never seeing, much as the piped music of Christmas carols in a crowded store is supposed to relax the tension of our senseless Christmas shopping, yet without for a minute interrupting the shopping. For the

4. L. Wittgenstein, *Philosophical Investigations*, trans. G. E. M. Anscombe (New York: Macmillan, 1953), § 66.

curious thing about this purported Wittgenstein critique of the doctrine of essences is that while it is quite unmistakably a critique of something, one wonders whether it is really a critique of the doctrine of essences.

Thus suppose someone were to enjoin us not just to look at the above-quoted passage from Wittgenstein, but to think about it as well, would it not become clear that what Wittgenstein is really criticizing is not so much the ontological doctrine of essences, or even the epistemological doctrine of the possibility of our knowing essences, but rather the some-what different philosophical doctrine that wherever there is one word or one name for many things there must be one essence common to them all? But this latter doctrine, while it may have often been associated with a doctrine of essences, is by no means the same as that doctrine, or even necessarily connected with it.

For example, suppose that we again call Aristotle to witness, particularly in his celebrated discussion of things or beings or entities that are things or beings or entities in the way in which "a white man" or "a pale man" might be said to be a thing or an entity.[5] As everyone knows, Aristotle would hold that a thing or entity of this sort was composite, being a com-pound of a substance (in this case, man) and of some other thing belonging to a different category (in this case, the quality of whiteness or paleness). Now suppose, Aristotle suggests, that we were to call such a composite being or entity by a single name, say "cloak." That thing, then, and any other like it would then be known as a "cloak." Does this mean, that since all cloaks will thus have the same name, there must be one essence which is common to them all? Aristotle answers, "Of course not." For the name "cloak" as here defined was not a name given to any thing that was properly one in the first place, any more than the *Iliad* could be said to be the name of anything that in any proper sense could be considered one single being or entity. However, if the thing or being that is under consideration is not one thing in the proper sense at all, but only an accidental unity,[6] then "it" does not have any essence or nature of its own at all. There is no

5. *Metaphysics*, Book VII, Chap. 4. See the references made to the same passage and the same doctrine in Chapter III above, note 14.

6. In Scholastic philosophy — e.g., in Aquinas — this distinction between things that are one in the sense that each has a single essence or *what*, and things that are one in the sense that each enjoys only an accidental unity, is characterized in terms of the distinction between *ens per se* and *ens per accidens*. See, for example, the edition of St. Thomas' *On Being and Essence*, ed. A. A. Maurer (Toronto: Pontifical Institute of Mediaeval Studies, 1949), p. 26, n. 2.

essence of white man or of the thing labeled "cloak," [7] any more than there is an essence of the *Iliad*.

Accordingly, when we set down as our basic principle that each thing is what it is and therefore has its proper nature or essence or character, it is important to recognize that, following Aristotle, this principle holds only if the thing in question is truly one thing or one being. Indeed, if it is not one thing or one being as presumably, to use Wittgenstein's example, a game is not, then it clearly does not have any single nature or essence that makes it that kind of thing and nothing else. And Aristotle would be no less emphatic than Wittgenstein in repudiating any contention that because all games are called by the same name, "game," or all cloaks (in Aristotle's sense) by the same name, "cloak," they therefore must have a common nature or essence. Indeed, we can even imagine that with respect to purely accidental unities like games or cloaks Aristotle might readily applaud Wittgenstein's suggestion that it is only by virtue of certain "family resemblances" [8] that we call all instances of such things by the same name, and not at all by virtue of any common nature or essence that they all have or share.[9]

Very well, then, going simply by what Wittgenstein says in the oft-cited sections of the *Investigations* (§§ 66 ff.), we would suggest that he really isn't arguing against a doctrine of essences at all, but only against

7. Alas, like all passages from Aristotle, this one is subject to divergent interpretations. For example, in Tricot's superb French edition and commentary on the *Metaphysics* (Aristote, *La Métaphysique* [Paris: Vrin, 1964], I, 359), the editor remarks that "rien ne s'oppose à ce qu'un terme composé, comme *homme blanc*, soit, dans une certaine mesure, une essence." But then Tricot hastens to add: "Ce ne sera pas une essence proprement dite."

Actually, we scarcely think there is any radical divergence of Tricot's interpretation from the one we are following. For while it is true that a pale man is one thing and in this sense even is what it is and has an essence, still it is not one and does not have an essence, "proprement dite." And this last is as much as is needed to sustain our argument in the text.

8. Wittgenstein, § 67.

9. It might be objected that in the argument of this paragraph we have confused two quite different considerations. Thus Aristotle, in arguing that "pale man" has no essence, is talking about the essential unity of a single individual thing. In contrast, Wittgenstein, in arguing against there being any single essence of "games," is talking about a common essence that could be shared by any number of different individual things. Nevertheless, even though the two considerations are indeed quite different, there is still a pertinent connection between them. To use Aristotle's example, if a "cloak" is not really one thing at all, then clearly there could be no common essence shared by all cloaks either. On the contrary, it could well be that what justifies our calling all cloaks by the same name rests on no more than their family resemblances.

what we might call the one word–one essence fallacy. If you then counter with the suggestion that whatever Wittgenstein may have said that he was against, we all know that what he really was against was the very doctrine of essences, we can only retort, "Perhaps so, but then what were his arguments? One can only speculate as to Wittgenstein's intended arguments, whereas his expressed arguments seem to show that he was not arguing against essences as such, but rather against quite another doctrine."

Moreover, if either Wittgenstein or any of his disciples should have wished to question not merely whether there must always be a common nature or essence corresponding to any universal, categorematic term, but also whether anything under any circumstances can ever be said to be what it is or the kind of thing it is and not something else, then that would have been a very difficult philosophical undertaking indeed. For is it even thinkable to suppose that a thing itself is never anything — not this kind of thing, or that, or the other? You may ask, "But why could not things be what they are only accidentally, and never essentially?" The answer obviously is, "But what would those things be that are now this and now that, but never anything just in themselves? Presumably they would be of no determinate nature, and hence could not be said to be anything at all."

Even the notion of family resemblances would seem to presuppose that at least some things or beings are the kinds of things they are. Thus as Wittgenstein puts it, "I can think of no better expression to characterize these similarities than 'family resemblances'; for the various resemblances between members of a family: build, features, colour of eyes, gait, temperament, etc., etc. overlap and criss-cross in the same way." [10] Very well, let us suppose it is the eminent family of Wittgenstein that we are talking about. It has already been conceded that to be recognizable as a member of that family it is not necessary that everyone in the family exhibit a specific set of common traits — the same build, the same color of eyes, the same temperament, etc. It might also be conceded that for a particular member of the family, say Ludwig himself, it was scarcely essential to him that he have the particular build that he did have, or the particular color of eyes, or the particular temperament, etc. And yet even though it may not have been essential to Ludwig that he have just that build, still the build that he did have was that kind of build and not another. Or it may

10. Wittgenstein, § 67.

not have been essential that he have just the color of eyes that he did, say blue; and yet, clearly, the blue of his eyes was blue and not red, it was a color and not a sound, a quality and not a quantity, etc.

If we shift to the Aristotelian example of a pale man, which we simply designate by the name "cloak," it is certainly true that cloak has no essence, and also that pallor is not of the essence of an individual man who happens to be pale. Yet surely the pallor of a particular man will certainly be what *it* essentially is, viz., pallor and not ruddiness, a skin color and not a kind of temperament, a quality and not a quantity or a substance, etc.

Accordingly, in the face of these rather more thoroughgoing logical and linguistic analyses, it is hard to believe that any Wittgensteinian, or any man in his senses, would have ever wanted really to deny that anything is ever essentially anything. If some Wittgensteinian should nonetheless persist in such a denial, then perhaps the only pertinent comment would be that philosophy is not only "a battle against the bewitchment of our intelligence by means of language,"[11] but also a battle against the abandonment of intelligence in favor of language.

"But," someone might say, "all this talk about things simply having to be what they essentially are would seem to leave us in a very sorry plight epistemologically. For how can we be sure that we have truly recognized what various types and kinds of things are essentially? Or for that matter, in view of the immediately foregoing discussion, how is one to know for sure in a given case whether one is dealing with the sort of thing that even has an essence? Thus how do we know that things in the everyday world about us — trees, sunshine, the color blue, oxygen, the height of a building — are what they are in the sense of having their own distinctive natures or essences? Why might not each of them turn out to be things on the order of a pale man or games, which don't properly have any nature or essence of their own?"

The answer is that we don't *know* such things, if by "knowing" one means "knowing for sure" or "knowing infallibly." This brings us back again to that frank recognition of falliblism in respect to a knowledge of essences which we remarked on in our discussion of criteria in Chapter IV. For it is indeed odd to what extent it is generally supposed that any recognition of essences in things, coupled as it is with a logic of what-statements and necessary truths about the world, etc., must inevitably

---

11. *Ibid.*, § 109.

bring in its train an extreme philosophical dogmatism, claiming an absolute certainty for its pronouncements on what is necessarily the case. However, as we hope we have made sufficiently clear in Chapter IV, neither essentialism [12] in philosophy, nor the what-logic that is associated with it, necessarily involves any such pretensions to infallibility in knowledge.[13] But to fall short of certain knowledge does not mean that one thereby falls short of all knowledge. This, undoubtedly, the ordinary language philosophers would be the first to insist upon. Surely, then, old-fashioned essentialist philosophers may claim a fallible and corrigible knowledge of essences, much as new-fashioned analytic philosophers claim a fallible and corrigible knowledge of contingent fact.

Outflanking Hume and Kant

Now we must come round to our long-promised confrontation with Hume and Kant. It will be remembered that we were nothing if not pretentious in our earlier pronouncements that if what-statements could be shown to be epistemologically possible as well as logically feasible then Hume and Kant would immediately be reduced to little more than historical curiosities in philosophy. Clearly though, the hour for such arrogance is now past, and we must get down to the more modest and serious business of showing how we would propose, if not to assault Hume and Kant directly, then at least to outflank them.

To this latter end, we should like to pose a question as to whether both Hume and Kant may not have worked with a dogmatic and somewhat

12. We use the label "essentialism" with misgivings, simply because it has been used in so many senses that it can hardly fail to be misleading. For example, Professor Gilson in *Being and Some Philosophers* (Toronto: Pontifical Institute of Mediaeval Studies, 1959) has used it as a general term, covering nearly all those tendencies in Western thought which are at variance with what he calls the "existentialism" of St. Thomas. Nevertheless, we are using the term in such a different sense that we see no incompatibility between essentialism as we are defending it and Professor Gilson's own brand of existentialism. Thus see Gilson, esp. Chaps. 4 and 5.

13. Thus it might be noted that Professor Popper, in his essay "Three Views Concerning Human Knowledge" (*Conjectures and Refutations* [New York: Basic Books, 1962], pp. 103 7), simply lays down, as one of the criteria of what he calls "essentialism," the conviction that "The scientist can succeed in finally establishing the truth of such theories beyond all reasonable doubt." We should not wish to deny that in the history of Western science and philosophy this conviction may indeed have often been associated with what Professor Popper calls essentialism. But whatever may have been the case historically, philosophically there is no necessary connection between the two.

uncritical notion of what it is that is given or presented in experience, with the result that the sort of knowledge that might be supposed to be mediated in and through what-statements is rendered impossible *ab initio*. Thus for Hume, all that may be said to be given or presented to us in experience are mere "impressions," nothing more. And while it would be misleading to say that such impressions are utterly characterless (they are, after all, specifically colors, sounds, odors, flavors, etc., of varying duration and of varying sizes, shapes, etc.), they nevertheless are not presented to us as being the colors or shapes or sounds of anything, or as being in any proper sense causally connected, either with each other, or with anything else. Likewise, for Kant the manifold of experience,[14] while it could hardly be said to present us with nothing at all, still does not present us with anything of sufficient determinateness or order that we can in any way describe it or say what it is. Kant's whole point is that the so-called matter of our experience, or that which we are literally given or presented with, is quite literally only the matter of experience and hence not experience as such; for the latter — i.e., for experience — our own human contribution is indispensable as serving both to complement what is simply given in experience and to so order and dispose the given as to make of it an experience.

In other words, for Hume and for Kant alike, the everyday world in which we find ourselves — the thick world of people and things, of real changes and their causes, of forces and powers — is not, strictly speaking, given to us as such in experience. Rather it must be in some way or another either inferred from or constituted out of what is given. One need merely mention the word "inference" or "constitution" in this connection, and thereby hangs a tale! For any such inference, Hume would insist, is unwarranted; and some such constitution, Kant would insist, is unavoidable, if there is even to be any world of experience at all.

So we at last come around to the general question that we should like to put to both Hume and Kant as to why the given element in experience must be understood and explicated in the peculiar way that both philosophers chose to follow, albeit each in his own way. Why must the model that is operative in such an understanding and explication be the model of what we might call the minimally given, from which the flesh

14. Or even prior to the manifold, the bare materials of experience as they are before they are formed and structured by either the a priori forms of intuition or the pure concepts of the understanding.

and blood character of the things in the world about us can only be inferred, or out of which it must somehow be constructed and constituted? Instead, we might avail ourselves of a model of the sort that Francis Parker has suggested,[15] in which the role of the senses in knowledge is compared to that of a soldier who brings a coded message from the front to the commanding officers in the rear, the latter, in turn, functioning in a role comparable to that of the intellect in knowledge: the soldier brings the message, but he cannot read it or interpret it; and yet the message is all there, given in full as it were, and nowise needing either to be inferred from or constituted out of what is given. Likewise, instead of supposing that it is but a minimally given with which we are presented in sensation and perception, why not suppose that the very things of our everyday world are given to us in their very substance, and as both active and being acted upon? True, it is not the eye alone, as such, that sees the tree; yet what is seen through the eyes is recognized by our intellect and understanding as being a tree.

In other words, to point up in a still different way the question which we would put to Hume and Kant, we might simply ask: why not consider the human understanding to be an apprehensive faculty quite as much as are the senses? Or, alternatively, why suppose that the only role which the understanding can have in knowledge is an exclusively inferring role, or perhaps an ordering role, or maybe even a constructive and fabricative role, with respect to the data which it finds itself presented with in sensation? Why should not its primary role be, rather, one of apprehension and description? True, the understanding can only discern and make out the character of something that is presented to it in sensation, just as the officers cannot read the dispatch unless and until it has been brought to them. Still, just as it is the business of the officers to read the message that is delivered, so also the business of the understanding in this particular

15. See his essay "Traditional Reason and Modern Reason," in *Faith and Philosophy*, ed. Alvin Plantinga (Grand Rapids: Eerdmans Publishing Company, 1964), pp. 40–41. The entire essay deserves to be read as a succinct statement of much the same thesis which we are trying to defend in this book. We flatter ourselves that what Professor Parker refers to as "traditional reason" is not unlike what we are calling a "what-logic," and what he refers to as "modern reason" is largely a "relating-logic," in our sense of the term. (Incidentally, Professor Parker's proposed model of the soldier relaying a message is reminiscent of a suggestion originally made by Gilson in *Réalisme Thomiste et critique de la connaissance* [Paris: Vrin, 1939], p. 218.)

context is simply to discern, to recognize, and to describe[16] the things and events of the everyday world that are given in sensation and perception.

Moreover, when one recognizes the plausibility of such an epistemological sketch of the given element in experience and of the proper function of the understanding with respect to it, then one can also see how this fits in with our earlier account of the logical character of what-statements. For so far from such statements being able to dispense with empirical evidence in their support, it is precisely because such judgments bear directly upon the things and happenings that are presented to us in experience that they must be judgments based upon such experience. At the same time, because they are judgments as to what these things are and why they are, they must equally be seen to be evident in the light of the very natures and characters of those same things with which they are concerned and which they are about.

One further point. In our earlier discussion of the logical character of what-statements, we put forward the somewhat paradoxical contention that even though such statements purport to be necessary truths, they are nevertheless subject to error and hence constantly in need of correction and revision. But now in the light of the epistemological setting which we are suggesting is proper to such statements, is not this seeming paradox rendered natural and plausible? For supposing that it is the function of the understanding to recognize what is presented in sensation for what it is, is there any reason to imagine that the understanding must be infallible in such judgments? On the contrary, there is every reason to suppose that something may well turn out not to be what we take it to be. Thus the thing that I judge to be an apple, or the man that I judge to be a lecherous, treacherous, bawdy villain may prove not to be so at all. Even my judgments as to what logicians, or planets, or time, or hydrogen, or men, or even analytic philosophy are (or is) might well turn out to be mistaken!

The Confusion of Epistemological with Ontological Ultimates

But enough by way of a preliminary sketch or crude working model of an epistemology that might well serve as an alternative to that of either Hume or Kant and that certainly does provide a congenial setting for a

16. Once again, it should be noted that such intellectual apprehension and recognition need not necessarily be infallible.

logic of what-statements. However, rather than undertake the requisite, but far too ambitious, task of working out such an epistemology in detail, we must limit ourselves to a few illustrations of how any logic on the order of a what-logic, without such a congenial epistemology but with the characteristic and somewhat arbitrary notion of the given element in experience that has come to be dominant in modern philosophy, is bound to become largely inoperative.

Our first illustration will be taken from Bertrand Russell. In the *Analysis of Mind* there is an interesting and rather amusing passage[17] in which Russell makes considerable sport of the old Aristotelian doctrine of substance-accident. Or, rather, Russell is not making sport of the doctrine so much as of the cogency of its application in a given concrete case. For superficially, what could be more cogent than the obvious fact that there cannot well be such a thing as walking without there being anything that is doing the walking? It pertains to the very nature of an activity such as walking that it be an activity of something — or, to use the technical Aristotelian terms, "an accident" of "a substance."

To this, a Russell might reply[18] that while it could well be the case that in the context of Aristotelian philosophy the word or concept "accident" (or even "activity") is necessarily associated with the further notion of being "of a substance," this is at best a mere verbal definition, or possibly an analytic truth — and such things, of course, tell us nothing about the world. In other words, while it would readily be conceded that an Aristotelian might not wish to use the word "activity" to designate anything that was not in or of a substance, that has no bearing whatever on the general question as to whether there are any such things as either activities or substances anywhere in the world. It also has no bearing on the question of whether the particular event that Russell presumably is now observing, and which he has simply labeled "walking," is or is not an activity of some substance.

Faced with such a rejoinder, one who would exploit a what-logic might in turn reply that for him the judgment that "Accidents (activities) can

17. This passage is reprinted in *Selected Papers of Bertrand Russell* (New York: Modern Library, n.d.), pp. 355–56.
18. It must be admitted that this reply may sound more Lewisean than Russellian in character. For the purposes of our present argument, however, though indeed not for their personal reputations, it would scarcely make too much difference if these two thinkers were simply conflated.

only be accidents (activities) of substances" is no mere verbal or analytic truth, but a necessary truth about the world. Indeed, in the very concrete instance of walking which Russell would admit that he is observing, it can be recognized what sort of a thing this is, viz., an activity; and an activity, necessarily and self-evidently, is the sort of thing that simply cannot be or take place save as the activity of something.

In other words, we can here see just how the issue between a what-logic and a relating-logic comes directly to a head. To one who is using a what-logic, it is what-statements that come into play in such an instance as that of walking, which Russell cites; and on the basis of these what-statements it is impossible that there should be any such thing as walking without there being anything that is doing the walking. But to one who is using a relating-logic, a what-statement, viz., a necessary truth about the world, is a veritable contradiction in terms — as if one could have a proposition that was both analytic and synthetic at the same time! Little wonder, then, that the partisan of such a logic, since he simply throws up his hands in horror at the very idea of a what-statement, will, of course, feel quite free to claim, with a perfectly straight face, that he sees no impossibility in there being such a thing as walking without there being anything that does the walking.

All the same, one cannot entirely escape the impression that there may be just a bit of play-acting in these professions of not being able to see any impossibility in such situations. Certainly, in our earlier discussion of the analytic-synthetic distinction we did try to make it clear that there is no reason in the nature of the case — i.e., of the logical case — why there might not be propositions that were at once necessary truths and factual truths, and that required not one but two truth-conditions, viz., both self-evidence and empirical evidence. Accordingly, to refuse to recognize a factual impossibility such as there being an activity of walking without anything that walks, merely on the ground that one will not admit what-statements into the precincts of one's logic, is just a bit arbitrary and does bring one under the suspicion that perhaps one is merely putting on an act.

We have already suggested that behind a partiality for a relating-logic there are probably deep-seated epistemological fixations, and it is these that we doubtless need to uncover if we are really to understand the casualness with which a thinker like Russell professes to see no impossibility, where everyone else — particularly every non-philosopher — would suppose that there certainly was one. With this we must recur to those assumptions in regard to the given which are so current and general in nearly all post-Humean philosophy. Thus in Russell's view, as everyone knows, all that is given or presented to us in sensory perception are mere sense data — momentary patches of color, sounds, odors, tastes, etc. These we can be sure are given to us; and, indeed, they are the only things that we can be sure of, all else being a matter of inference or construction. In fact, whereas we can certainly be deceived in regard to any and all inferred entities, in regard to just the bare given data we are not deceived; these are infallible; these are our epistemological ultimates.[19]

In such an epistemological setting, when Russell sees a man walking down the street, he cannot do other than insist that he (Russell) really doesn't see a man at all. All that he sees are patches of color arranged in various patterns and succeeding one another in various ways. If one protests that even colors have to be the colors of something, Russell would answer that nothing like this is given to him in sensation: all that is given is just the datum of color; if there is in addition something that is so colored, that is a matter of inference and hence capable of being doubted. Thus colors, shapes, sizes, motions, even activities, considered as mere sense data, are not given or presented as being accidents of anything or as in any way dependent in their being on anything else.

Why and how can Russell deny what would seem so obvious to anyone else, viz., that qualities, motions, sizes, and activities are immediately presented and given to us as being (and are immediately recognized by us as being) of or in other things, as dependent in their being? The answer is that quite apart from a doctrinaire epistemology that, on purely a priori grounds, would exclude any and all things from the given other than bare sense data,[20] Russell was probably led to such a position by a regard for what we earlier called the supposed epistemological ultimacy of bare sense data. Thus while I cannot possibly be deceived as to my having this visual

19. For example, consider a typical statement like the following: "Although we are doubting the physical existence of the table, we are not doubting the existence of the sense-data which made us think there was a table; we are not doubting that, while we look, a certain color and shape appear to us, and while we press, a certain sensation of hardness is experienced by us." Bertrand Russell, *The Problems of Philosophy* (New York: Henry Holt, n.d.), p. 27.

20. Having chosen Russell as our example, our critique tends naturally to be couched in terms of sense data. However, the scope of our argument is, we believe, sufficiently broad to encompass any number of philosophers who would repudiate anything like sense data in the strict sense — e.g., thinkers as divergent as Lewis, Husserl, and Waismann, to mention but a few.

datum of green right now, I can be deceived as to whether it is a leaf or not. Or Russell might say that while he cannot be deceived as to his seeing certain moving colored shapes in front of him, he can be deceived as to whether what he is seeing is a man walking.

But surely there is something amiss here. For is not Russell in effect confusing an epistemological ultimate with an ontological or metaphysical ultimate? Just because I can be sure that a certain sense datum exists even when I can't be sure about anything else, does it follow that such a datum can exist without anything else? Put a little more abstractly, even supposing that I do not need to *know* about anything other than X in order to *know* that X exists, does it follow that nothing other than X need *exist* for X to *exist*? This surely is a *non sequitur*.

Whatever the validity of this final criticism may be, the foregoing illustration, drawn from Russell's repudiation of the substance-accident principle, should at least serve to show how the peculiar epistemological position which Russell assumes in regard to what is given in experience has the effect of rendering what-statements at once groundless and pointless. Moreover, once one begins to appreciate the very tenuous grounds that Russell or anyone else has for subscribing to such a theory of the given, then it will also begin to look as if what-statements could be made not only logically respectable, but epistemologically respectable as well.

Now let us turn to our second illustration, which is drawn from Hume's repudiation of the causal principle. As is well known, although the greater part of Hume's argument against causation in the *Treatise* is directed against the notion that we have any evidence for particular causal connections in nature (i.e., they are evident neither a priori nor a posteriori), he does nonetheless face squarely up to the issue of the general causal principle, "Every effect must have a cause." [21] Now Hume says that when stated in this way the principle cannot be denied, simply for the reason that it is purely verbal: obviously, by the very meaning of the word "effect," every effect must have a cause. But getting away from such purely verbal considerations, what about the causal principle considered as a genuinely substantive principle? Is it the case that everything that begins to exist, and whose existence is thus contingent, requires a cause of its existence? Hume answers "No." For it is perfectly possible to conceive of a thing as not existing one moment and existing the next, without having to

---

21. *A Treatise of Human Nature*, ed. L. A. Selby-Bigge (Oxford: Clarendon Press, 1888), see especially Bk. I, Pt. III, Sect. 3, "Why a cause is always necessary?"

suppose that there must have been a cause of its having come into existence.

Once again, just as with Russell's argument against substance, there seems to be something rather puzzling about what Hume is saying here. For would not most of us — again, supposing that we put aside for the moment our philosophical sophistications or superstitions — be inclined to respond to Hume's question in just the opposite way? "Why, of course," we would say, "if something that did not exist were suddenly to come into existence, there must be some reason or cause for its having done so. Anything else is simply inconceivable."

Such a common-sense answer, we would suggest, reflects the very natural use on the part of all of us of something like a what-logic, as well as the even more natural assumption or recognition of a general epistemological setting that is congenial to such a logic. Put in more figurative language, it is as if all of us, when our thinking was not all "sicklied o'er with the pale cast" of modern philosophical thought, would consider that written on the very face of any contingent event or happening is its very dependence on at least some outside cause or causes. That is just what such an event or happening is, namely, one that is dependent for its being on some cause outside itself. Here, in short, is an unmistakable and unequivocal example of a what-statement at work, at once self-evident and empirically evident.

How, then, is Hume able to disregard the testimony of such a typical and, as we would suggest, such an inescapable human judgment? How can he say that it is perfectly possible to conceive a thing as being non-existent one moment and existent the next without supposing any sort of cause of its coming into existence? Merely to affirm such a possibility is not enough, for this is the very thing that our natural human judgment would call into question: "It is not possible, nor is it conceivable, that something could just come into existence without a cause." Nor could Hume at this point merely invoke his favorite principle to the effect that as all distinct ideas are separable, and as whatever is separable is capable of separate existence, and as the ideas of cause and effect are evidently distinct, etc., etc.[22] This will not do, because it is just such a principle that is in question and that is implicitly denied by any number of our ordinary, everyday what-statements. For that matter, it really would never do for Hume to

22. *Ibid.*, pp. 79, 233.

regard this principle as being in the strict sense a principle, i.e., a necessary truth. Were he to do so, he would in effect be propounding a what-statement in regard to the sorts of things he calls "ideas." But what-statements, as we have seen, purport to be truths that are factual and necessary at the same time — and such a thing would ill befit the philosophy of David Hume! At the most, therefore, Hume's principle about the distinctness of ideas and the separability of existence could only be a sort of summary statement of what on other grounds we may have learned about the particular events and happenings of our world.

What, though, might these other grounds be? We can only imagine that they might be various epistemological considerations in regard to the nature of the given, the like of which we have already met with in Russell. That is to say, harkening back to Hume's doctrine of impressions and ideas, there is little doubt that Russell's sense data are very like Hume's impressions. And what is it that we are presented with in a Humean impression or a Russellian sense datum? Surely nothing that could be reckoned in the class of natures or essences or *whats*. For that would introduce into the world, and provide a foundation for, those very necessary connections in nature that Hume denies we have the slightest evidence for. Yet how is Hume able to avoid recognizing that what we are presented with in our impressions are just the sorts of things that are not self-subsistent, but are dependent in their being — for example, effects upon causes, or accidents upon substances, etc.? Once more, we would suggest that Hume manages to blind himself to this very patent nature and character of his own impressions, precisely through the same confusion of an epistemological ultimate with an ontological ultimate that we found Russell guilty of. Because Hume has supposed that we cannot be deceived as regards the impressions that we do have, even though we may be in doubt as to everything else, he therefore concludes that such impressions require, in order to be or to exist, nothing whatever other than themselves. It may sound preposterous, but it certainly is Humean. Indeed, one might even say that this is the very foundation stone of Hume's epistemology, as it also is, in a sense, of Kant's. For it would seem that in this respect at least, while Hume may have awakened Kant from certain of his dogmatic slumbers, he at the same time lulled him into still others, even more slumberous and more dogmatic!

163

Chapter VIII

Induction As Conceived *by a*

Relating-Logic *and a*

What-Logic

WITH THE EPISTEMOLOGICAL CONSIDERATIONS of the last chapter safely behind us, let us once again turn our attention to more specifically logical issues. We have discussed propositions; what now of arguments, inductive or deductive? Will it be possible for us to show that, just as propositions appear to take on a different character and function, depending upon whether they are operative in the context of a what-logic or of a relating-logic, so likewise induction and deduction will each tend to assume a different character and play a different role in the two logics?

First, let us consider induction. Or perhaps it might be well for us to follow the lead of many contemporary philosophers of science and speak to the supposedly more general issue of the relation of facts to theories. For induction, as we all know, has fallen into some disrepute nowadays, at least so far as the logic of scientific discovery is concerned. Nor would it be amiss, perhaps, were we to look into some of the reasons for this currently fashionable tendency to dismiss induction out of hand, as being both incompetent and irrelevant in the matter of scientific discovery. Here we could surely do no better than to look for guidance to one who would surely not deny himself to be the reigning pontiff of the logic of scientific discovery, Sir Karl Popper. For he constantly avers that there is no way — at least no way involving any properly logical procedures — for deriving scientific theories from observed facts. He supports his contention by citing Newton with disapproval and Kant with approval. Thus "Newton," Popper notes, "asserted that the truth of his *theory* could be logically derived from the truth of certain *observation-statements*." [1] That is to say, Newton was quite explicit in his belief that "he had wrested [the] functional principles" of his theory of gravitation "from experience" and "by induction." [2]

But in this Newton was dead wrong, Popper thinks. And he was wrong not just in fact — i.e., in the mere historical fact of how he arrived at his theory of gravitation — but also in principle, it being "logically impossible to derive theories from observations." [3]

In contrast, it is an entirely different view of the relation of facts to theories that Kant suggests in the Preface to the second edition of the first *Critique* and that Popper cites with an approval, marked not merely by a Jovian nod, but also by the human, all-too-human, device of italics.

When Galileo let his balls run down an inclined plane with a gravity which he had chosen himself; when Torricelli caused the air to sustain a weight which he had calculated beforehand to be equal to that of a column of water of known height; . . . then a light dawned upon all natural philosophers. They learnt that our reason can understand only *what it creates according to its own design*: *that we must compel Nature to answer our questions*, rather than cling to Nature's apron strings and allow her to guide us. *For purely accidental observations, made without any plan having been thought out in advance, cannot be connected by a . . . law — which is what reason is searching for.* [4]

Popper's italics, needless to say, are designed to pay Kant the singular compliment of having anticipated — to be sure, in a somewhat confused and hesitant way — certain of the more remarkable insights of Popper himself. Still, these insights may, in some respects at least, be not so much remarkable as commonplace, it having become an ever recurrent theme among contemporary scientists and philosophers of science that, (1) it being impossible to derive scientific theories either inductively or by any other logical

1. *Conjectures and Refutations* (New York: Basic Books, 1962), p. 185.
2. *Ibid.*   3. *Ibid.*, p. 189.   4. *Ibid.*

means from the facts of observation, (2) the only alternative would seem to be to regard such theories as being on the order of things which "the mind freely creates according to its own design."

On the latter score, it is not unusual for current writers to give their imaginations free rein and to compare the devising of explanatory theories in science to the inventing of "musical themes," of "dramatic conflicts," [5] and even of fairy tales.[6] Einstein himself apparently had no hesitation in speaking of "the purely fictitious character of the fundamentals of scientific theory," and in declaring that "the fundamental concepts and postulates of physics [being] in the logical sense free inventions of the human mind, [they could nowise] be deduced from experience by 'abstraction' — that is to say by logical means." [7]

Still, the palm for such extravagance should perhaps go to the late Norman Campbell, who says of Newton:

His theory of universal gravitation, suggested to him by the trivial fall of an apple, was a product of his individual mind, just as much as the Fifth Symphony (said to have been suggested by another trivial incident, the knocking at a door) was a product of Beethoven's. The analogy seems to me exact. Beethoven's music did not exist before he thought of it. Neither resulted from a mere discovery of something that was already there; both were brought into being by the creative imagination of a great artist.[8]

It is time, though, to draw the curtain on such romantic flights of fancy respecting the scientific imagination and turn our attention to the more down-to-earth logical considerations that may be supposed to have given rise to this currently fashionable view of science as involving procedures that are held to be quite literally creative rather than inductive. Once more, if we are to credit Popper's explanation, it is the patent logical inadequacy of induction as a method of inference that is the real ground for its having fallen

5. These are both terms which Popper uses in *The Logic of Scientific Discovery* (New York: Science Editions, 1961), p. 31.

6. The likening of the devising of scientific theories to the inventions of fairy tales is developed at some length by Norman Campbell, *What Is Science?* (New York: Dover Publications, 1952), pp. 106–7. Moreover, as if not to be outdone in the matter of metaphors, similes, and flights of fancy, Thomas Kuhn (*The Structure of Scientific Revolutions* [Chicago: University of Chicago Press, Phoenix Books, 1964], pp. 91–92) likens scientific revolutions to political revolutions.

7. See Albert Einstein, *Essays in Science* (New York: Philosophical Library, n.d.), pp. 15–16.

8. *What Is Science?*, p. 102

into comparative disuse among scientists: to try to infer a universal law from observed particular cases just cannot be done; it is not a logically warranted inference.

Induction as a Natural Instrument of Everyday Life

As over against this view, however, we should like to suggest that it is not so much the logical insufficiency of induction, but rather the increasing reliance of modern science upon the ways of a relating-logic as contrasted with those of a what-logic that is responsible for the comparative disuse of induction on the part of scientists, particularly physicists. To indicate in just a rough, preliminary way why we think this, consider the following. Traditionally, one might suppose, induction was regarded as little more than a common, everyday logical procedure which human beings found ready at hand and naturally availed themselves of in attempting to learn what the natures and ways of things in the world are. Thus to take a seemingly almost trivial Aristotelian example, just how do we come by the distinction in type or kind between being a substance and being of a certain size, or between actively doing something and being somewhere, and so on for the other category distinctions? For many more pedestrian souls it is hard to stomach either the Platonic or the rationalist notion that such ideas are literally innate or inborn; and even Kant's notion of the categories as pure forms of the understanding seems, at least prima facie, a bit over-sophisticated, to say the least. Yet does the distinction in kind between being a substance and being of a certain size strike us as the kind of thing that could ever have been a "new idea" in Popper's sense? True, if the distinction is not an innate idea, in the literal sense, it could only be an acquired notion, and acquired in some way or other and at some time or other either in the life of the individual or, indeed, in that of the culture as a whole. But this hardly implies that such acquisition would have had to be on the order of a free creation or invention of the kind that we associate with the composition of musical themes or of dramatic conflicts, or even of scientific theories in the modern sense.

In other words, let us forget about modern scientific theories for the moment, or, rather, let us simply concede that they are, as Einstein suggested, "free inventions of the human mind." Instead, let us consider the rudimentary and quite naive judgments that we make simply as human beings about the natures of things in the world about us. Is it plausible in this context to suppose that a distinction such as that involved in judging that something is a piece of wood, as contrasted with judging that it is two feet long, is one that we human beings have invented or created or dreamed up? Is it not rather one that we have found and encountered in our experience of the everyday world? And so is it not by some such process as that of abstraction or induction from experience that we have learned what it is for something to be a substance as over against being of a certain size?

To take another and very different sort of example from common life, is it not from experience or, more accurately, by induction from experience that we come to learn what manner of men our fellow human beings are, and are capable of being? Thus consider two character sketches drawn at random from C. V. Wedgwood's *The King's Peace*, the one of Thomas Wentworth, later Earl of Strafford, and the other of Archibald Johnston, Laird of Warriston:

Wentworth was a tall, spare, formidable Yorkshireman, with a notoriously bad temper and no personal charm. His dictatorial manner, which reflected his sense of his own position, generally inspired dislike, but he had strong and tender affections and depths of simple loyalty and gratitude in his nature which made him truly beloved by those who knew him best. As a practical administrator he had done well in the North of England, and more than well in Ireland. He was efficient, just and fearless, and he worked with a violent methodical energy at every task he took in hand. Like the King, like Laud, he believed in the establishment of unquestioned authority as the foundation of good government.[9]

As for Johnston:

He came of a border family of small gentry, but his father had prospered in trade and Warriston inherited a shrewd business head. On the mother's side he had ancestors distinguished in the law and he himself had chosen that profession. Well under thirty, he was already one of the leading advocates at the Edinburgh bar. Warriston was not simply a religious fanatic; the spiritual diary which he kept reveals a man walking on the dizzy edge of madness. His exceptional gifts of logic, of memory, of concentration and calculation, were supported by no broadening wisdom and no human understanding. He could analyse a legal text or extract every particle of verbal meaning from a passage of Scripture, but he was lacking in ordinary powers of criticism; he was credulous to the point of silliness, intolerant from a rabid ignorance, unable fairly to examine his own heart or motives. For so narrow and hard a mind the long hours of prayer common to the Presbyterians meant a daily exercise in self-deception. "For the

9. (New York: Macmillan, 1955), pp. 151-52.

space of two or three hours I got an exceeding great liberty, freedom and familiarity with my God," he would write; and again, "the Lord all this time was powerfully, sensibly, speaking in me and to me, praying in me and answering to me." In a cold sweat of terror and devotion he learnt that "I was appointed for eternal salvation and my name written in the Book of Life" and was inexpressibly uplifted by the conviction that he would not only be glorified after death, which was "too little favour and common to all His saints and chosen, but He would even in this life glorify Himself visibly and sensibly in my life and death." He knew, no less, that unworthy as he was, he was God's chief instrument for the "welfare of His Church, Satan's overthrow, Antichrist's ruin, and comfort of the godly." The dazzling revelation of his mission made him reel "like a man drunken." His intoxication lasted a melancholy and bitter life time.[10]

Now who can read such descriptions without recognizing in each case a not unfamiliar type and manner of man — the one an efficient, arrogant, yet exceedingly loyal and devoted, man of affairs, the other an emotionally unstable fanatic, self-righteous and self-tormented, of brilliant intellect, but narrow, bigoted, and miserable? Must we not further acknowledge that, in our ready recognition of such types, our understanding of and our relative familiarity with them are the fruit of our own experience, and not at all a function of any creative invention on our part of purely hypothetical types from our own imaginations? In other words, so far as our everyday experience as human beings is concerned, we do seem to learn from the facts of such experience; and it is precisely by inductions from particular instances that we come to learn what manner of men our fellow human beings are, as well as what the various types and kinds of things and the various ways and modes of being are that we encounter in our everyday experience.[11]

Induction as an Anomaly in a Relating-Logic

Now let us abruptly eject ourselves from this everyday world of experience, where induction would seem to be quite naturally operative on every hand, and instead project ourselves into that rather bizarre world of experience as it is understood in the Humean or Kantian manner described in the preceding chapter. At once, we wonder if in these changed circum-

10. *Ibid.*, pp. 185–86.

11. In the foregoing discussion we have tended to confound inductions from experience with abstractions from experience. However, in a what-logic the two processes are decidedly analogous. Cf. F. Parker and H. Veatch, *Logic as a Human Instrument* (New York: Harper, 1959), pp. 245–46.

stances induction will begin to appear not so much logically indefensible as simply irrelevant and beside the point.

Thus take Hume first. For him, as we have seen, experience was to be understood in terms of the distinction between impressions and ideas, all of our ideas, at least simple ones, having to be derived from prior impressions.[12] And what are impressions? Again, suppose that we simplify the matter by identifying Humean impressions with the sorts of things which later English philosophers were wont to call sense data — colors, sounds, tastes, odors, even such cherished items as have more lately come to be designated by the somewhat suggestive title of "raw feels."

Now granted that we do have such impressions or data, and granted that they are epistemologically primary, still our everyday human experience is certainly not an experience of color patches, sounds, odors, and raw feels. Instead, it is an experience of tables and chairs, of trees and flowers, of men and animals, of light and shade, of summer and winter — in short, of the everyday world itself. How, then, is this transition made from an experience of what initially consists only of sense impressions to the full-bodied awareness of things and objects in everyday experience?

To such a question, Hume would surely reply that in one sense we never make such a transition, for the simple reason that there literally is no experience of things and objects in the sense of substances:

We have no idea of substance of any kind since we have no idea but what is derived from some impression, and we have no impression of any substance either material or spiritual. We know nothing but particular qualities and perceptions. As our idea of any body, a peach, for instance, is only that of a particular taste, color, figure, size, consistency, etc., so our idea of any mind is only that of particular perceptions without the notion of anything we call substance, either simple or compound.[13]

Indeed, "our ideas of bodies are nothing but collections formed by the mind of the ideas of the several distinct sensible qualities, of which objects are composed, and which we find to have a constant union with each other."[14] Moreover, as we know, this sort of dissolution which Hume effects

---

12. We are of course omitting from consideration the one apparent exception to this principle which Hume examines in *A Treatise of Human Nature*, ed. L. A. Selby-Bigge (Oxford: Clarendon Press, 1888), Bk. I, Pt. I, § 1, p. 6.

13. "An Abstract of A Treatise on Human Nature," printed as an appendix to C. W. Hendel's edition of Hume, *An Inquiry Concerning Human Understanding* (Indianapolis and New York: Bobbs-Merrill, 1955), p. 194. See also the *Treatise*, p. 16.

14. *Treatise*, p. 219.

of any supposed ideas of objects or substances into mere collections of ideas of sensible qualities is the forerunner of a whole spate of such reductions and dissolutions in contemporary philosophy. Of these, we have already cited a number of examples, and yet we cannot resist adding one more which is distinguished by an arrogance such as only a Bertrand Russell could muster:

Since the "thing" cannot, without indefensible partiality, be identified with any single one of its appearances, it came to be thought of as something distinct from all of them and underlying them. But by the principle of Occam's razor, if the class of appearances will fulfil the purposes for the sake of which the thing was invented by the prehistoric metaphysicians to whom common sense is due, economy demands that we should identify the thing with the class of its appearances. It is not necessary to *deny* a substance or substratum underlying these appearances; it is merely expedient to abstain from asserting this unnecessary entity. Our procedure here is precisely analogous to that which has swept away from the philosophy of mathematics the useless menagerie of metaphysical monsters with which it used to be infected.[15]

But what immediately interests us in the present connection is not the question of the legitimacy of such a Humean dissolution of substances into sense data, but rather the somewhat unnoticed implications of such a sense-data philosophy, so far as the traditional operation of induction is concerned. For just consider how, once the idea of a collection of sense data is made to do duty for the idea of substance, the operative question in our efforts to know and understand ceases to be "What is this which I am now experiencing (i.e., seeing or tasting or touching or what not)?", and becomes "How is this sensory datum which I am now experiencing to be ordered or related to other, further data?" or, more simply, "What further data is this present datum to be correlated with?" In other words, what we observe here is the phenomenon of a what-logic being displaced by a relating-logic.

Or suppose we shift our example to Lewis for a minute, and specifically to his famous account of his perceptions of an apple:

At the moment, a certain "that" which I can only describe (in terms of concepts) as a round, ruddy, tangy-smelling some-what, means to me an "edible apple." . . . An object such as an apple is never given; between the real apple in all its complexity and this fragmentary presentation lies that interval which only interpretation can bridge. The "objectivity" of this experience means *the verifiability of a further possible experience which is attributed by this interpretation.*[16]

15. *Mysticism and Logic* (New York: Doubleday Anchor Books, n.d.), pp. 149–50.
16. *Mind and the World Order* (New York: Dover Publications, n.d.), pp. 119–20.

Now suppose that the realities involved in such a situation are just what Lewis says they are; does this not somehow force us into a shift from a what-logic to a relating-logic? If asked such a question, Lewis might well answer "No." For he would say that when one is presented with a bare sense *quale*, say, a particular "round, ruddy presentation," so far from this precluding one from posing a what-question, this is precisely the question that is called for: "What is this that I see (or am presented with)?" "It's an apple." Yet note that the context of the what-question as it is here put is rather different from the ordinary, common-sense context of such a question. For normally, and apart from the sophistications of modern epistemology, we all suppose that the real apple, the actual substance, is there before us, and that it is this that we see and are presented with. To be sure, when we reflect a moment, we no doubt would acknowledge that the visual datum as such could be no more than a round, reddish patch. But though we might thus acknowledge that, simply to the organ of vision at a particular moment the apple doubtless appeared as no more than a round, reddish patch, we should never for a moment question that it was the apple itself and as a whole that was there before us and that was being presented to our eyes in the momentary guise of a round patch of red.

In contrast, in the cognitive situation as Lewis envisages it, "an object such as an apple is never given." Instead, all that is ever given is a mere series or set of sense qualities— "round," "ruddy," "tangy," "sweet-smelling," etc. Moreover, for Lewis, as for Hume, there never are such things as apples and peaches, in the sense of substances actually existing in the real world. The real apple is nothing but a collection of sense data or sense qualities, and the notion or concept of "apple" is but a name given to such a set or series of qualities, ordered to one another in a certain pattern.

Hence, when I am presented with something in experience that, considered simply as a visual datum, is but a round, red patch, and I am asked what it is, I can properly answer — either in a Lewisean or in a common-sense context — "It's an apple." But, clearly, the answer will mean something quite different in the two contexts. In the common-sense case, I shall simply be stating what the presented thing or substance is essentially, whereas in the Lewisean case, I shall, in effect, in using the word "apple," be relating or connecting or tying up an immediately presented datum with a more or less determinate set or series of data that I can experience in the future and that would serve to verify my use of the concept "apple" in the first place. In other words, the concept "apple" has, for Lewis, a purely connecting or relating function: it is a conceptual go-cart that gets me from the one immediate presentation to the others in the same set or series. It is thus not a what-concept of the ordinary, unsophisticated sort at all. Rather we might say that it is what, for want of a better term, can only be designated a relating-concept.

But to return to the issue of induction. In what we have been calling the more traditional view, induction is altogether integral to a what-logic and is aimed at establishing conclusions as to what the various things and items are that we encounter in our experience. While in Lewis' view "an object such as an apple is never given" in experience, in a more everyday, unsophisticated view it is precisely objects such as apples that are given in experience. Also, it is just because objects such as apples are presented to us in experience that it makes sense to suppose that by a process of induction from such experiences we can come to learn what such objects as apples are. A single experience with an apple may not suffice to tell us what the thing really is, but given several such experiences of similar objects we can eventually come to have some notion as to what is common and essential to them all, in other words, what an apple essentially is.

But not so in Lewis' theory. Indeed, in any theory that is tributary to Hume, induction in the sense just described is not merely a logical anomaly; it is a downright impossibility. For one thing, since full-bodied objects like apples are never given in experience, then it is clearly impossible that from repeated experiences of objects like these one could ever by a process of induction arrive at a knowledge of what such objects are. Also, when one considers the sorts of things which in Lewis' view are given in experience, viz., sense impressions or sensory qualities, then it is no doubt possible for us to have repeated experiences of the same or similar sense *qualia* — e.g., a round, ruddy patch. But then it goes without saying that any induction from experiences of this sort to the "what" of the same repeated sense *quale* as such would be, if not out of the question, then certainly pointless.

Two Senses of "Induction"

If induction is to enter into the picture at all in any Humean view, it must be induction of a quite different sort and aimed at a quite different end. For while the Humean would insist that only sense impressions (and never substantial objects) are given in experience, he would be equally insistent that there is a sense in which "constant conjunctions" of sensory qualities might be said to be given. Moreover, from repeated experiences of *qualia* thus constantly conjoined, we may well be inclined to infer that the next time *quale* "x" occurs, it will be accompanied by *quale* "y". And such an inference, if it is a legitimate inference at all, could only be an inductive one.

Note how different the situation in regard to induction is in the Humean context from what it was in the more ordinary and unsophisticated context described earlier. In the more everyday sense of induction, it is repeated experiences of the same or similar things that are supposed to provide us with the basis for drawing conclusions as to what these things are essentially, or what their natures are. From countless experiences with apples, or with substances and their accidents, or with human beings of the type of Archibald Johnston, I come to infer what the nature of apples is, as over against peaches or pears, or what substances are as contrasted with accidents, or what manner of man an Archibald Johnston is as over against men of other types and kinds.

But how different is Humean induction. It is not from repeated observations of sensory qualities that I come to infer what the nature of each of these various qualities is. Rather it is from a repeated experience of the conjunction of certain qualities that I tend to infer from the appearance of the one that the other will be conjoined with it. "Thus we remember to have seen that species of object we call *flame*, and to have felt that species of sensation we call *heat*. We likewise call to mind their constant conjunction in all past instances." [17] From such experience, then, do we seek by induction to draw a conclusion as to what flame is or what heat is? Not at all. "Without further ceremony, we call the one *cause* and the other *effect*, and infer the existence of the one from that of the other." [18] In other words, the purpose of induction conceived in this way is to relate things to others as "causes" to "effects," [19] rather than to lead to an understanding of things for what they are in their very natures.

Moreover, no sooner does such a shift occur in the understanding of induction than all possible logical warrant for such an inductive process is

17. *Treatise*, p. 87.   18. *Ibid*.

19. The reason for setting the terms in quotes is that inferences from causes to effects are conceived very differently in a relating-logic than in a what-logic. See below, Chapters XI and XII.

thereby removed. For while it is not implausible to suppose that from repeated experience with the same or similar things we should eventually come to some understanding of what such things are,[20] from a repeated experience of a constant conjunction of sensory qualities there is no warrant whatever for supposing that any sort of cause-effect relation holds between them. There is nothing, absolutely nothing, in the nature and character of the one such sensory quality or datum which would indicate that it bears any necessary relation or connection with the other such quality. "Adam, though his rational faculties be supposed, at the very first, entirely perfect, could not have inferred from the fluidity and transparency of water that it would suffocate him, or from the light and warmth of fire that it would consume him. No object ever discovers, by the qualities which appear to the senses, either the causes which produced it or the effects which will arise from it. . . ."[21] In short, the question as to what things are having been displaced in favor of the question as to what other things a given thing is necessarily related to, the latter question becomes simply unanswerable — at least on any logically warranted basis.

Accordingly, returning to the question of the relation of facts to theories, since such theories are not designed to tell what the facts are, but rather to provide a pattern of necessary relations into which such facts are to be fitted, there can be no possible way in which such theories can be derived from the facts, either inductively or in any other way. In this respect Popper is quite right. And, in a measure, he is right too in his strictures with regard to induction. At the same time it needs to be borne in mind that induction as Popper criticizes it is scarcely the same as induction of the more traditional, everyday sort. Nor is the weakness of induction taken in the former sense quite what Popper takes it to be. The trouble is not that such induction attempts to derive "universal statements" from "singular statements."[22] Instead, the trouble is that in a general setting of Humean empiricism it is a relating-logic rather than a what-logic that tends to put itself forward as the only appropriate *organon*. But in such a logic the only possible way of conceiving the function of induction is to think of it as a procedure for

20. There is no claim involved here to the effect that such understanding must be infallible. See our earlier discussion in Chapter IV above.

21. Hume, *Human Understanding*, p. 42.

22. Popper's critique of induction is couched in these terms in *The Logic of Scientific Discovery*, p. 27.

deriving necessary connections from observed constant conjunctions. However, such a derivation—i.e., supposing it to be a logical derivation—is simply impossible. Thus it presumably is one thing to say that there is some logical warrant for supposing that from repeated experiences of the same thing one can come to some knowledge of what such a thing is. But it is an entirely different thing to say that from observing two sensory qualities to be constantly conjoined there is some logical warrant for supposing them to be necessarily connected.

Chapter IX

The Picture *of the* World

Derived *from the* Inductions

in a Relating-Logic

THERE ARE FURTHER CONSEQUENCES for induction of the use of a relating-logic which need to be explored. Suppose that we now undertake to consider just what the character of universal propositions must be — i.e., propositions that are constitutive of scientific theories and hypotheses, but that nevertheless in the context of a relating-logic are not to be regarded as having been derived by any sort of induction from experience. However such propositions, considered as explanatory principles, may have been arrived at — whether by a free invention of the mind or by retroduction [1] or by whatever means — just what is it that they may be taken to assert? In the light of our foregoing analyses, if such principles are taken to be necessary truths, then they cannot possibly be truths about the world —

---

1. This is a type of inference which Norwood Hanson has argued for most persuasively as being an alternative both to induction and to deduction. See *Patterns of Discovery* (Cambridge: University Press, 1958), pp. 85–90.

i.e., they tell us nothing about natural events and happenings, or real causes or forces in nature. On the other hand, if they are taken to be synthetic truths, there is still a sense in which, within the context of a relating-logic, such statements and propositions cannot be regarded as describing what is in the world at all. For such propositions are composed of concepts whose meaning or sense can only be determined analytically. However, to unpack the various notes that are analytically contained within a concept gives no information whatever about the nature and character of objects in the world. Even when such concepts are "applied," as we were at pains to show in Chapter VI, there would seem to be no way in which those things that have been acknowledged to pertain to "men" (to revert to our former example) can be made to pertain to men. In other words, within the context of a relating-logic, synthetic propositions would appear to be no more informative as to the way the world is than are analytic propositions. Instead, the only option that would seem to be open is the one which we sought to describe in Chapter V, where the entire body of scientific propositions, whether analytic or synthetic, whether the mere laying down of grammatical rules or their actual application, must be regarded as a closed-system language game. All references and all significations point only to elements within the game and to nothing outside the game, or at least to nothing of a recognizable specificity and definiteness.

Clearly, though, such reflections have a strange ring to them. They are not the sorts of things that one hears about, at least not in so many words, when one turns to current discussions in the philosophy of science regarding the relation of facts to theories. Accordingly, let us for the moment occupy ourselves more directly with such current discussions, in order to see whether in the long run they may not lead to a conception of the interrelation of facts and theories in science that amounts to just such a closed-system language game. To this end, we will trace our steps back to Kant, just as in the preceding chapter we had recourse primarily to Hume.

Variation on a Kantian Theme

If we were to characterize the philosophical situation confronting Kant in language drawn from the discussion of the preceding chapter, we might put it in some such way as this: Since the given data of experience do not come to us in intelligible patterns (i.e., in patterns of connection marked by universality and necessity), and since there is in principle no way in which such patterns can be abstracted or induced from the presented data, there would appear to be no alternative but to consider the order of nature, which modern science most certainly does disclose to us, as being not an order which characterizes nature in itself, but rather an order which we human beings bestow upon and endow nature with. Such at any rate is the alternative which Kant seized upon. Nor did he feel that it was an alternative that was merely seized upon, *faute de mieux*; rather it was one that he felt could be justified in the manner of what he called a transcendental deduction of the categories. Moreover, what such a justification amounts to, in sum, is an insistence that, save for our human activity of imposing an order upon nature, there simply would be no such thing as a world of nature, or a world of experience at all. As Kant remarks, "We can extract clear concepts of them [i.e., of such basic ordering principles of nature and of experience as cause-effect] from experience, only because experience is thus itself brought about only by their means."[2]

Now unless we are much mistaken, such a principle of justification — let us call it a transcendental[3] principle of justification — might perhaps be considered the very foundation stone of almost the entire edifice of contemporary philosophy of science. True, it is a stone that is not always acknowledged or even recognized. Yet surely this need occasion no surprise, considering the not uncommon fate of "the stone which the builders refused." Moreover, the reason for its rejection may be traceable to the fact that modern philosophers of science have departed from Kant so markedly in one respect that they have tended to forget their continuing indebtedness to him with regard to this far more fundamental notion of a transcendental principle of justification and even of an entire transcendental logic. Thus we are all aware that where most contemporary thinkers would depart from Kant is in his assumption that the basic categories of explanation, which form the core of any explanatory theory of the events and happenings of nature, must be fixed and unchanging.

Everyone knows of Kant's conviction that such a unifying and ordering of the sensuous manifold as would make possible an ordered world of experience could only proceed from certain stable and invariant forms of judg-

2. *Critique of Pure Reason*, trans. Norman Kemp Smith (London: Macmillan, 1929), A196 = B241. Cf. also the citations given in note 2 of Chapter IV above.
3. Unless we have thoroughly misunderstood Kant — which is by no means unlikely — we intend to use the term "transcendental" in its precise Kantian sense.

ment characteristic of the human mind, or, as he would say, of "the transcendental unity of apperception":

In order to show the possibility of experience in so far as it rests on pure concepts of the understanding *a priori*, we must first represent what belongs to judgments in general, and the different moments of the understanding in them, in a complete table. For the pure concepts of the understanding will fall exactly parallel to them, being nothing more than concepts of intuitions in general which are determined in themselves as judgments, necessarily and with universal validity, in respect of one or other of these moments. Through this the principles *a priori* of the possibility of all experience, will also be exactly determined. For they are nothing other than propositions which subsume all perception under the said pure concepts of the understanding.[4]

Now take away this settled conviction of Kant's that the basic categories and principles for the explanation of nature are fixed and invariant, and one comes out with the familiar modern notion that explanatory theories in science are not of one type only; rather, they are infinitely many and diverse, and, far from being rigidly determined in their nature and structure by the necessary forms of judgment of the human mind, such theories are in the nature of free creations and inventions of the human mind. In this modern view, then, the basic categories (to use a Kantian term) — through which we order our world and thus render it intelligible, and indeed even constitute it a world in the first place — are held to be variable and subject to change, one set being used at one time and in one age, perhaps, and another at a different time and in a different age.[5]

4. Immanuel Kant, *Prolegomena to Any Future Metaphysics,* trans. and ed. P. G. Lucas (Manchester: Manchester University Press, 1953), p. 61. See also p. 65.

5. In this connection it might be illuminating to refer to Waismann's notion of what might be called "visionary metaphysics." Thus G. J. Warnock (*English Philosophy Since 1900* [London: Oxford University Press, 1958], pp. 136-37) gives this account of it: "What roughly at any rate, are we to understand by the notion of metaphysical 'vision'? Dr. Waismann writes that 'what is decisive is a new way of seeing and, what goes with it, the will to transform the whole intellectual scene. This is the real thing and everything else is subservient to it.' It is essential here, first of all, to distinguish carefully between a new way of seeing, and the seeing of something new. To see something new, to find out what was not known before, is not an exercise of *metaphysical* vision — even though the effect of this new knowledge may even be to 'transform the whole intellectual scene.' It may be, for example, that the theory of evolution has done as much as anything in the last hundred years to alter our ways of thinking, of seeing the world and our own place in it; but this of course was a scientific and not a metaphysical theory, supported not so much by arguments or would-be arguments as by an immense variety and range of empirical facts. It is by contrast characteristic of a metaphysical theory that facts should neither be cited in its support nor be brought in evidence against it; it was for this reason that the Positivists were able to object that metaphysical doctrines were 'unverifiable'; such

Thus to recur to our own obvious, if hackneyed, illustrations, how is one to compare Ptolemaic astronomy with Copernican, or Newtonian physics with Einsteinian? Is it not the case that such differing scientific theories or systems simply represent so many different ways of viewing the world,[6] or, better, different ways of organizing the data of our experience to make them fit into a particular ordered pattern of a universe? True, the choice between such rival theories is held not to be arbitrary, but as being guided by a reference to the data. For it is the data themselves, which a particular explanatory theory is put forward to explain, that are supposed to serve as the ultimate arbiters in terms of which that same theory may be considered to be either verified or falsified.

But there is a difficulty here which has only begun to be recognized by philosophers of science in comparatively recent years. Stated succinctly, the difficulty is this: how can one appeal to observed facts and independently given data in verification or falsification of a scientific theory, when these same facts or data can presumably have no independent status, and for that matter no character, apart from the particular theory which explains them and renders them intelligible? After all — so the contention runs — there just would not be any facts, were they not in the context of some theory or other. Consequently, if the over-all explanatory theories are different, then the facts must be different as well.

Professor Hanson has attempted to bring home this point in an almost literally dramatic way:

Let us consider Johannes Kepler: imagine him on a hill watching the dawn. With him is Tycho Brahe. Kepler regarded the sun as fixed: it was the earth that moved. But Tycho followed Ptolemy and Aristotle in this much at least:

---

a theory consists not in an account of any new facts but in a new account of familiar facts, a new reading, so to speak, of what has already been agreed upon."

6. It is true that Waismann would want to distinguish sharply between a metaphysical vision and a scientific theory, no matter how sweeping the scope of the latter. Indeed, the difference between the two, he thinks, lies just in the fact that the former is perforce "all-embracing" whereas the latter never is (see Warnock, p. 138). Moreover, it is presumably in consequence of this difference in scope that metaphysics is thought always to involve only "a new way of seeing," and hence never "the seeing of something new." However, as we shall note in the course of this chapter, this way of distinguishing metaphysical visions from mere scientific theories is by no means universally honored by philosophers of science. For many of them would insist that a new scientific theory does offer a new way of seeing, just as does a new metaphysics. Thus in our discussion we shall make no sharp distinction between scientific and philosophical theories in illustrating the peculiar logical problems that are connected with determining the relations between facts and theories in the context of a relating-logic.

181

the earth was fixed and all other celestial bodies moved around it. *Do Kepler and Tycho see the same thing in the east at dawn?*[7]

The answer which Hanson eventually gives is "No," but it is given only after a considerable spinning out of pages filled with all sorts of lore from Gestalt psychology, with ingenious logico-linguistic speculations, and with many fascinating dialectical somersaults.

But for all of its padding and procedural pyrotechnics, Professor Hanson's discussion is obviously aimed at criticizing the more standard and traditional view of the relation between facts and theories, the chief tenets of which a recent expositor has aptly summed up as follows:

Test of a scientific theory can be accomplished if and only if there are at least some terms, or at least some distinguishable components of the meanings of some terms occurring in the theory, that, by reference to theory-independent elements of experience, have a meaning independent of their theoretical context; and comparison of different scientific theories can be accomplished if and only if there are at least some such terms (or components) that have the *same* meaning in both of those different theories. If there is no such common meaning, the theories are not talking about the same things, and hence cannot be compared with respect to their adequacy.[8]

Clearly, if Professor Hanson were really to follow through with the thrust of his earlier quoted remarks, he could hardly stop short of denying outright that there are any "theory-independent elements of experience," or that there are any terms that have the same meaning in two such different theories as, say, the Ptolemaic and the Copernican. For Kepler and Tycho, he has suggested, simply did not see the same thing in the east at dawn. Thus, even though they might have used the same term, "sun," it would not have been a term that had the same meaning in the two different theories. Hence, Kepler and Tycho could not, strictly speaking, have been talking about the same thing, nor could their respective theories have even been compared to one another with respect to their adequacy.

Nevertheless, it is to Professor Kuhn that we should turn for a still more extreme statement of the view that there are no facts independent of the theories that explain them or that fit them into a particular context of intelligibility. For he rather dashingly concludes that there really is no way in which one can properly speak of scientific theories being either confirmed

7. *Patterns of Discovery*, p. 5.

8. Dudley Shapere, *Philosophical Problems of Natural Science* (New York: Macmillan, 1965), p. 15.

or falsified by any supposed appeal to the facts. After all, given the perspective of a different scientific theory, the facts themselves must look entirely different, and indeed must be entirely different:

During the seventeenth century, when their research was guided by one or another effluvium theory, electricians repeatedly saw chaff particles rebound from, or fall off, the electrified bodies that had attracted them. At least that is what seventeenth-century observers said they saw, and we have no more reason to doubt their reports of perception than our own. Placed before the same apparatus, a modern observer would see electrostatic repulsion (rather than mechanical or gravitational rebounding), but historically, with one universally ignored exception, electrostatic repulsion was not seen as such until Hauksbee's large-scale apparatus had greatly magnified its effects.[9]

And, still more generally, Professor Kuhn observes:

Examining the record of past research from the vantage of contemporary historiography, the historian of science may be tempted to exclaim that when paradigms change, the world itself changes with them. Led by a new paradigm, scientists adopt new instruments and look in new places. Even more important, during revolutions scientists see new and different things when looking with familiar instruments in places they have looked before. It is rather as if the professional community had been suddenly transported to another planet where familiar objects are seen in a different light and are joined by unfamiliar ones as well. Of course, nothing of quite that sort does occur: there is no geographical transplantation; outside the laboratory everyday affairs usually continue as before. Nevertheless, paradigm changes do cause scientists to see the world of their research-engagement differently. In so far as their only recourse to that world is through what they see and do, we may want to say that after a revolution scientists are responding to a different world.[10]

Extreme though these recent views of Kuhn and Hanson and others may seem regarding the relation between theory and fact in modern science, they ought not to occasion too great surprise if one stops to consider their philosophical background in Hume and in Kant. On the one hand, as we have seen, the Humean background of contemporary philosophy of science has so conditioned these philosophers that they are unable to see how theories can ever be derived from observed facts by way of induction. Nor does the problem which they experience in this regard arise from any mere difficulty as to how one can derive universal principles from particular cases. Rather the difficulty arises from the fact that the task of science is understood to be

9. Thomas S. Kuhn, *The Structure of Scientific Revolutions* (Chicago: University of Chicago Press, Phoenix Books, 1964), p. 116.

10. *Ibid.*, p. 110.

one of relating the data of observation to one another in ordered patterns of connection and relation; and yet at the same time it is assumed that there is nothing in the given data as such to suggest a relation or necessary connection of any kind between one such datum and another. Hence, any use on our part of a relating-logic to achieve intelligibility through bringing the data of sense into necessary connections with one another must, from a Humean standpoint, be regarded as at once gratuitous and logically unwarranted.

On the other hand, turning to the Kantian background of modern philosophy of science, it is Kant who encouraged modern thinkers to suppose that if ordered patterns of connection and relation in terms of which the data of observation might be made intelligible could not be found in the data then they must be imposed upon the data by human beings in our very acts of knowing: Hitherto men had assumed that all our knowledge must conform to objects; we shall now assume that objects must conform to our knowledge.[11]

Moreover, Kant did not mean to imply that his assumption was an arbitrary one. On the contrary, as we have already remarked, he was convinced that the assumption was justified, although the justification could only be a transcendental one. As such, it turned on the general consideration — to put it in non-Kantian language — that save insofar as human beings lay down and prescribe the most general laws and principles beforehand, to which the objects of our experience must conform, there would not be any experience of objects at all. In other words, if, following Hume, one says that what we are presented with in sense experience is not in itself ordered and disposed so as to constitute intelligible objects of experience or an intelligible world of nature, then Kant would respond that it can only be human beings — or the human mind as such — that bestow such order and intelligibility upon the given data of our experience as to constitute them a world of objects.

Note, though, that given such a transcendental justification for the human mind's creative role in knowledge, there would seem to be no possible opening for any sort of verification or falsification in experience of those fundamental ordering principles which we prescribe to nature and to which all natural objects must conform. For what sort of experience could we possibly have that might either verify or falsify principles such as those of

11. *Critique of Pure Reason*, B xvi.

Kant's categories? None, for the simple reason that any possible experience we might have would first have to conform to our basic categories of understanding before it could even qualify as an experience.

There should be no mistaking the fact that this Kantian transcendental principle of justification is quite general in its scope — much more general, perhaps, than even Kant seems to have suspected. For let us just suppose for purposes of argument — as most contemporary philosophers, particularly philosophers of science, do suppose — that Kant's attempt to provide a transcendental deduction of his own specific list of categories, and only those, was a failure — that, for example, the categories of inherence and subsistence, of causality and dependence, of community and all the rest, are not the only conceivable set of categories, and that there is no possible way of proving that they are. Let us go still further and assume that no set of categories or theoretical principles, whether Kant's or any other set, can be shown in principle to be the only possible set. What we will then be faced with is a situation not unlike that which prevails today, in which it is held that there are any number of conceivable alternative sets of ordering principles or basic scientific theories.[12]

Nevertheless, Kant's transcendental principle of justification is still of sufficient generality to be relevant even in such a situation. For whichever set of categories or ordering principles, of whichever basic scientific theory, we select as the one in terms of which the happenings of nature are to be made intelligible, the only ultimate ground for advancing any theory or set of categories at all must lie in the transcendental consideration that apart from at least some such basic theory or set of categories there would be no ordered world of experience and no intelligible objects of experience of any kind. How, then, could such a theory or set of categories be verified or falsified in experience? Once more, the answer is the same: There would seem to be no possible way for such verification or falsification to be brought off, simply because apart from the context of the basic theory that is supposed to be

12. In other words, the notion of metaphysics as vision, such as we found Waismann to be an advocate of (see above notes 5 and 6), is viable only within the context of Kantian transcendental philosophy. True, Kant was convinced that there was but one set of categories and hence only one possible "metaphysical vision" open to human beings, whereas Waismann is convinced that countless alternative visions are open to us. However, whether our possible sets of categories, and hence our possible metaphysical visions, are one or many, it remains true that the universal and necessary propositions that structure such basic "ways of seeing" are neither self-evident nor capable of being supported by inductive evidence. Hence their justification can only be of the sort that may be termed "transcendental" in the Kantian sense.

verified or falsified, there could not be any experience, at least not any experience of sufficient determinateness and intelligibility, to make possible anything on the order of verification or falsification.

This brings us again to the very point which we earlier saw had already been approached, if not actually reached, by philosophers of science like Hanson and Kuhn. The only difference is that we have reached this point through purely philosophical considerations stemming from Hume and Kant, whereas the philosophers of science tended to approach the same point from considerations more directly germane to science.

However, the significant thing to emerge from this whole discussion is, or should be, a clear recognition of how the tendency to repudiate induction and the tendency to rely upon a transcendental method of justification for our scientific world views would seem to be mutually reinforcing. Thus, on the one hand, the conviction grows that what may be said to be presented to us through our senses is scarcely anything determinate at all, since it is only in virtue of such relations as these sensory presentations have to other and further presentations that they can even become intelligible, there being nothing in their nature and character that could give the slightest ground for supposing that they do stand in such relations to one another. On the other hand, the complementary conviction grows that since intelligibility cannot be found in, or derived logically from, the sensory data themselves, the only alternative is to suppose that any and all intelligible relationships pertaining to the sensuous manifold must have been conjured up and imposed upon it by the mind. But then the further consequence seems inescapable: if what our senses present us with is not sufficiently determinate to warrant at least some sort of induction to its nature and causes, then neither can it be sufficiently determinate to serve the purposes of verifying or falsifying the various theories and hypotheses which the mind propounds in order to explain the data and render them intelligible.

Either Induction or Transcendental Justification

Further, any attempt to justify our categories and first principles through a transcendental method is simply incompatible with any and all attempts of whatever kind to induce or derive such principles from experience or to verify or falsify them in experience. Indeed, to affirm the one is to deny the other; and to deny the one is to affirm the other.

Yet, curiously enough, this seems to have been a hard lesson for modern

186

epistemologists to learn. Instead, they are forever trying to have it both ways, or neither way. To illustrate and confirm this last statement, let us examine, by way of brief case studies, the respective views of Lewis and Popper. Lewis, we shall find, wants to avail himself of a kind of transcendental justification and at the same time to insist that a complementary inductive procedure is both valid and indispensable. On the other hand, Popper, while he explicitly and vigorously repudiates induction, at the same time seems to feel that he has no need to fall back on any sort of transcendental justification in compensation.

First, then, as to Lewis. Rather early in *Mind and the World Order*, Lewis formulates what sounds very like a transcendental principle of justification: "Objects do not classify themselves and come into experience with their tickets on them. The classifying attitude or mode of behavior which the mind brings to given experience and which represents its meaning, dictates the explicit concept and implicitly possesses it already." [13] Moreover, correlated with such enunciations of what would seem to amount to a transcendental mode of justification are repeated assertions that the given element in experience — i.e., that element which is merely presented and given apart from all interpretation and classification by the mind — is in a way simply "ineffable." True, "The given is presentation of something real, in the normal case at least." [14] Yet,

Obviously, we must distinguish the given from the *object which* is given. . . *what* is given (given in part) is this real object. But the whatness of this object involves its categorial interpretation; the real object, as known, is a construction put upon this experience of it, and includes much which is not, at the moment, given in the presentation. [15]

And just what is left when the "much which is not, at the moment, given in the presentation" is eliminated? Naturally, Lewis finds this hard to characterize since it is, strictly speaking, ineffable, and since any characterization of it must already involve that element of construction and interpretation which the mind brings to the given. Thus, to refer once more to Lewis' example of an apple, when I am presented with such an object, what in the strict sense may be said to be given or presented to me are certain sense *qualia* — sensations of redness, roundness, perhaps of smoothness, and a certain tangy fragrance. Yet to characterize any one of these

13. (New York: Dover Publications, n.d.), p. 88.
14. *Ibid.*, p. 58.
15. *Ibid.*, pp. 57–58.

data as being red or round or smooth or tangy-smelling is to go beyond the given and to add something in the way of interpretation, classification, and construction, which only the mind can contribute.

One feels as if it were almost in desperation that Lewis flounders into saying that the sensuous given is almost like Bergson's *durée*:

When we remember that even the delimitation of that in which we are interested, the singling out of the presentation of our object from other accompanying consciousness is, in some part at least, a work of excision or abstraction wrought by the mind, we may be led to remark that there is, in all strictness, only one given, the Bergsonian real duration or the stream of consciousness. This, I take it, is at least approximately correct. The absolutely given is a specious present, fading into the past and growing into the future with no genuine boundaries. The breaking of this up into the presentation of things marks already the activity of the interested mind.[16]

Finally, when at the conclusion of the chapter from which these quotations have been drawn Lewis attempts to state in so many words the explicit criteria of givenness, all that he can do is to cite first the "specific sensuous or feeling character" of the given, and then to fall back upon a purely negative characterization: the given is that which "the mode of thought can neither create nor alter," which "remains unaffected by any change of mental attitude or interest."[17]

From passages such as these one might conclude that Lewis' position in epistemology was one from which all reliance upon induction or upon the verification or falsification of our theories by experience had been eliminated. True, the purely given element in experience is such that thought can neither create nor even alter it. Yet, at the same time, it is so characterless as presumably to be quite incapable of giving any indication either as to what interpretation or construction the mind should put upon it in the first place, or as to whether, once such an interpretation has been put upon it, that interpretation is correct or incorrect.

But this is not so at all. Rather it is as if Lewis wished deliberately to fly in the face of the logic of his own position and to insist that the given is, after all, sufficiently determinate to serve as a "cue" and to provide a "clue" for its own proper interpretation. Indeed, in a passage immediately following the one quoted above, where Lewis likens the given to the purely undifferentiated *durée* of Bergson, he quickly takes back with his left hand what he has just given with his right: "On the other hand, we should beware of con-

16. *Ibid.*, p. 58.   17. *Ibid.*, p. 66.

ceiving the given as a smooth undifferentiated flux; that would be wholly fictitious. Experience, when it comes, contains within it just those disjunctions which, when they are made explicit by our attention, mark the boundaries of events, 'experiences' and things." [18]

How strange this is, coming from Lewis. For if the distinctions between events, experiences, and things, and so their respective natures and characters, are already implicit in what is given to us in experience, and if it requires only our attention to them to make them explicit, then this surely bespeaks an epistemology of the old-fashioned, Aristotelian, realistic type, according to which our knowledge of the real world is derived by abstraction and by induction from what we experience through the senses. Where, then, is there room for anything like a transcendental principle of justification? How, indeed, can Lewis speak of its being the mind that "dictates the explicit concept" and that "implicitly possesses it already"? If the proper interpretation is already implicit in the data, then the mind has no business trying to function transcendentally and creatively to bestow an interpretation on the data.

On the other hand, if the interpretive concepts are only in the mind — if it is there that they are implicit and not in the data — then any such thing as an induction of meanings and interpretations from what is given in experience is rendered gratuitous, if not downright impossible. Nor would it make any sense to speak — as Lewis repeatedly does speak — of sensory cues and clues to the meaning of experience. In short, we have here reached the point in Lewis' epistemology where it would appear that he must either fish or cut bait. But he still wants to have it both ways — both induction and transcendental justification. Yet a "both . . . and" in this case is simply an impossibility; it has to be an "either . . . or."

Popper as Compared to Lewis

Now let us move directly from Lewis to Popper. For the interesting thing is that in contrast to Lewis, Popper's doctrine might be characterized as one of "neither . . . nor," rather than "both . . . and." Thus, on the one hand, Popper's repudiation of induction as a method in science is so well known as scarcely to need documentation.[19] On the other hand, he is equally

18. *Ibid.*, pp. 58–59.

19. Thus see *The Logic of Scientific Discovery* (New York: Science Editions, 1961), esp. Pt. 1, Chap. 1.

insistent that no such thing as a transcendental method of justification is either needed or appropriate, so far as explanatory theories in science are concerned. It is true that Popper, to our knowledge, makes no explicit mention of any such thing as a transcendental justification. Instead, he directs his fire at what he calls "instrumentalism." Nevertheless, what he terms "instrumentalism," we feel sure, can be shown ultimately to involve the use of at least some kind of a transcendental method of justification in regard to scientific theories. For briefly, instrumentalism as Popper represents it is the view that (1) since explanatory theories in science cannot be derived from the observed facts by any logical means, (2) such theories must therefore be regarded as mere "computation rules" which scientists have devised to enable them to order and predict the observable data. But, clearly, if such theories amount to no more than computation rules, then they cannot in any sense be regarded as descriptive of the way the world is. Instead, they are mere mathematical devices that serve us as instruments for dealing with the data.

To illustrate the import of such instrumentalism, Popper uses the example of Newtonian dynamics, and shows how it would be interpreted in the instrumentalist view:

[Let] a and b be taken to be two positions of two spots of light (or two positions of the planet Mars). [Let] α and β be the corresponding formulae of the formalism, and ϵ the [explanatory] theory strengthened by a general description of the solar system (or by a "model" of the solar system). [Now in the instrumentalist view] nothing would correspond to ϵ in the world . . . : there simply are no such things as attractive forces, for example. Newtonian forces are not entities which determine the acceleration of bodies: they are nothing but mathematical tools whose function is to allow us to deduce β from α.[20]

Clearly, though, if an explanatory theory like ϵ in the above example is nowise derived from the facts, and if it is not even supposed to be descriptive of the facts or to set forth any feature or aspect of the real world at all, then what possible justification is there for introducing it in the first place? To such a question the instrumentalist answer would be that the theory is justified as a mere matter of convenience; it is but a tool or an instrument that enables the scientist to order the data in certain ways, thus rendering them at once manageable and intelligible in terms of their deducibility and

20. *Conjectures and Refutations* (New York: Basic Books, 1962), p. 108. We have changed the wording slightly and inserted a couple of emendations in order to fit this quoted passage into the context of our present discussion.

predictability. Surely, though, a justification of scientific theory simply on grounds of convenience and as a necessary tool for ordering and handling the data of observation would seem to be, if not the same as, then certainly germane to what we have called a transcendental justification. For in the latter case, scientific theories are justified merely on the ground that they make possible an ordered world of experience. But what is such a ground, if not ultimately one of convenience? Likewise, theories that are transcendentally justified, no less than theories introduced on an instrumentalist basis, are never held to be descriptive of the real world, considered as a *Ding an sich*. Indeed, for all practical purposes an instrumentalist philosophy of science is but a particular case of philosophy conceived of as having a transcendental function.

It is well known that Popper makes no secret of the fact that he will have none of any such instrumentalist or transcendental philosophy. When confronted by a direct question as to whether science is "descriptive or instrumental," Popper would answer unhesitatingly, "Descriptive!" And citing the example of Galileo, one of his great heroes in the history of thought, Popper roundly declares that Galileo was not willing to settle for the superiority of the Copernican system merely on the ground of its being a superior "instrument of calculation," as Cardinal Bellarmine had suggested that he might do. Galileo insisted upon its superiority as "a true description of the world," [21] and for his resoluteness he receives a resounding pat on the back from his latter-day admirer. Moreover, Popper even goes so far as to try to range Einstein alongside Galileo as one who, while at first inclined to a purely instrumentalist interpretation of his own theory of relativity, "later repented." Unfortunately, such repentance Popper can document only by referring somewhat cryptically to a conversation which he had with Einstein back in 1950. But at least we do have his word for it that the great man's repentance amounted to a repudiation of instrumentalism and a conversion to realism. We are further assured, albeit only implicitly, that, while Einstein did not die until 1955, he presumably departed this life in a state of grace such as could only have dated from the most fortunate meeting some years earlier, when a repentant Einstein chanced upon a truly understanding confessor, Sir Karl Popper.

What is so interesting about Popper's position is that he blithely supposes that he can combine an uncompromising repudiation of both instrumen-

21. *Ibid.*, p. 98

talism and transcendentalism with an equally uncompromising repudiation of induction. Yet surely this is passing strange even on the face of it. For if there is nothing in our experience that could in any way be said to lead us to see, or even to suggest to us, what the laws of nature are, or even whether there are any such laws or any order of nature of any kind, then what possible reason could we have for supposing that the explanatory theories which we propound would have any relevance to what we experience, much less that they would be correct or incorrect? It is true perhaps that we might suppose the human mind to be a faculty of limitless inventiveness and creativity. Yet the problem is not one of the invention of so-called theories; rather the problem is why it should ever be supposed that such invented theories are theories — i.e., are schemes and patterns that somehow have a relevance and bearing beyond themselves, in the sense of being schemes and patterns *of* events in nature, or *of* the order and connection of sense data, or *of* anything at all.

To this, Popper would no doubt reply that there is no logically cogent reason for supposing in advance that our inventions and mental constructs have any relevance of any kind to anything — to experience, to nature, to sense data, etc. And yet, Popper would say, it is not necessary to have a reason in advance for thinking such theories relevant; all that is required is that with no reason and in all arbitrariness we may simply suppose them to be relevant. Do this much, and it will be found that there are "severe critical tests" to which these theories may be put and in terms of which they will be either corroborated or falsified.

But surely this is far-fetched. For would I ever propound a theory in the first place, if there were literally no reason, either inductive or transcendental, for doing so? Again, Popper's response would be that I do not need a reason for my procedure; I need only be guessing. Yet even a guess is not made in an utter vacuum as regards intelligibility. I only make guesses in contexts where I feel I have at least some reason to believe that my guesses may be right.

Besides, if I have no reason at all for propounding a theory in the first place, if there is literally nothing in my experience to make me think that one theory might be more in accord with the facts than some other, then how could such experience eventually prove to be either a corroboration or falsification of such a theory once the latter has been proposed? We have seen how there must be a certain comparability in determinateness in the experience which serves to corroborate or falsify a theory and in the experience which serves to provide inductive evidence of the theory in the first place. Hence, if what is given in our experience is not sufficiently determinate to provide grounds for induction, neither will it be of sufficient determinateness for purposes of corroboration or falsification.

In fact, one almost wonders whether Popper may perhaps have been led astray in this connection by purely formal logical considerations. For suppose that the logical relation between an explanatory theory and its *explanandum* is simply that of "If p, then q"; we then know, of course, on purely formal logical grounds that to affirm the consequent in such a case does not give us sufficient basis for inferring the truth of the explanatory theory. On the other hand, to know the consequent, q, to be false is a sufficient basis for inferring the falsity of p. However, suppose that my experience is sufficiently determinate to enable me to recognize whether the state of affairs represented in q does or does not occur; then my awareness of q's being the case would seem to provide me with just as much inductive evidence of the truth of p as my awareness of q's not being the case would provide me with deductive evidence of the falsity of p.

What we hope may have become clear from our discussion of both Popper and Lewis is that there would seem to be an incompatibility between an inductive method of knowing and a transcendental method of knowing that amounts almost to an opposition of excluded middle; not only are these methods incompatible, but there is a further opposition between them by which repudiation of the one would seem to commit us to acceptance of the other — not "both . . . and," and not "neither . . . nor."

The Alternative of the Closed-System Language Game

Our discussion has even broader implications, which we will briefly sum up as follows. Once the problem of the relation between facts and theories is approached from the standpoint of a relating-logic, it soon becomes apparent that inductive procedures, as well as procedures of verification and falsification, have to be ruled out as simply not feasible. However, if philosophical or scientific theories can be neither inductively justified nor experientially verified or falsified, then there would seem to be no possible justification of such theories, other than the sort that is vouchsafed by some sort of Kantian transcendental method. In other words, there apparently can be no consistent use of a relating-logic, either in science or in philosophy, without one's having to take what has sometimes been called the

"Kantian turn" in philosophy. There is nothing particularly shocking or horrendous about this. Yet it is amusing, not to say ironical, to contemplate the spectacle of our countless contemporary analytic philosophers, busily "doing philosophy," as they are wont to call it, without realizing that each and every one of them is really but a little Kantian *malgré lui!*

Still, this conclusion may be overhasty. For even if in principle there can be no consistent use of a relating-logic without taking the Kantian turn, it is nevertheless remarkable that in practice so few analytic philosophers and almost no scientists think of themselves as ever having made this turn, or as being in any way obliged to make it. This suggests that there might be a possible alternative to such Kantianism. It is true that the alternative may be somewhat fanciful and would appear, to us at least, to be hardly justifiable philosophically; yet its widespread practice seems to lend it not merely a certain plausibility, but even a considerable respectability.

Thus suppose that one takes certain of Wittgenstein's cryptic utterances in regard to meaning and use, and proceeds to invest them with some such interpretation as the following. For example, Quinton flatly states that "The fundamental point of Wittgenstein's new theory of meaning is that the meaning of a word is not any sort of *object* for which the word stands." [22] And then a bit further on he observes that "To talk about the meaning of a word is to talk about its use." Very well, translating this into the language of a what-logic, such an interpretation of Wittgenstein's meaning-is-use doctrine would appear to be tantamount to the contention that there just are not any *whats,* or any natures or essences of things, for our what-statements to be about and that instead of there being any "objects" of this sort in the world which our what-concepts might be said to mean, the meaning of such notions is to be identified with their behavior or their correct use in the particular language game of which they are a part. It is much as if one were to ask what was the "meaning" of a bishop in a game of chess. To suppose that there was some object in the world that might be said to be "meant by" a bishop is, of course, ridiculous. But to say that such a piece takes on a certain meaning within the game, in virtue of the particular kinds of moves that one makes with it, does make sense.

Transferring this notion of "meaning," which is quite properly the sort of meaning which the various pieces in a game of chess may be said to

---

22. A. M. Quinton, "Excerpt from 'Contemporary British Philosophy,'" reprinted in *Wittgenstein: The Philosophical Investigations,* ed. George Pitcher (New York: Doubleday Anchor Books, 1966), p. 11. The stress on the word "object" is ours.

have, and applying it to the words and phrases of a language game, one can begin to see how at least one possible interpretation of Wittgenstein's amorphous meaning-as-use doctrine begins to take on a certain form and substance. Moreover, the form and substance are those of a meaning which is proper to what we have called a closed-system language game, or, better, a language game of indeterminate reference. In such a game, or, rather, once language is taken to be a game in this sense, then to play the game is not to mean or signify or refer to anything else; it is just to follow the rules of the game itself. And although these same rules may indeed be said to determine the meaning and significance of the various moves or plays that are made within the game, it of course makes no sense to talk about their meaning or signifying or intending anything outside the game. Similarly, knowing how to play the game amounts simply to knowing how to "go on," [23] in the sense already indicated, and to nothing more.

It is not hard to see how and why such a way of conceiving the language game might appear to obviate any sort of transcendental method or Kantian turn in philosophy. For, presumably, the decisive reason for invoking any such transcendental method or justification in the first place is in order to explain how a proposition or set of propositions or an entire theory can be regarded as being about the world when it has not in any way been devised or induced from a consideration of the world. But suppose that we have a language game in which the terms and propositions and theories constituting it are held not to be about the world in the usual sense at all: they do not describe or represent or signify anything outside the language game of which they are a part; instead, their sole function is to gesture and point beyond themselves to other elements within the game (but not outside it), and in such a way as to enable the players or language-users to keep "going-on." And with this, presto! Do not all the numberless dif-

---

23. So far as we have been able to understand it, Wittgenstein's meaning-as-use doctrine seems to have had two rather different objectives, which unhappily are not always kept clearly distinguished from one another. On the one hand, Wittgenstein apparently wanted to show that since knowing the meaning of a word may be simply a matter of knowing how to use it, it is not necessary that such a knowledge of meanings involve any mysterious mental happenings or mental events. On the other hand, he was equally concerned to show that knowing the meaning of a word does not necessarily involve knowing "any sort of object for which the word stands" (Quinton).

For our purposes we can simply disregard Wittgenstein's concern as to whether the act of knowing involves some sort of mental occurrence or not. However, the question as to whether the object of knowledge is perhaps nothing on the order of a *what* or quiddity is indeed one that any partisan of a what-logic must take quite seriously.

ficulties connected with induction and the relation of theories to facts simply vanish into thin air?

Still, there is the comparatively minor detail of verification and falsification. For surely, even in a Wittgensteinian language game the indicative sentences and factual statements must be of a kind that may be either true or false. And with truth and falsity, it is no longer just meaning that one need take account of, but reference as well. While meanings may well be confined to the closed system of the language game, the minute it becomes a question of reference, surely the reference must be to entities and realities outside the game.

However, even this difficulty in regard to reference can be got round by a really resolute and ingenious Wittgensteinian, if he is determined not to compromise his relating-logic by any dubious association with Kantianism. For why not simply admit that no matter how much of a closed system one's language game is conceived to be, it still need not be collapsed into anything like a coherence theory of truth. The language will be a language involving reference all right, and the references will be to reality or realities outside the language game itself. And yet why not get around the obvious difficulties that would seem to be involved by simply leaving all such references studiously and systematically indeterminate?

Thus take even the famous example of "The cat is on the mat." Certainly everyone would agree that the so-called syncategorematic or logical words in this statement do not refer to anything. Why not, then, go one step further and stipulate that even the categorematic or supposedly descriptive words do not refer to anything, at least singly and individually? Thus there need be no real object, cat, which the single word "cat" might be said to mean or refer to. On the other hand, the words of the sentence taken as a whole perhaps refer to something; or, better, the words of this sentence, taken together with the words of other sentences in the language, do indeed have reference. But what the reference is we will simply leave indeterminate. That is to say, the meaning of a word, or for that matter the meaning of all the words of a language, will never be any object or set of objects for which the words stand. Reference, in short, does not commit us to anything of this sort.[24] Instead, all that such reference does is either to reassure us in our activity of going-on in the context of a given language game, or else to draw us up sharp and make us realize that it is a time for a change, i.e.,

24. We shall have still more to say in our Conclusion regarding this topic of reference. See esp. note 6 of our concluding chapter.

for a shift to an altogether different conceptual scheme, or for what Professor Kuhn might wish to call a "scientific revolution," or Professor Waismann a new "metaphysical vision."

In other words, by this mere device of indeterminacy of reference it is supposed that our going-on within a given language game is subject to at least some sort of check, and yet not one that amounts to actual verification or falsification in the usual sense. Instead, it is simply a case of our going-on in a given language game until we find ourselves either blocked or slowed down in our on-going procedures; and then it is time for us to shift to another game. Here, surely, there is no question of a theory being quite literally not "in accord with" the facts; rather, it is a case of interferences, hindrances, and difficulties preventing certain prescribed procedures from being carried out. So the sooner one shifts to another game or another set of procedures the better.

Now isn't this ingenious? All one has to do is to avail oneself of the idea of a language game, being careful, of course, to leave all extra-linguistic references indeterminate, and one will presumably have disposed of all problems in connection with the relation of facts to theories — no inductive leaps, no induction substitutes, no verifications or falsifications, no transcendental deductions, no philosophical clouds of any kind in the sky. Indeed, the more one reflects upon this specimen, or at least supposed specimen, of Wittgensteinian ingenuity, the more one tends to suspect that the best way to understand the relation of facts to theories is not in terms of the language-game model, but rather the model of the pin-ball machine. Propounding a scientific theory or hypothesis would then be rather like pulling the lever and releasing the ball. The resulting shot is not designed to mean or signify something outside the game, but rather is directed at nothing more than keeping the ball going, avoiding pitfalls, picking up points, skirting obstacles that would involve a loss of points, careening on in its course until, finally and hopefully, the maximum of points. It is true that there probably are no ultimate pay-offs in science, the theory that seemingly pays off today being replaced by another tomorrow. But come to think about it, there may not be any ultimate pay-offs in pin-ball games either. Still, while our pin-ball example may not offer an analogy, it would surely seem to provide us with an allegory of what happens in the so-called verification and falsification of scientific theories. Accept this allegory, and one can be rid of no end of embarrassment: no longer will there be a problem of how theories are to be regarded as derived from, or even in accord or disaccord with, the facts. And verification and falsification take on a new sense and meaning: no longer do they have to be interpreted in terms of whether a theory discloses things as they really are or not; rather they may be interpreted simply as facilitations or obstructions with respect to a given, specified, on-going procedure.

To summarize, we might say that a relating-logic can easily avoid falling into the fallacy of inverted intentionality by simply renouncing intentionality altogether. But is that such a price to pay, after all? Well, philosophically the price could well be utter bankruptcy; but scientifically, as we shall suggest later on, the price is one which many contemporary scientists and philosophers of science not only do not mind paying, but pay without apparently realizing that they are paying a price at all! It is something that would appear to come easy to users of a spider-logic.

Chapter X

Deductive Explanation:

A Likely Case Study *in* Surrealism?

WHAT NOW OF DEDUCTION and deductive explanation? For just as one may seek to understand how it is possible to arrive at explanatory theories from a consideration of the facts that presumably demand and require such explanation, so also one can seek to understand just how it is that so-called explanatory theories actually manage to explain the facts that are generally thought to be so in need of explanation. But on this latter score, unfortunately, when one turns to the usual explanations of explanation that tend to be propounded in a relating-logic, one wonders if one is not being treated to a spectacle reminiscent of surrealism in the arts.

It is true that surrealism in art might be considered largely as a movement of protest and revolt, whereas modern theories of deduction in logic remind one not so much of protests as of complacent registers of triumph over all opposition. Even so, the fact should not be lost sight of that one of the rallying cries of the surrealists was "freedom from the control of reason."

It was reason, they exclaimed — not thought, but reason! — that exercised its dictatorship upon men, forcing them to observe and abide by a supposed rational order in things. But such order is not really there; it is only imposed by reason, which does the ordering and effects the connections, which are then said to be "rational," and so manage to palm themselves off as being somehow enshrined in the nature of things. Let man free himself from this dictatorship of reason. Take a T-square, a woman's breast, a battered wagon wheel. Who says that these don't belong together? Does their conjunction seem absurd or irrational? But in dreams, in intoxication, in "madness," it is just such conjunctions and juxtapositions that we are constantly encountering. Indeed, it is thus that "the language of the soul" speaks; for this language is the expression of one's deep and profound self, in its very nudity, and stripped of all logical apparatus. Thus as a recent historian and commentator on the surrealist movement has remarked:

Imagination, folly, dream, surrender to the dark forces of the unconscious and recourse to the marvellous are here opposed, and preferred, to all that arises from necessity, from a logical order, from the reasonable. . . . Folly, or at least what reasonable men designate by this word, is considered by Breton to be a manner of understanding reality which is as valid as that of ordinary men, if not more so. "Hallucinations, illusions," he said, "are not a negligible source of pleasure. . . . The confidences of madmen: I would spend my life in provoking them. They are people of a scrupulous honesty, and whose innocence is equalled only by mine. Columbus had to sail with madmen to discover America. And see how that folly has taken form and endured."

The dream — and recognition of the omnipotence of the dream — will comprise one of the strongholds of the surrealist position. And homage will be paid to Freud, who was the first to lift the veil of consciousness and to systematize the analysis of dreams as a means of knowing man. The Freudian dynamic will become an article of faith for the surrealists. "From the moment when . . . we will succeed in realizing the dream in its integrity . . . when its contour will develop with unequalled regularity and breadth, we can hope that mysteries — which are not really mysteries — will yield to the great Mystery. I believe in the future resolution of those two states, so contradictory in appearance — dream and reality — into a kind of absolute reality, of *surreality*, if one may call it so." [1]

1. Patrick Waldberg, *Surrealism*, trans. Stuart Gilbert (New York: McGraw-Hill [1966?]); London: Thames and Hudson, 1965), p. 16. From certain parts of this passage one might wonder whether it was the intent of the theorists of surrealism to deny the existence of any intelligible or rational order in reality, or to admit such an order but to insist at the same time that the sheer madness and irrationality of the dream world must be equally reckoned with and eventually taken up into the higher synthesis of a surreality. Unfortunately, we are not competent to determine and assess such subtler intentions on the part of

Now far be it from us to claim that modern logic, either overtly or covertly wishes to proclaim any such message of "surreality"! We certainly would not wish to suggest either that modern logicians have ever banded together in quite the manner of the surrealist artists, not simply "for the purpose of experimenting with a manner of painting, but rather with a manner of living." [2] Nor have they — so far as we know — "drunk with a youthful liberty," exclaimed with André Breton:

"Drop everything. Sow your children in the corner of a wood. . . . Let go the prey, for the shadow. . . . Set out on the road." Philippe Soupault, looking somewhat haggard, would ring doorbells, and ask the concierges "if Philippe Soupault did not live there." Benjamin Peret would insult priests on the street. Paul Eluard, without warning, sailed for the Orient, where he was soon joined by Max Ernst. Robert Desnos went into trances at Breton's house. Georges Limbour, famished and simulating Desnos' trance, would get down on all fours, bark, and eat the dog's food [*s'en allait tranquillement manger la pâtée du chien*]. Louis Aragon sang softly: "No, I won't go home." Jacques Prévert, at night dressed as a hooligan, would lead astray [*malmenait*] the innocent passerby in the bourgeois quarters. Tanguy captured spiders which he ate [*araignées qu'il dévorait vivantes*] to terrify the neighborhood. Dali, whose moustache was still young [*dont la moustache n'avait encore que deux ou trois centimètres d'âge*], gave lectures at the Sorbonne with his bare right foot soaking in a pan of milk.[3]

It must be admitted that antics such as these have never been reported of our revered contemporary logicians — not even of Bertrand Russell, to say nothing of the more staid Carnap or Popper or Hempel or Quine or Strawson *et al.* This is not to suggest that they are for that reason surrealists *manqués*. What we do suggest is that there is a sense in which the picture of the world which is congenial to the account that a relating-logic tends to give of deductive explanation and demonstration is one which simply divests reality of all rational or logical connections. That there is any real order in things, or any necessary connections between things, or any sort of dependence of things on real causes, in terms of which the things and events and happenings of our world can be explained and made intel-

---

the surrealists. Instead, for purposes of our own argument, we are simply interpreting the movement as a revolt against reason and a denial of any objective order in things.

2. *Ibid.*, p. 34.

3. *Ibid.*, pp. 34–35. We could not forbear pointing out that in the French edition of this same work of Waldberg's (*Chemins du Surréalisme* [Bruxelles: Editions de la Connaissance, 1965], p. 34), the language would appear to involve rather less of an understatement than the English translation indulges in.

ligible — all this is not so much explicitly denied in a relating-logic,[4] as it is brushed aside as being irrelevant to any properly logical explanations or demonstrations or giving reasons for things. But if our logical understanding of why things are as they are, or of why things happen as they do is nowise dependent upon things being really connected with or causally dependent upon other things, then isn't the very notion of a real order as over against chaos, of commonplace reality as over against dreams and hallucinations, of the necessary and the reasonable as over against the crazy and the mad, not merely so much stuff and nonsense but actually a snare and a delusion? Why not, then, liberate ourselves from all such superstitions, and "drunk with our new liberty" simply defy or deny the laws of God and man? For is it not the logicians themselves who, if not by their practice, at least by their theory, point the way to this new-found freedom and realism, which in very truth is not a realism at all, so much as a surrealism?

Causal Explanations and What-Statements

Now let us return to an actual analysis of just what it is that logical explanation and/or demonstration may be taken to involve in a what-logic on the one hand and in a relating-logic on the other. In the case of an ordinary, everyday what-logic, it is fairly obvious what sort of thing explanations are usually taken to involve. Thus if I ask for an explanation of why ice floats on water, the stock answer would be, "The density of ice is less than that of water." This explanation in turn harks back to the more fundamental Archimedean law that a fluid buoys up a body immersed in it with a force equal to the weight of the fluid displaced by the body.

Looking at this latter principle in a quite uncritical, common-sense sort of way, would not almost anyone take it to be a statement more or less on

4. Sometimes it is denied quite explicitly. Cf., for example, "Atomic facts are independent of one another. From the existence or non-existence of an atomic fact we cannot infer the existence or non-existence of another" (Wittgenstein, *Tractatus Logico-Philosophicus* [London: Kegan Paul, Trench, Trubner & Co., 1922], 2.061, 2.062). No doubt, underlying this stark pronouncement of Wittgenstein's is the still more basic consideration that, so far as *PM* logic is concerned, at least as interpreted by Russell, although the relational structure of atomic propositions corresponds to the relational structure of facts in the world, the relational structure of molecular propositions corresponds to nothing in reality. Cf. Russell's celebrated dictum: "You must not look about the real world for an object which you can call 'or,' and say, 'Now, look at this. This is "or."' There is no such thing, and if you try to analyze 'p or q' in that way you get into trouble" ("The Philosophy of Logical Atomism," in *Logic and Knowledge*, ed. R. C. Marsh [New York: Macmillan, 1956], pp. 209–10).

the order of a what-statement? [5] What the principle or law appears to be saying is that it pertains to the very nature of fluids to exercise this sort of force, once bodies come to be immersed in them. Accordingly, the explanation of ice's floating on water turns on the fact that, ice being of less density than water, the natural buoyant force of the fluid will be sufficient to keep ice afloat, whereas it would hardly suffice to keep substances like iron or rock afloat. It is because there is a real causal force that thus buoys up the ice that it becomes understandable why the ice is kept afloat. More generally still, it would seem that such an explanation explains because it succeeds in disclosing or pointing to a real cause in nature which is responsible for the natural happening that needed explanation.

Let us take another example, from an altogether different domain. Many of us will recall how early in Book I of his *History*, Thucydides asks "why the Athenians and the Peloponnesians violated the thirty years' truce concluded by them after the capture of Euboea," and "what were the grounds of the war." His answer is, "The real though unavowed cause I believe to have been the growth of the Athenian power, which terrified the Lacedaemonians and forced them into war." [6] Once again, just as in the case of why ice floats on water, what is here being sought is an explanation of a certain happening or occurrence. [7] Moreover, the presupposition in both cases would appear to be that such an explanation can be effected only through a discernment of the cause or grounds of the event. In fact, Thucydides is far from repudiating anything like real necessity or a logical order in things, in the manner of the surrealists; it is precisely to such a necessity that he appeals for purposes of explanation — viz., "The real though unavowed cause . . . which . . . forced" the Lacedaemonians into war.

5. This approximation of statements of causes to what-statements demands considerably more explanation and justification than we can afford to devote to it here. Indeed, at first glance it would seem to involve going directly counter to Hume's generally accepted pronouncement that "the mind can never possibly find the effect in the supposed cause by the most accurate scrutiny and examination. For the effect is totally different from the cause" (*An Inquiry concerning Human Understanding*, ed. C. W. Hendel [Indianapolis and New York: Bobbs-Merrill, 1955], p. 43). For a preliminary but by no means sufficient discussion of the issue, we must refer to our earlier book, *Intentional Logic* (New Haven: Yale University Press, 1952), pp. 306–12. Cf. also our comments in note 11 below.

6. Thucydides 1.17.

7. Of course, there is a very important difference between the two cases: Thucydides is seeking an explanation of a particular occurrence or event, whereas in the case of "Ice floats on water" what is sought is an explanation of what might be called a law of nature. This difference, however, important though it is in other contexts, is of no relevance to the present discussion.

We might go beyond Thucydides' actual words and suggest that insofar as he does regard the growth of Athenian power as a real cause and not just a chance concomitant event or process, then the implied major premise of his explanation can only be some such principle as: "Any city-state that becomes terrified by the growth in power of a rival will sooner or later make war on that rival." And what is a principle of this sort if not a what-statement or necessary truth? [8] Moreover, as such it purports to state what in the very nature of the case a city-state in terror of a rival is impelled to do, viz., make war on that rival. Accordingly, we would here again appear to have an explanatory principle or what-statement that is, *mutatis mutandis*, quite comparable with the example cited above, viz., "A fluid buoys up a body immersed in it with a force equal to the weight of the fluid displaced by the body."

So much, then, by way of a preliminary account of explanation as it functions in a what-logic. The explanation is effected through an appeal to real causes in the world, such necessary causal connections being expressed in what-statements that serve as the major premises for the requisite causal explanations or demonstrations.

Causal Explanation in a Relating-Logic

What now of a relating-logic? If we may rely for the moment upon our earlier analyses, it would certainly seem that since in such a logic there are no what-statements, these could never play any sort of a role in logical explanation or demonstration. Even more generally, just as in such a logic no appeal is made to the real *whats* or essences of things in attempting to understand necessary truth, so likewise it would seem that in attempting to understand causal explanations, a relating-logic must rely on purely linguistic and logical connections without making any appeal to real causal connections in nature or in the world.

Still, these mere suspicions or hypotheses as to how explanation must be understood in a relating-logic need to be worked out in more detail. By way of introduction let us again call to mind that invidious comparison of Aristotelian with Galilean modes of thought on which Lewin seems to

---

8. In many recent discussions of the philosophy of history questions have been raised as to whether there is either point or purpose even to adduce general laws as major premises in explanations of historical events, not to mention what-statements or necessary truths. Questions of this sort, however, we must postpone until the following chapter.

have prided himself. It will be remembered that with respect to induction, Lewin liked to insist that it is not by observing the things and happenings of nature that we learn the truth about them. Such a way of doing things is Aristotelian. "For thousands of years man's everyday experience with falling objects did not suffice to bring him to a correct theory of gravity." [9] Instead of just looking at nature, the proper procedure in "induction" is one of idealized constructions, inventions, *Gedankenexperimente*: "It is essentially a process of creative invention which constructs a picture of the underlying reality that must be assumed to account for the observed behavior of the object." [10]

Very well, then, passing from matters of induction to those of deduction, it is just this accounting for the observed behavior of an object that is now at stake. How precisely does one of these "pictures of the underlying reality" that has been "constructed by a process of creative invention" serve to explain or account for a given phenomenon or phenomena? And it is just here that Lewin would no doubt wish to exploit his distinction between Aristotelian and Galilean modes of thought. For the characteristic Aristotelian mode of explanation, he would say, is always in terms of what a thing is, its nature, its essence, the kind of thing it is. By an appeal to something more or less on this order the Aristotelian attempts to understand or explain why a thing behaves or acts as it does. We ourselves saw that this was the way in which Aristotle sought to explain the motion of the planets. We also, in any number of earlier examples, put it forward as being an almost undeniably obvious principle that the way to explain or understand a human being's conduct must be largely in terms of what manner of man he is. But no, says Lewin: "The kind and direction of the physical vectors in Aristotelian dynamics are completely detemined in advance by the nature of the object concerned. In modern physics on the contrary, the existence of a physical vector always depends upon the mutual relations of several physical facts, especially the relation of the object to its environment." [11]

9. Quoted from John William Atkinson, *An Introduction to Motivation* (Princeton, N. J.: Van Nostrand, 1964), p. 66.

10. *Ibid.*, p. 69.

11. *Ibid.*, p. 71. We might remark in passing that Lewin's assessment here is misleading, if not actually erroneous, on two counts. First, his account of Aristotelian dynamics might lead one to suppose that Aristotle acknowledged only the intrinsic causality of formal causes and completely disregarded the extrinsic causality of efficient causes. But, of course, this is not so. Still, Lewin is right to the extent that for Aristotle the causality of both formal and efficient

It is almost as if we were hearing echoes of Professor Hanson inveighing against "causal chains": "The elements of [a physicist's] research are less like links in a chain and more like the legs of a table or the hooks of a clothes pole." [12] For that matter, every term or concept that is used in science is so theory-laden as to remind one indeed of "the flower in the crannied wall," in that it has relational links with everything else in the system and simply cannot be understood save in the context of the entire relevant scientific system or scheme.

Yet unhappily, when brought face to face with the issue of whether this network of interrelationships in a given body of scientific doctrine is a physical network [13] or only a linguistic or logical one, Professor Hanson does not so much look the other way, as begin to squint. Thus to the question, "What guarantees our inferences from cause to effect?", he roundly replies, "A body of theory and information guarantees inferences from cause-*words* to effect-*words*." [14] He continues:

This is the whole story about necessary connection. "Effect" and "cause," so far from naming links in a queue of events, gesture towards webs of criss-crossed theoretical notions, information and patterns of experiment. In a context and by way of a theory, certain effect-words inevitably follow the utterance of certain cause-words: "mainspring uncoils — hands move," "lightning flashes — thunder rumbles," "rain falls — wet pavement," "summer — heat," "fire — destruction." [15]

"Yes," we can imagine a puzzled reader of Professor Hanson saying, "I can easily understand how words of this sort can get connected with one another through various grammatical rules and other conventions of a given language game, but what about the things that the words are supposed to stand for?" Here we find him giving the squinting answer that we have

---

causes tends to be understood in terms of the natures or *whats* of the things involved. To use our own example, that ice should float on water is understood in terms of an extrinsic cause, namely the buoyancy of the water; yet it is considered to pertain to the very nature of water that it should have a buoyancy sufficient to keep ice afloat. Cf. note 5 above. In a second respect, what Lewin says is misleading inasmuch as in a Galilean mode of explanation the object, as contrasted with the relations that it enters into, is not itself a factor in explanation but tends to be dissolved into its relations. Cf. the quotation from Nagel in Chapter VI above, pp. 143–44.

12. *Patterns of Discovery* (Cambridge: University Press, 1958), p. 52.

13. If it were a physical network, then the logic proper to its cognition would be a what-logic — i.e., a logic which effects understanding through an understanding of what the various interrelationships are.

14. *Patterns of Discovery*, p. 62.

15. *Ibid.*, p. 64.

already quoted in a previous chapter: "Causes certainly are connected with effects; but this is because our theories connect them, not because the world is held together by cosmic glue. The world *may* be glued together by imponderables, but that is irrelevant for causal explanation." [16]

Apparently, what Professor Hanson wants to say here is that causal connections, necessary connections, are merely verbal and linguistic, nothing more. Yet he doesn't quite seem to have the courage to say it. Indeed, the consequence of such courage would amount to the frank admission that it is only "summer" that is connected with "heat" and not summer with heat, or only "rain falls" with "wet pavement" and not the falling of rain with a wet pavement. Or to revert to our own earlier example, what Professor Hanson seems to be saying is that scientific explanation contents itself with explaining merely how the word "ice" comes to be used in conjunction with the expression "floats on water"; explaining how ice comes to float on water would appear to be something quite irrelevant so far as scientific explanation is concerned.

Yet Professor Hanson is apparently reluctant to go quite this far. And it is just here that the real squinting begins, or perhaps a better metaphor would be: talking out of both sides of the mouth at once. In any case, Professor Hanson is in goodly and numerous company. For his is but a repetition or reenactment of the same sort of ambiguity and equivocation that we have already found to attach to Ryle's talk about inference-tickets or Waismann's cryptic references to the "application" of linguistic rules, or Lewis' heroic efforts to bring his analytic truths to bear upon the real world. In all such cases, what would seem to be operative is just that curious inversion of intentionality which we sought to expose in Chapter V. Nor, in Professor Hanson's case, is the enormity of the inversion necessarily reduced by his invoking various Delphic-sounding utterances by way of justification: "Treat of the network, not of what the network describes." Alas, one wonders if he would not have done well to think of what befell Croesus from trusting overmuch in oracular pronouncements!

Nevertheless, our present concern is not with such twentieth-century versions of trust in oracles. Rather, we want to try to expose, if we can, the inner workings of a relating-logic, which result in logical explanations coming to be construed as something to be achieved in terms of mere linguistic or conceptual or second-intentional connections and in apparent indiffer-

16. *Ibid.*

ence to anything like real causal connections or relations of dependence in nature and in the world. As we have already suggested, the first step toward such an understanding of explanation can be recognized in the sort of move which Lewin makes: to explain and understand why events in nature happen as they do, it is misleading to appeal to the *nature* of the objects involved; rather it is the complex *relations* of objects to other objects in the situation that determine what happens and how it happens. Yet a mere appeal to relations of things to other things, as contrasted with an appeal to the natures and *whats* of such things, still falls short of what is most characteristic of a relati*ng*-logic, as contrasted with any mere logic of relati*ons*. For in a relating-logic the relations that are the resource of intelligibility are mere linguistic or second-intentional relations, i.e., relations that we ourselves effect, or in which the relating is done by us.

In our earlier discussion of analytic truth we saw how such a relating is effected and exploited for purposes of logic. To recall our example of "logimilk" [17] as a paradigm, it is we who determine arbitrarily and by convention which notes are to be packed into our concept of "logimilk," viz., those of being "a logician" and being "filled with the milk of human kindness." On the basis, then, of such a purely conventional relating of properties to one another in single concepts, we are able to formulate analytic truths which will be quite typical of logically necessary truths as these are conceived in a relating-logic — e.g., "Any logimilk is necessarily filled with the milk of human kindness."

Very well, then, when it comes to the business of logical explanation, and more specifically of the explanations of facts in terms of theories, will it not be just such logically necessary, and yet conventionally determined, truths that will make up the warp and woof of our explanatory theories and hypotheses? Once more, we need only call Professor Hanson to witness:

The properties of particles are discovered and, in a way, determined by the physicist. Certain phenomena are observed which are surprising and require explanation: the observations may be of the tracks left by microparticles in a cloud chamber, or in a photographic emulsion, or they may be the scintillations excited when particles strike certain sensitive screens, or any one of a number of their other indirect effects. The theoretician seeks concepts from which he can generate explanations of the phenomena. From the properties which he ascribes to atomic entities he hopes to infer to [*sic*] what has been encountered in the laboratory; he aspires to fix the data into an intelligible conceptual pattern.

17. Cf. above, Chapter III.

When this is achieved he will know what properties fundamental entities do have.

For example, electrons scintillate, and "veer away" from negatively charged matter, so they must be somewhat like particles. But electron beams also diffract like beams of light, so they must resemble waves too. In order to explain such phenomena as these, the physicist must fashion his concept of the electron so as to facilitate inferences both to its particle and to its wave behaviour; and a conception so fashioned is unavoidably unpicturable.

Observations may multiply. Further properties may be pushed back into the concept "electron," properties from which each new explanation of each new observation follows as a consequence. That theory which depends on the particle being assumed to have these properties will naturally be taken to explain the observations. . . .

In general, if A, B and C can be explained only by assuming some other phenomenon to have properties a, β and γ, then this is the *best possible reason* for taking this other phenomenon to possess a, β and γ. . . . The cluster of properties, a, β and γ, may constitute an unpicturable conceptual entity to begin with. As new properties δ, ϵ and ϕ are "worked into" our idea of the particle the unpicturability can become profound. This does not matter: there will never be any atomic particles we will fail to recognize just because we failed to form an identification picture of them in advance. The main point about fundamental particles is that they show themselves to have just those properties which they must have if they are to explain the larger-scale phenomena requiring explanation. Thus, discovering the properties of elementary particles consists in a logical complex which is, in principle, like the very one within which Democritus found himself. Unless they are taken to have certain abstract properties the elementary particles cannot explain the phenomena they were invoked to explain.

Professor Fermi illustrated this: "The existence of the neutrino has been suggested . . . as an alternative to the apparent lack of conservation of energy in beta disintegrations. It is neutral. Its mass appears to be either zero or extremely small." . . . Its spin is believed to be ½; its magnetic moment either zero or very small. . . . Our concepts of the properties of the neutrino are determined by there being gross phenomena A, B and C, which defy explanation unless an entity exists having the properties a, β and γ: just those which the neutrino has. The idea of the neutrino, like those of other atomic particles, is a conceptual construction "backwards" from what we observe in the large. The principles which guarantee the neutrino's existence are like those which guarantee the existence of electrons, particles, and even atoms.[18]

In other words, it is just some such activity as that which Professor Hanson so aptly describes as "conceptual construction 'backwards'" that would

18. N. R. Hanson, *The Concept of the Positron* (New York: Cambridge University Press, 1963), pp. 45–47. Cf. an almost identical passage from *Patterns of Discovery*, pp. 123–25.

appear to be the source both of the basic concepts that enter into the very make-up of explanatory theories (the "intelligible conceptual patterns") in modern physics and of those analytically necessary truths [19] from which explanations of the phenomena may be "generated." However, is this kind of "conceptual construction 'backwards'" any different in principle from the sort of construction that leads to a concept like that of "logimilk"? And will not the theoretical explanatory principles that incorporate such backwardly constructed concepts be in the manner of "All logimilks are filled with the milk of human kindness"? If so, then we would wonder whether the explanations which thus come to be effected through the medium of a relating-logic would in fact turn out not to be explanations of actual phenomena in nature, such as tracks left by microparticles in a cloud chamber, or scintillations excited when particles strike certain sensitive screens, or even more generally of clusters of properties a, β, and γ. Instead, they would seem to be explanations of how certain linguistic expressions come to be used in connection with other expressions, e.g., "tracks left by microparticles in a cloud chamber," or "scintillations excited when particles strike certain sensitive screens," or "the cluster of properties a, β, and γ."

The Paradox of How Explanations Explain

Even with this rather odd conclusion, however, we still have not got to the end of the story of explanation and deductive demonstration in a relating-logic. For it is not merely a question of how such explanations can be explanations of real phenomena and happenings in nature if the very principles on which such explanation depends are no more than verbal or linguistic truths; in addition, there is a question as to just how in a relating-logic a particular *explanandum* is to be understood as following from or being deducible from a given *explanans*.

19. Of course, it might be questioned whether the explanatory principles from which explanations are generated necessarily have to be analytic truths. However, we find it difficult to understand how explanatory principles could ever have the requisite universality and necessity to enable the phenomena to be deduced from them if they were not analytic (assuming, of course, that there are no synthetic a priori principles from which the phenomena might be deduced). Besides, it is quite generally recognized in the history of science that scientific laws and principles not only may start out by being mere empirical generalizations and end by being analytic, but also at a given period of scientific development the same principle may be used now as an empirical generalization, now as something "functionally a priori," and then again as something analytic. Cf. *Patterns of Discovery*, pp. 97–98.

As we have already said, in a what-logic it is only by a reference to real causes in nature that one can ever hope to explain an *explanandum* by means of an *explanans*. In contrast, in a relating-logic such a reference to real causes would seem to be quite irrelevant to a logical explanation as such. Instead, what nearly all contemporary writers on the subject would take to be of the essence of such explanation is a particular feature referred to by the term "logical deducibility": the *explanandum* must be shown to be logically deducible from an *explanans*. Thus to cite accounts of scientific explanation that in other respects are as widely divergent as Kneale's on the one hand, and Hempel's (or perhaps Popper/Hempel's) on the other, we find Kneale saying: "When a natural law is explained, we can say that it has been shown to be a necessary consequence of some other proposition or propositions." [20] And a little further on, "necessary consequences" is construed in terms of logical entailment or logical deducibility. Hempel, in the rather more painstaking and pedantic mode that is so characteristic of him, says:

Scientific explanation, prediction, and postdiction all have the same logical character; they show that the fact under consideration can be inferred from certain other facts by means of specified general laws. In the simplest case, this type of argument may be schematised as a deductive inference of the following form:

$$C_1, C_2 \ldots\ldots\ldots C_k$$
$$L_1, L_2 \ldots\ldots\ldots L_r$$
$$E$$

Here, C_1, C_2, C_k are statements of particular occurrences (e.g., of the position and momenta of certain celestial bodies at a specified time), and $L_1, L_2 \ldots L_r$ are general laws (e.g., those of Newtonian mechanics); finally, E is a sentence stating whatever is being explained, predicted, and postdicted. And the argument has its intended force only if its conclusion, E, follows deductively from the premises.[21]

But just what is to be understood by "following deductively from the premises"? Apparently, what is meant is nothing more than a purely formal consequence, whose validity or soundness is in no way dependent upon the content of the propositions involved or upon what the propositions are about. Indeed, the situation here in regard to formally valid deductive arguments is quite analogous to what we have already seen to be the case

20. William Kneale, *Probability and Induction* (Oxford: Clarendon Press, 1949), p. 92.
21. Carl G. Hempel, "The Theoretician's Dilemma," quoted in Dudley Shapere, *Philosophical Problems of Natural Science* (New York: Macmillan, 1965), pp. 31-32.

211

in regard to analytic truths — at least when such truths are judged in the light of that third criterion of analyticity which we mentioned in Chapter III.

Thus to bring the issue directly to the fore, we will quote a rather well-known passage from Professor Quine regarding truths that are analytic in the sense of our third criterion. Such truths, he suggests, are *logically true* and are typified by:

No unmarried man is married.
The relevant feature of this example is that it not merely is true as it stands, but remains true under any and all reinterpretations of "man" and "married." If we suppose a prior inventory of *logical* particles, comprising "no," "un," "not," "if," "then," "and," etc., then in general a logical truth is a statement which is true and remains true under all reinterpretations of its components other than the logical particles." [22]

Moreover, everything which Quine here says pertains to formal truths or logical truths could also be said to pertain, *mutatis mutandis,* to arguments that are formally valid and whose conclusions are "logically deducible" from their premises. Thus, for example, when Hempel in the above-quoted passage speaks of the ability of a certain fact to be "inferred from other facts by means of specified general laws," it is solely by virtue of the logical particles involved that such an inference is able to be effected, and not at all by virtue of any real (i.e., factual or non-logical) dependence of the one fact upon the others.

Or suppose we illustrate the point in terms of still another of our examples, viz., the one based upon Thucydides, which purports to be an explanation of why the Lacedaemonians made war on the Athenians. Setting up this explanation in crude syllogistic form, we would have something like the following:

I. Any city-state that becomes terrified by the growth in power of a rival will make war on that rival.

The Lacedaemonians became terrified by the growth in power of their rivals, the Athenians.

∴ The Lacedaemonians made war on the Athenians.

Paraphrasing Professor Quine, we might say that this argument not only is valid, but remains valid under all reinterpretations of its components other than the logical particles. Very well, suppose we effect such a reinter-

22. W. V. Quine, *From a Logical Point of View* (Cambridge: Harvard University Press, 1953), pp. 22–23.

pretation of certain of the components other than the logical particles, and we could come out with the following:

II. Any city-state that goes to war against a rival makes war on that rival.

The Lacedaemonians went to war against their rivals, the Athenians.

∴ The Lacedaemonians made war on the Athenians.

Quite patently, in II no less than in I, the conclusion is logically deducible from the premises. Also, the logical form by which the conclusion is deduced in II is exactly the same as it is in I. Accordingly, if the criterion of logical explanation is mere logical deducibility, then II provides a logical explanation of why the Lacedaemonians made war on the Athenians just as much as does I.

Some of us might be inclined to wonder a bit whether, if "explanation" as defined in terms of "logical deducibility" is a term properly applicable to what is achieved in II, it is any longer possible to regard such "explanations" as being explanations.[23] However that may be, our more immediate task is simply this. Suppose that the notion of logical deducibility as manifested in a relating-logic makes for, or even compels, a type of explanation which proceeds in complete independence of all reference to real causes,

23. A number of modern logicians have questioned whether explanation really should be construed according to the Hempelian model of logical entailment or logical deducibility. Thus Strawson, for example (cf. *Introduction to Logical Theory* [New York: John Wiley, 1952], Chap. 9), suggests that on many occasions when we might be said to be explaining something — e.g., "He's been travelling for eight hours, so he'll be tired" — what is involved is not a deductive inference at all, but only an inductive one (inductive inference being defined as one in which it is possible to accept the premises and yet deny the conclusion without self-contradiction). On the other hand, Toulmin (cf. *The Uses of Argument* [Cambridge: University Press, 1958], esp. Chaps. 3 and 4) would appear to be saying that many explanatory arguments may quite properly be regarded as "field-dependent" rather than "field-invariant," and at the same time as being "formally valid," even though they are not "analytic."

Unfortunately, we have not bothered in the text to take note of these deviations from the norm among relating-logicians. For, clearly, such deviant logicians are not opting for any sort of a what-logic in place of a relating-logic. Instead, they would appear only to be insisting that among the uses of language there are uses of the word "explanation," in which we may be said to explain things, even though we do not avail ourselves of the instrument of strict logical entailment (call it, instead, with Strawson, a case of "induction," or, with Toulmin, a non-analytic and yet formally valid argument). Now this may be all very well as regards certain uses of "explain" or "explanation." The only trouble is that one does not see just how such explanations work or what their logical justification is. To be sure, even to raise such an issue may involve looking for the meaning rather than the use, or perhaps even hankering after what the network describes rather than just the network. To such a charge, we fear we can do no more than plead guilty and accept sentence.

or forces, or grounds in nature, for the facts or occurrences in nature that demand explanation. Is it possible to develop in the context of a what-logic an alternative notion of logical deducibility that will make for a very different and much more familiar type of explanation and demonstration? We believe that this is possible, and furthermore we believe that such an alternative account of logical deducibility can be worked out more or less analogously to the way in which we sought to show earlier that construing necessary truths as what-statements is a quite defensible alternative to construing them as analytic.

The Analogy between Logical Deducibility and Logically True Statements

To this end, then, let us begin by considering more closely the so-called purely formal character of logical deducibility. For it is this that has led modern logicians to insist, almost to a man, that a conclusion which is logically deducible from certain premises tells us absolutely nothing about the world; at most, it tells us only about the disposition of the various logical words or logical particles appearing in the different sentences making up the argument. For example, Strawson observes, in a well-known passage, that there is a difference,

between the criticism we offer when we declare a man's remarks to be untrue and the criticism we offer when we declare them to be inconsistent. In the first case we criticize his remarks on the ground that they fail to square with the facts; in the second case we criticize them on the ground that they fail to square with one another. The charge of untruth refers beyond the words and sentences the man uses to that in the world about which he talks. . . . But the charge of inconsistency does not in this way refer to anything outside the statements that the man makes. We simply consider the way his statements hang together.[24]

Moreover, what Strawson says here about inconsistency and invalidity would apply equally well, *mutatis mutandis*, to consistency and validity and logical deducibility. In other words, recalling Hempel's account of explanation in term of logical deducibility, it should now be clear just how and why it is that to be able to infer "the fact under consideration . . . from certain other facts by means of general laws" tells us nothing whatever about those *facts* and the way they hang together, but only about our *statements* and the way they hang together.

24. *Introduction to Logical Theory*, p. 1.

Yet just how cogent is this sort of contention? Does it not remind us of a similar argument in connection with analytic truths? It will be remembered that, relying upon what we earlier designated as the third criterion of analytic truth, the proposition "All bodies are extended" was true not by virtue of the nature and character of bodies but by virtue of what such a proposition is ostensibly about. Since the proposition is taken to be an analytic truth, and since an analytic truth merely analyzes out in the predicate what is already contained in the subject, its true character as a proposition is: "All bodies that are extended are extended." In other words, the proposition is true by virtue of the purely formal principle, "All *A*'s that are *B*'s are *B*'s." And so the conclusion is drawn that since we do not have to know anything about bodies or extension or anything else in order to know that "All extended bodies are extended," it follows that the proposition is not about bodies or about extension, but rather is a purely formal truth.

Nevertheless, as we saw earlier, such a conclusion in regard to analytic truths is surely dubious, simply because it would seem to involve a serious confusion of use with mention.[25] For even if I may be said to use the purely formal principle "Any *A* that is *B* is *B*" in asserting that "All bodies are extended," my assertion is nonetheless about bodies; it is not an assertion of the purely formal principle.

Applying the same sorts of considerations to logical deductions and arguments, when we say that ice floats on water because it is lighter than water, it may well be that we use a purely formal argument to deduce our conclusion from the premises; yet surely this should not be taken to mean that such an argument in no way tells us that the one fact (that ice floats on water) is really and causally dependent upon certain other facts (such as the one that ice is lighter than water), but only that our respective statements hang together in a certain way. No, for the argument or demonstration in question is about the facts in the case and not about the statements which we use to express those facts. In other words, the logical prohibition against a confusion of use with mention would certainly seem to be applicable, *mutatis mutandis*, to logical arguments and demonstrations quite as much as to individual statements and propositions.

At this point still another difficulty might naturally be raised. For presumably it is our present purpose to show that logical deducibility need

25. Cf. above, Chapter III, pp. 82 ff.

not be construed in the characteristic fashion of a relating-logic, as being able to demonstrate nothing other than purely formal relationships between propositions, but rather that such relations of deducibility between propositions can be used to demonstrate real causal relations and dependencies between the things in the world which those propositions are about. But someone might raise an objection along some such lines as the following:

"Even if it is admitted that a deductive argument might be used as a means to demonstrate real causal connections in nature, still, supposing that in a given case we were mistaken about such connections, our logical argument considered as such would not be rendered invalid. Thus let us imagine ourselves to have constructed an argument showing that the conclusion, 'Ice floats on water,' was logically deducible from certain further propositions to the effect that ice has less density than water, a fluid buoys up a body immersed in it with a force equal to the weight of the fluid displaced by the body, etc. But now suppose that one of these latter propositions should turn out to be false — that ice does not necessarily have less density than water, or that fluids do not always have a buoyancy of the sort specified — would our conclusion then be invalidated, in the sense that it would have ceased to be logically deducible from those particular premises as originally stated? Of course not. But would this not simply cut the ground out from under all contentions to the effect that the logical deducibility of a conclusion from premises somehow involves a reference to real causes or real dependencies in nature?"

Once again, we would propose to meet this difficulty in a way similar to that in which we attempted to deal with a somewhat analogous difficulty in regard to what-statements. It will be remembered that in Chapter IV above we suggested that what-statements, even though they would presumably have to be necessary truths, might still turn out to be false. For example, such statements as "Hydrogen is an element," or "Human beings are a species of animal," or "Motion is a transition of something from something to something else" are clearly what-statements, in that each merely attempts to state in the predicate what its subject is. If this is so, then it would seem that the evidence for the truth of such statements would have to be a self-evidence — i.e., it is only through a consideration of hydrogen itself that we come to know what it is. On the other hand, for all of their seeming self-evidence, we also noted that such statements might well turn out to be false. Chemists might decide that hydrogen was not an element after all, or motion might turn out to be an entirely different sort of thing than the Aristotelians had thought it was, etc.

Very well, then, in the light of such considerations, what could possibly be the criterion for the truth of what-statements? On the one hand, it would seem that such truths cannot be other than self-evident — i.e., to suppose them false would seem to be self-contradictory. On the other hand, these same truths which appear to be self-evident often turn out to be false in the light of further experience. Does this mean, then, that they are subject both to the criterion of self-evidence and to that of empirical evidence? How can this be?

Now this difficulty, it will be remembered from our earlier discussion, we sought to resolve by pointing out that in the case of what-statements the criterion of self-evidence, or of the opposite's being self-contradictory, was only a necessary and not a sufficient condition for the truth of such statements. In fact, we even put it somewhat paradoxically in saying that a presumed what-statement like "Hydrogen is an element" is the sort of statement which, if it is true, is necessarily true, in the sense that being an element would pertain to the very nature of hydrogen, so that to deny it would be self-contradictory. On the other hand, it does not work the other way around. The fact that I consider "Hydrogen is an element" to be a necessary truth — in the sense that this is what I take hydrogen to be, so that if I were to deny that hydrogen was an element, I simply wouldn't be talking about hydrogen any more — is only a necessary and not a sufficient condition for the truth of my what-statement. For it could perfectly well turn out that hydrogen was not of the character that I had thought it was, and then my what-statement would turn out to be false, and I would have to recognize that hydrogen was not an element after all.

"But," someone might retort, "however you may later change your mind as to what hydrogen is, your original statement, 'Hydrogen is an element,' is and remains a necessary truth. For given your understanding and definition of the term 'hydrogen,' it was then, and still is, impossible to deny *that* predicate of just *that* subject."

To this, however, the obvious answer is that while such a retort might not be altogether false, it is very misleading. For if one is going to say that given my meaning of the term "hydrogen," the statement, "Hydrogen is an element," is and remains a necessary truth, this would be to radically alter the character of my assertion. It would turn it into a statement about "hydrogen," whereas in fact it was a statement about hydrogen.

The Discrepancy between Explanation and Deducibility

All right, then, let us now undertake to apply considerations, more or less analogous to these regarding what-statements, to the case of explanation and logical deducibility. The result, we suggest, will be to introduce a certain distinction between the notion of explanation and that of logical deducibility, much as we earlier sought to effect a distinction between the notion of a what-statement and that of a statement the opposite of which is self-contradictory. Also, just as it was found in the earlier context that for a statement to be such that its opposite was self-contradictory was but a necessary and not a sufficient condition of its being a true what-statement, so here, we suggest, it will turn out that for a conclusion to be logically deducible from its premises is only a necessary and not a sufficient condition of so-called logical explanation.

Thus, have we managed to explain why ice floats on water by showing that a statement to this effect follows logically from various other statements such as that ice has less density than water and that water buoys up a body immersed in it with a force equal to the weight of the water displaced by the body, etc.? The answer must surely be that we have explained this only if in fact there is such a buoyancy in water as to have this particular effect. And if one were to question such an answer on the ground that whether water had this sort of buoyancy or not, the conclusion would still follow from the premises, then the exact pertinence of such an objection would not be easy to determine. Of course, the statement, "Ice floats on water," is logically deducible from the various other statements, "Ice has less density than water," etc.; and it is thus logically deducible regardless of whether these other statements are true or false, or whether the buoyancy of water really does operate causally in the specified manner. Yet granting all this, just what bearing does it have on the question at issue, which was a question of explanation? For the explanation that was being sought was an explanation of why ice floats on water, not of any mere sentence or statement, "Ice floats on water." Accordingly, if you merely succeed in showing that the statement, "Ice floats on water," follows from certain other statements, not only have you failed to explain why ice floats on water, but there is even a sense in which you have not shown what the original conclusion

218

you were trying to prove is deducible from. For that conclusion was no mere statement taken in second intention, but rather a statement taken in first intention. But to demonstrate such a statement amounts to demonstrating a fact about the world. To do this, you must surely do more than make reference to the mere arrangement and disposition of statements or propositions considered in second intention; instead, reference has to be made to the real cause or causes of the fact that is being explained or demonstrated.

Apparently, then, to state the matter in terms of our example, not only does one fail to explain why ice floats on water by adducing evidence to the effect that ice is lighter than water and that water has a certain buoyancy, etc., if these latter are not in fact the case, but in addition the statement, "Ice floats on water," considered precisely in its first intention, is not even logically deducible from these other statements, if the latter do not exhibit the real cause or causes of ice's floating on water. Again, the situation here would seem to be strictly analogous to what it was in the case of what-statements and analytic truths. For there too we found that it does not suffice to show that hydrogen is an element merely by showing that one's concept of "hydrogen" involves the further note of "being an element." Nor, if it should turn out that hydrogen was not in fact an element, could one maintain that the statement "Hydrogen is an element" is still an analytic truth; that statement was never an analytic truth, since an analytic truth could perforce only be about "hydrogen," not about hydrogen.

At long last, then, we hope that we have not just scotched our snake but killed it. It's a snake that would seem to have got its coils around so much of modern logic, and as a result it has come to be almost universally taken for granted that all such things as the logical necessity of propositions, the logical deducibility of conclusions from premises, the deductive demonstration of propositions in the light of other propositions, and the logical explanation of propositions by means of others have no bearing on the real world, indicate nothing whatever in the way of real necessities or real causal connections in the world, and are nowise dependent for their own truth or validity upon the real natures of things, or the necessary causal connections and relations between things. Given this modern drama, not of the old Eve, but of the new logic and the old serpent, it is little wonder that our latter-day, wild-eyed surrealist artists and poets should have suddenly felt themselves justified in their all-out preferences for "imagination, folly, dream, surrender to the dark forces of the unconscious, recourse to the marvellous," etc., as opposed "to all that arises from necessity, from a logical order, from the reasonable." In a way, one might even say that there is a certain irony in the fact that these devotees of surreality are doing little more than drawing a very logical conclusion from what so many modern logicians have been saying. The only thing is — and this rather compounds the irony — the conclusion which the surrealists appear to have drawn is one that could only have been drawn in the context of a what-logic; and yet it must have been something like a relating-logic that prompted them to draw it!

But why conjure up fanciful affinities between a relating-logic and surrealism in the arts, when all one has to do is to be serious and literal, and the consequences with which a relating-logic would appear to be fraught will turn out to be embarrassing enough? For if the analyses of this chapter are sound, then surely there is no escaping the impression that when modern logicians undertake to explain just how explanatory theories explain their *explananda*, they seem to skate on very thin ice indeed. Often the *explanans* is so characterized as to appear to explain only our use of certain terms and words in connection with the phenomena, and not the phenomena themselves. Moreover, the very notion of the deducibility of *explanandum* from *explanans* is understood in such a way as seemingly to fall afoul once again of that same confusion of use and mention or, rather more accurately, of the fallacy of inverted intentionality that we have already had occasion to expose as being a characteristic and recurring weakness of a relating-logic.

Once More the Device of a Language Game without Intentionality

Nevertheless, for all of its disabilities, there is a respect in which a relating-logic can be made to serve the purposes of scientific knowledge sufficiently well, at least for practical purposes. In the preceding chapter we noted that, when it is a question of trying to understand how scientific theories might be derived from the facts, contemporary philosophers of science seem to suggest that the fallacy of an inverted intentionality may be avoided by the simple device of renouncing intentionality altogether. Similarly, in the present context of trying to understand just how scientific theories can serve to explain the facts they are supposed to explain, it is just possible that an inversion of intentionality may be avoided by a studious unconcern for intentionality itself. One has only to place a certain interpretation on the Wittgensteinian injunction to treat of the network and not of what the network describes, and one will find oneself in a happy, idyllic state not unlike that which we described in the last chapter under the heading of a closed-system language game. For so far as modern science, particularly modern physics, is concerned, there is no dearth of networks. Quite the contrary; any number of elaborate but alternative deductive networks are there ready at hand from the mathematicians' workshop. Accordingly, it is not too difficult a matter to insert one's *explananda* into such a network, and then proceed just to label other portions of the same network as *explanans* or *explanantia*, with the result that the *explananda* are thereby rendered logically deducible from the *explanantia*, and the whole business of one's continuing to "go on" comes to be determined by the particular features of one's deductive network.

True, one cannot obey the injunctions altogether and treat only of the network and never of what the network describes, any more than, as we saw in the preceding chapter, one can manage to keep one's language game an absolutely closed system. For there is always the bothersome question of reference. Still, if in one's scientific activity one eschews being philosophically scrupulous and contents oneself with a mere easygoing pragmatism, then one can more or less sweep the question of reference under the carpet. All one has to do is to admit that, of course, one's network does refer, but then hasten to add that one is indifferent to the question of whether the network actually gives anything like a literal description of that to which it refers. Indeed, it is just this divorce of description from reference that the injunction to treat only of the network, not of what the network describes, really imports. This metaphor of the network must presumably be construed in the way our earlier metaphor of the closed-system language game was to be construed: the system is not absolutely closed; it does have reference, but the reference is kept deliberately vague and indeterminate. Such a *modus operandi* should suffice quite well for spiders, for it is indeed characteristic of them to be concerned only with their networks, and not with what their networks describe.

Chapter XI

From Deductive Explanation in

General to Historical

Explanation in Particular

IT IS HIGH TIME that we cut short our discussion of logical explanation in general and move to a consideration of what at the moment, in the Anglo-American philosophical world at least, would appear to be at once the more relevant and interesting question, that of historical explanation. Just what is the logic of this type of explanation? Is it an explanation that is somehow *sui generis*, or at any rate markedly different from scientific explanation? As we all know, there are a number of young men today who would answer this question with a cheery "Yes"; and ranged over against them are a number of older, rather more heavily-weighted philosophers who would answer the same question with a ponderous and pedantic "No."

So far as we are concerned, would it not seem that the distinction which we have been seeking so laboriously to draw between a what-logic and a relating-logic might have a very direct bearing on the current issue of whether or not historical explanation is of a fundamentally different type from scientific explanation? Moreover, does not our insistence that the proper domain of a what-logic is our ordinary, everyday knowledge of the world mean that something on the order of a what-logic must surely be the proper tool for historical explanation, as contrasted with the more sophisticated sort of explanation that is proper to the sciences and that would seem to require something more on the order of a relating-logic?

To both of these questions our answer is "Yes." But this answer must be set in the context of the current controversy over the so-called covering-law thesis in regard to historical explanation, as propounded by Popper and Hempel. Put succinctly, what that thesis amounts to is the contention (1) that historical explanation is not in principle different from scientific explanation, and (2) that in the case of both scientific and historical explanation, the explanation can only be effected by subsuming the *explanandum* under a proper *explanans*, which latter must ultimately take the form of a so-called general law or covering law. As over against this, Professor Dray — to cite the example of one of the more extreme, but also one of the more provocative, opponents of the Popper-Hempel thesis — would maintain that so far as historical explanation is concerned, subsumption of the *explanandum* under a general law is neither a necessary nor a sufficient condition of such explanation.[1]

It is not a necessary condition because, taking any such general law you like, it is always possible to question the law and yet accept the explanation. Thus consider our earlier example from Thucydides, who sought to explain the violation of the thirty years' truce in terms of the growth of Athenian power, which, he suggests, terrified the Lacedaemonians and forced them into war. According to the Popper-Hempel theory, such an explanation must turn on some implicit general law or other, which might be roughly formulated in some such fashion as we attempted earlier: "Any city-state that becomes terrified by the growth in power of a rival will sooner or later make war on that rival."

Presented with an example of this sort, Professor Dray would have little difficulty in making sport of it. For who in his right mind would maintain that the law cited above is really and truly a law? It is so easy to think of

1. William Dray, *Laws and Explanation in History* (Oxford: Oxford University Press, 1957). See Chap. 1 for a statement of the Popper-Hempel "covering-law model," the relevance of which for historical explanation Dray wishes to question.

exceptions. And if the so-called law is but a generalization to which there are admitted exceptions, then it is surely no properly universal and necessary connection that is being asserted between a city-state's becoming thus terrified and its being forced into war. But if the connection is not universal and necessary, then why should it be supposed to be a necessary condition of the explanation which Thucydides wished to give of the Peloponnesian War? It is obvious that someone might perfectly well deny the law and yet stand by the explanation.

Nor, Dray argues, will it do any good to try to tailor the proposed general law to make it a truly necessary condition of the explanation. For such a tailoring could move in either of two directions, as it were. One might try to exclude the exceptions to the law by making it more and more general, thus eventually turning it into little more than a truism. For example, in this case, one might try something like, "Extreme fear tends to generate an extreme fear-response." But while such a tailoring of the law might thus tend in the direction of excluding all exceptions, it does so in such a way that, as Dray remarks, "The farther the generalizing process is taken, the harder it becomes to conceive of anything which the truth of the law would rule out."[2] And how can such a thing contribute to, much less be a significant necessary condition of, an explanation of why the Spartans went to war against the Athenians?

In contrast, the tailoring process that moves in the other direction tends to pack into the *explanans* or general law more and more of the details that are relevant to the particular case of the *explanandum*. Thus while it might not be the case that just any city-state that became terrified at the growth in power of its rival would go to war, still it might be true with a city-state in the peculiar circumstances of Sparta. And while not necessarily any and every city-state like Sparta would go to war as a result of being alarmed over the growth of a rival, still it might be that this would necessarily follow if its alarm were occasioned in just such a situation as that of Sparta vis-à-vis Athens. But, clearly, to tailor the covering law in this way leads in the direction of eventually eliminating all generality from the law entirely; it would thus become nothing more than a detailed description of the particular circumstances of the original *explanandum*. Or, as Dray puts it, "Such

---

2. *Ibid.*, p. 29. In other words, Dray is suggesting that the generalizing process thus approximates to a mere analytic truth, which, being no more than linguistic, can hardly be relevant to an explanation of happenings in the real world.

a general 'law' is, no doubt, no more than a vacuous limiting case of a covering law." [3]

Hence Dray's conclusion: the citing of so-called covering laws or general laws is nowise a necessary condition of giving a historical explanation. Dray is no less severe as regards the other aspect of the Popper-Hempel thesis. For on their thesis a covering law is not only a necessary but also a sufficient condition of historical explanation. But Dray disposes of the latter part of the thesis in short order. For what is it to explain an *explanandum* through a general law, he asks, if not simply to subsume a particular case under a general law? And what, in turn, is a general law? For Popper and Hempel, Dray implies, a general law is but a statement of what always happens. And yet it is surely not difficult to think of cases from everyday affairs, Dray remarks, where to subsume a particular case under a general law in this sense would hardly be considered an explanation of such a case:

When puzzled by something, we do not ordinarily find it enlightening to be told: "That's what always happens." Indeed, although such a remark appears to be just an idiomatic, incomplete way of subsuming what happened under a general law, we should often feel justified in protesting: "That's no explanation at all."

What, for instance, is the explanatory force of the common-sense generalization, "Red sky in the morning is followed by rain"? Does the fact that the sky was red this morning *explain* the fact that rain fell before lunch? Surely not. . . . Having a good reason for expecting something is not necessarily being able to explain why it occurs. [4]

Accordingly, in the light of considerations such as these Dray feels that he has pretty well scuttled the principal claim of the Popper-Hempel thesis; to subsume an *explanandum* under a so-called covering law can be regarded as neither a necessary nor a sufficient condition for explaining historical events. But does this mean, then, that there cannot be any explanation of historical events? Far from it, Dray insists. Rather, his conclusion would appear to be that while historical events cannot be explained after the manner of explanations in science (i.e., through subsuming them under covering laws), they nevertheless are entirely susceptible of explanation, but of an explanation that is somehow *sui generis*, of a sort that is proper to history and that thus serves to distinguish history from science. Dray suggests that such a properly historical type of explanation is on "the model of the con-

---

3. *Ibid.*, p. 36.   4. *Ibid.*, p. 61.

tinuous series."[5] And presumably — though we are far from sure — this model is supposed to show that a historical explanation is a proper explanation even though it seems not to involve the subsumption of the particular case (the *explanandum*) under a universal or covering law.

However, our present concern is not with the details of how Dray would wish to distinguish historical from scientific explanation. Rather, we would like to push the question as to whether, with the recognition of some such distinction as the one we have been trying to draw between a what-logic and a relating-logic, the general sort of distinction which Dray is trying to make between historical explanation and scientific explanation may not appear in a quite different light. More specifically, we shall argue that if scientific explanation is to be construed in the manner of a relating-logic, then certainly the explanations which men give of events in history, or of happenings in their everyday lives, simply cannot be interpreted in the manner prescribed by the Popper-Hempel thesis. On the other hand, that historical explanations do not involve the subsumption of their *explananda* under so-called general laws by no means implies that they may not look toward, or desiderate, a subsumption of their *explananda* under something on the order of what-statements. For as we have been at pains to show, what-statements in a what-logic are not to be confounded with universal propositions or general laws in a relating-logic; nor is explanation in the content of a what-logic to be confused with explanation in a relating-logic.

What-Statements vs. *General Laws in Historical Explanation*

Let us return to Professor Dray's contention that to subsume a historical event or happening under a general law just isn't sufficient when it comes to giving an explanation of that event. From the standpoint of a what-logic, of course it is not sufficient, because, in addition to the mere formal deducibility of *explanandum* from *explanans*, there is the further condition that the *explanans* must signify or intend the real causes of the event that is to be explained. Or, to put it a little differently, in a what-logic it is a con-

---

5. Cf. *ibid.*, p. 66 ff. It should be noted, however, that Professor Dray does not subscribe to "the model of the continuous series" as if it were *the* distinctive model of historical explanations. Indeed, it would seem that he is reluctant to accept any model as being *the* model. On this whole question, see the assessment of Dray's position by Arthur C. Danto (*Analytical Philosophy of History* [Cambridge: University Press, 1965], pp. 213–15).

dition of explanation that something on the order of a what-statement be invoked as one of the premises of such explanation.

On the other hand, it appears that Dray wishes to be rather less specific as to just why mere formal deducibility is not a sufficient condition of historical explanation. He contents himself with citing examples to show how, when it comes to historical explanation as this is ordinarily understood, the mere subsuming of a particular case under a general law would not be considered a proper "explanation" at all. For that matter, Professor Dray might well have gone even further than this, although he didn't. He might have invoked those more general features of formal deducibility which we noted above and which clearly rule out the sufficiency of such formal deducibility for purposes of explanation even in the ordinary sense, to say nothing of the specific sense of historical explanation.

For one thing, such mere formal deducibility considered as a sufficient condition of explanation would not enable one to discriminate between explanations of substance and trivial explanations — e.g., an explanation of the Spartans making war on the Athenians in terms of their fear of the growth of Athenian power, as distinguished from an explanation of the Spartans making war on the Athenians simply in terms of their going to war with the Athenians. For another thing, and still more generally, such formal deducibility represents no more than a technique for "going on" linguistically, for linking up certain terms and expressions in a language with certain other terms and expressions in the same language.[6] Accordingly, while it may be perfectly proper to call this sort of thing "explanation" in a somewhat Pickwickian sense, it certainly does not suffice for

6. We should imagine that Professor Dray would be the last to repudiate this notion of explanation as a mere technique for "going on" linguistically. Rather, his concern would seem to be with merely making sure that the particular technique for thus "going on" that is provided by the covering-law model not be regarded as the only possible such technique, and particularly as the only technique proper to historical explanation. Thus he would surely regard his own model of the continuous series as nothing more than a kind of inference technique or explanation technique, which, however much it might differ from the technique of the covering-law model or from the specific inference technique proposed by Toulmin, for example (cf. Dray, p. 64), would nonetheless be but one more variety of those "inference licenses" which Professor Ryle talks of so glibly (cf. Dray, p. 41) and, in the eyes of some of us, so unsatisfactorily. In short, Dray moves entirely within the confines of a relating-logic, and does not appear to have any particular appreciation for the way historical explanation is to be understood in the context of a what-logic.

explanation in the more usual sense. And the more usual sense is surely the commonly accepted one in historical contexts.

From the standpoint of a what-logic, what is particularly interesting and challenging about Professor Dray's position is not so much his insistence that the mere formal deducibility of *explanandum* from *explanans*, as expounded by Popper-Hempel, can never serve as a sufficient condition of historical explanation, but rather his insistence that such deducibility is not even a necessary condition of such explanation. Now on this score a what-logic would seem at least superficially to go right down the line with the advocates of the Popper-Hempel thesis; in both cases, the explanation of a happening or an event would seem to require the deducibility of an *explanandum* from an *explanans*. Indeed, the case in regard to explanation would seem to be analogous to what it was in regard to necessary truth. For so far as a what-logic is concerned, we saw that a necessary condition of a what-statement was that the formal criteria of the opposite's being contradictory, or the predicate's being contained in the subject, be applicable to such a statement; now, likewise, it would seem that in the context of a what-logic, no less than in that of a relating-logic,[7] a necessary condition of causal explanation must be that of formal deducibility of *explanandum* from *explanans*.

What, then, may be said by way of reply to Professor Dray's strictures on this score? For all of his arguments as to the artificiality and dispensability of a principle such as "Any city-state that becomes terrified by the growth in power of its rival will sooner or later make war on that rival," to explain why Sparta made war on Athens, would seem to be just as telling against explanation as it is conceived in the context of a what-logic as they are against explanation as conceived by a relating-logic.

Yet not exactly so. It might be that in raising his telling considerations against the various specific instances of supposed covering laws (which covering-law theorists have suggested that historians must appeal to at least implicitly in their explanations), Professor Dray is really arguing only against a peculiarly narrow and straitened conception of such necessary conditions of historical explanation — a conception which perhaps is proper

7. In light of what was said in note 6 above, this last statement would seem to be in need of some qualification. For Professor Dray avails himself — at least in our view — of a relating-logic just as Popper and Hempel do. Nevertheless, he would contend that in historical explanation the formal deducibility of *explanandum* from *explanans* is not requisite, whereas Popper and Hempel would maintain that it is. Accordingly, such a requirement of formal deducibility could scarcely be said to be characteristic of a relating-logic *per se*.

only to a relating-logic. To see if such is the case, let us reexamine some of the relevant specific examples. In addition to our example of Thucydides, we might bring forward what has become a somewhat stock example in the literature, viz., the explanation of why Louis XIV died unpopular.[8] As Dray suggests, one might imagine a historian's explaining this situation on the ground that Louis pursued policies detrimental to French national interests. Finally, there is the example which Professor Danto exploits [9] of the explanation which C. V. Wedgwood gives of the radical change of mind on the part of Prince Charles and of the Duke of Buckingham toward the plans for Charles's marriage to the Infanta and toward the entire projected Spanish alliance. Miss Wedgwood's explanation simply reads: "[King James's] son and his favorite, Buckingham, indignant at their reception in Spain whither they had gone to hasten the negotiations, returned to England and declared themselves unwilling to participate further in the unholy alliance."

Now let us analyze each of these examples of historical explanation, first from the standpoint of a what-logic and then from that of a relating-logic. Clearly, so far as a what-logic is concerned, the explanation in each case must be seen to depend on a recognition of something like real forces or causes in the world that were presumably responsible for actually bringing about the changed state of affairs that in each example is enunciated in the *explanandum*. Thus in the case of the Spartans going to war with the Athenians, would not most of us recognize, at least on a common-sense basis, that fear over the growth in power of a rival might well drive a nation or a city-state into war with that rival? As for Louis XIV dying unpopular, is it not reasonable to suppose that the pursuit of policies that are detrimental to national interests would naturally make for a monarch's unpopularity? Likewise, as regards Charles's and Buckingham's change of mind toward Spain, it might very well have been the case that the indignation of these impressionable young men over the way the haughty Spaniards had treated them was indeed the thing that caused them to

8. This example, it seems, was originally given by P. L. Gardiner in *The Nature of Historical Explanation* (New York: Oxford University Press, 1952). Cf. Dray, pp. 25 ff., for his discussion of it.

9. Danto, pp. 240–41. The same example — though based on Trevelyan's account rather than on Wedgwood's — is discussed by Ernest Nagel in *The Structure of Science* (New York: Harcourt, Brace & World, 1961), pp. 564 ff. In turn, Danto sees fit to discuss not only the example, but Nagel's discussion of it as well (*Analytical Philosophy of History*, pp. 234–35).

change their minds as to the wisdom of the entire policy of the Spanish alliance. After all, don't things like this happen every day?

But we can readily imagine someone's making rejoinder to the effect that such considerations are all beside the point. After all, the issue which Dray's arguments pose for a what-logic is not the issue of whether real causes might be appealed to in historical explanations. Rather, Dray's challenge concerns whether such an appeal to real causes necessarily involves the use of covering laws and of the resultant formal deducibility of historical *explananda* from such covering laws. When the issue is viewed in this light, it would seem that a proponent of a what-logic, no less than of a relating-logic, would be hard put to specify the relevant covering laws in the above examples. Thus we have already had occasion to remark on the artificial and inadequate character of the covering law that presumably would have to be brought forward to cover the case which Thucydides is trying to explain. The presumed candidates for the role of covering laws in the other two examples would be just as farfetched and insufficient. One might try to explain Louis XIV's unpopularity on the basis of the general principle that any monarch who pursues policies detrimental to the national interests will tend to become unpopular. Yet this just isn't true; it isn't *always* the case that a monarch who pursues such policies tends to become unpopular. What about Francis I, or Louis XV, or, perhaps better still, Ludwig II of Bavaria? And if such a consequence isn't always the case, why should it be thought to be a sufficient condition of the explanation of Louis XIV's unpopularity?

Moreover, while we might appear to make the explanation of the change of mind of Charles and of Buckingham plausible by saying, "But don't things like this happen every day?", this would really seem to be little more than a dodge. For just try to formulate the relevant principle of explanation as a universal covering law — for example, "Politicians who become indignant over the way their prospective allies treat them will end by repudiating the projected alliance." Surely, attempts of this sort to formulate the relevant covering law can only produce results at once so clumsy and farfetched as to seem almost worthless for purposes of explanation.

Still, when we reflect on the matter a little more carefully, does it not become increasingly obvious that such criticisms of the covering-law thesis are telling only as it emerges in the context of a relating-logic? For so far as a what-logic is concerned, explanations are in terms of causes; and this means that a necessary condition of such explanation is that there be a reference to real causes that are either actually or potentially operative in nature and in the world. However, no sooner is it a question of reference to real causes in the world, that are outside of and independent of the mere logical structure of the argument or explanation itself, than it also becomes a question of possible error in regard to such causes. And it is not merely a question of error in the bald sense but also a question of possible confusion, of not seeing very clearly, and consequently of being somewhat hesitant and uncertain as to just what the relevant causes are and how they may be most properly articulated. Very well, then, against this sort of background it might well be the case, say, in regard to Louis XIV, that when as a historian I come to explain the fact of his having died unpopular, I readily recognize, from a study of the documents and the sources, that his policies were detrimental to French national interests, and that this did — to judge from the contemporary complaints and criticisms on the part of his subjects — have a direct bearing on his increasing unpopularity. Yet at the same time I might be far from clear as to just how and in what exact sense his policies contributed to his unpopularity; nor could I even hope to formulate with any precision the relevant causal law or laws that would be needed if the fact of Louis's unpopularity were to be made thoroughly intelligible in the light of its causes.

Vagueness in Causal Knowledge and Universality in Covering Laws

Yet what does all this betoken, save only the limitation and inadequacy of my knowledge and understanding of the relevant causes? It nowise shows that there are no such causes in the first place, or that for a complete explanation and understanding of Louis's unpopularity the formulation of a genuine covering law is really not a necessary condition after all. On the other hand, and at the other extreme, such limitations and inadequacies as afflict my rather feeble knowledge and understanding of the causes of things must not be taken to mean that I just do not have such causal knowledge at all, or that my attempted explanation of Louis's unpopularity amounts to no explanation. On the contrary, I may truly be said to recognize that the fact that Louis's policies were detrimental to French national interests did indeed have a real bearing on his unpopularity; and to the extent that I recognize that the one must have had such a real bearing on the other, I can bring forward the one fact in explanation of the other.[10] At the same time, not being able to formulate the precise causal laws that would make such an explanation thoroughly cogent, my explanation can scarcely claim to be more than imperfect and incomplete.[11]

Perhaps it would be illuminating if we could exhibit a certain analogy here between the situation in regard to causal explanations and that which we have already discussed in regard to what-statements. Thus with respect to the latter, remember St. Augustine's plaintive apostrophe on the subject of time.[12] Everyone, he says, knows what time is, but who is able to say just what it is? Moreover, such a situation, of knowing the *what* and yet not being able to formulate the appropriate what-statement, is normal in our everyday existence. For we all know what an apple is, and yet how many of us can say just what such a thing is? And similarly with respect to religion, or to the color green, or to sunshine, or to justice, or to a poem, or any

10. No sooner do we put the matter in words like these, as if it were possible simply to "put forward the one fact in explanation of the other," than a hostile critic might say that so far from meeting the specific sort of challenge which Dray wishes to raise, we are in fact only surrendering to it. For Dray might be interpreted as not wishing to deny the possibility, or even the necessity, of explanations in terms of causes — or, rather more accurately, in terms of "because's" — but rather as wishing only to deny that such an explanation in terms of a "because" must involve any sort of appeal or reference to a covering law. In other words, the fact of Louis's having pursued policies detrimental to French interests — or perhaps "a continuous series" of such facts — might indeed, so Dray would hold, explain the fact of his having died unpopular; and yet such an explanation nowise involves our having to trundle out an implausible and irrelevant covering law to the effect that any monarch who pursues policies detrimental to French national interests tends to become unpopular.

In response to this, we would merely say that we simply cannot understand how there can be causation without necessity, or necessity without universality. That the one fact, X, should be the cause of Y can only be understood as meaning that X necessarily and by its very nature is the cause of Y, and that therefore not just the one fact, X, but any X is causally productive of Y. Accordingly, where we would part company from Dray is in our insistence that an explanation in terms of a "because" necessarily involves a reference to a universal principle. And on the other hand, where we would part company from the covering-law theorists is in our insistence that the covering law must be a what-statement, and hence no mere general law or universal law as these are usually understood.

11. One must be careful not to interpret this suggestion as involving the sort of thing which Hempel calls a mere "explanation sketch" (on this, cf. Dray, p. 32). For Hempel's explanation sketch must be understood with reference to the full-bodied picture that is provided by an entire set of relevant universal laws; in contrast, our explanation sketch, if it may be called such, is to be understood with reference to a genuine what-statement whose self-evidence is apparent to us.

12. *Confessions* 11. 14.

number of things. True, not everything with respect to which we may ask the question "What?" is necessarily a genuine *what* or nature or essence in its own right.[13] For we can be deceived as to whether it is a genuine *what* or essence that we are considering, just as we can be deceived as to what specifically such a *what* or essence is, even supposing it to be genuine. Yet such possibilities of error and of ignorance, of confusion and lack of clarity, do not warrant the conclusion that there are no *whats* of things at all; nor do they warrant the conclusion that we can never know the *whats* of things; they do not even warrant the conclusion that when we can't say what a thing is, we therefore have no knowledge at all as to what it is. On the contrary, St. Augustine's testimony is decisive on this latter score: we frequently know, though we cannot say, what it is that something is.

This should not surprise us — at least insofar as we are thinking in the context of a what-logic. For if it is a condition of a true what-statement that its opposite is inconceivable or self-contradictory and also that it is a statement about what something really is in fact — i.e., that it refers to a real *what* or essence in things — then of course the possibility is always open that we may be deceived in such a what-statement, or that we may not be right as to what the thing in question is after all. It is also possible that we may be confused or unclear as to just what it is that we are considering, with the result that we can scarcely even formulate a proper what-statement in regard to it. But in the latter case it does not follow that we have no knowledge of the *what*, or that the eventual formulation of a true what-statement is in no sense a necessary condition of the full and proper knowledge of such a *what* or nature.

Now the analogy between a knowledge of *whats* and a knowledge of causes, or between what-statements and explanations, would appear to be complete. Since in both cases a reference to the real world is a necessary condition of such statements and explanations, it follows that in both cases our knowledge of such *whats* or of such causes may be so hazy and so imperfect as to prevent us from formulating in the one case a proper what-statement or in the other a proper covering law as the major premise of the explanation. At the same time, considered in the context of a what-logic, Dray's contention that the formulation of a covering law is nowise a necessary condition of historical explanation would seem to be quite as wrongheaded as if one were to say to St. Augustine, for example, that because

---

13. Cf. our earlier discussion of this point in connection with Wittgenstein's notion of "family resemblances" in Chapter IV above.

he in a sense knows what time is, even though he can't say what it is, the formulation of a proper what-statement is for that reason quite irrelevant to a full and complete understanding of what time is.

Interestingly enough, though, just as Dray's point would seem to be mistaken in the context of a what-logic, it would seem to be well taken in the context of a relating-logic. For in the latter type of logic, a reference to real causes in nature or in the world is not at all a condition of a proper explanation of the scientific kind. But if one thus eliminates external reference to real causes as a condition of explanation, then the criteria of such explanation must be considered as being almost entirely intrinsic or internal to the explanation. That is to say, such criteria are reducible pretty much to those of formal deducibility. However, formal deducibility in such cases is not merely hampered, but becomes downright impossible without a covering law to serve as a major premise. Hence the determination of the partisans of the Popper-Hempel thesis to foist covering laws upon all historical explanations — if not a genuine law, then a purely trivial one; and if not a full explanation, then an explanation sketch. Nor is it amiss of Dray to expose such *ersatz* covering laws and such supposititious explanation sketches as being neither necessary nor sufficient, so far as historical explanation is concerned (and he might have added, so far as explanation in everyday life is concerned).

Perhaps we can begin to see more clearly the full import of trying to understand historical explanation in the context of a what-logic, as over against that of a relating-logic. In the latter case, such explanation will not be conceived of as involving any sense of, or insight into, the actual causes that presumably were operative in bringing about this or that state of affairs, or in determining this or that decision. It will not even be an explanation that is concerned with the real forces and factors in historical change at all, or even with any real connections between historical events and happenings. Rather, its sole concern is with statements — in this case historical statements — and with how they can be linked up logically or linguistically with still other statements and these with still others, so as to enable us to keep "going on" from one statement to another, and yet with a reliance upon no more than the "grammatical" or logical connections among these statements.[14] Little wonder that in the context of such a logic there can be

14. Thus it should be possible to recognize how Dray, for all of his differences with the covering-law theorists, is nonetheless in the tradition of a relating-logic. For him explanation is not in terms of the real causes and natures of things, any more than it is for

no room and no tolerance for the kind of cognitive or logical situation that is involved in a historian's saying, for example: "I see clearly that the decisive reason for Charles's and Buckingham's change of mind was the treatment they received at the Spanish court, and yet I am far from understanding clearly enough just how treatment of this sort works on men's sensibilities in such a way as to make them give up their most cherished plans and projects. Hence I am not just reluctant, I will not even allow myself to try my hand at formulating universal laws or what-statements expressing a causal connection between haughty treatment and radical changes of heart and mind." No, in a relating-logic in which explanation is construed entirely in terms of purely logical or linguistic connections, either the necessary elements of such connections are all there and present, or there is no explanation at all. In contrast, in a what-logic where explanation involves, in addition to the purely formal and logical connections between statements, the further condition of an actual reference to real causes and factors in the world, it is entirely possible that our comprehension of such causal connections may be so approximate and so tentative as to lead us to stop short of actually formulating any relevant what-statements or causal laws at all. Yet such an inability to state the actual causal principle that is involved implies neither that we are completely lacking in any sort of knowledge of the relevant causes, nor that the formulation of such causal principles or covering laws is at once unnecessary and pointless, when it comes to a full understanding and explanation of the events and happenings in history.[15]

---

the covering-law theorists. Instead, all that Dray wishes to do is to argue for a different sort of linguistic or logical connection between *explanans* and *explanandum* from that which the covering-law theorists would contend for. While the latter would insist that a covering law is essential to the logical grammar of historical explanation, Dray would insist that it is dispensable.

15. It might be objected that what is said here quite misses the point, that the issue is not whether we are able sometimes to have only an inkling of the true causes of a given event, and therefore be at a loss as to how to formulate such a merely approximate knowledge in legitimate what-statements or causal laws. Rather, the point is whether, when it is acknowledged that our formulated what-statements and causal laws are thus imperfect, we can any longer be said to explain the *explanandum* by an appeal to such laws and statements.

It is just this sort of objection which, as we understand it, Professor Donagan has put very tellingly in his subtle and perceptive essay on "The Popper-Hempel Theory Reconsidered" (reprinted in *Philosophical Analysis and History*, ed. W. Dray [New York and London: Harper and Row, 1966], pp. 127–57). Briefly, Donagan's contention is that for any proper explanation of a given event one must recognize the truth of what he calls "the deductive thesis." And the reason for this, he thinks, is quite simple: "If your

The Integrity of Historical as Compared with Scientific Explanation

These same characteristic resources of a what-logic make it possible to provide historians and those who practice historical explanation with guarantees of a kind of integrity and autonomy for their discipline that it would lose entirely if it were set in the context of a relating-logic. Indeed, the very thing that disturbs Dray particularly, and justly so, about the Popper-Hempel thesis is that its proponents refuse to recognize any difference in principle between historical explanation and scientific explanation, the former being no more than a sort of fumbling, bumbling, imperfect instance of the latter. It is even suggested by the advocates of the thesis that there may one day dawn a golden age when the social sciences will have become so far advanced that history will amount to nothing more than the application of psychological, sociological, and economic laws in the explanation of historical events.

Approaching the matter from the standpoint of a what-logic, however, even if such a golden age for the social sciences should someday come about, the sorts of explanations of historical events that would be made possible through the use of covering laws drawn from these sciences would be explanations only in the sense of a relating-logic and not in the sense of a what-logic at all. That is to say, as explanations they would be mere devices for "going on" linguistically or grammatically or logically, and hence would nowise serve to disclose anything like the real causes of historical events; nor would the marshalling of such scientific explanations lead to the kind of understanding of historical events that the use of a what-logic has traditionally vouchsafed to historians using a more humanistic approach. Accordingly, historians might wish to think long and earnestly before deciding to settle for scientific explanations in this sense.

Moreover, while credence can hardly be given to Dray's thesis that his-

---

task is to explain why a given event E occurred, rather than did not occur, then your *explanans* must exclude the possibility that E did not occur; but, if your explanation is not deductive, i.e. if its *explanans* does not logically entail its *explanandum*, then it will not exclude that possibility, and so will not explain why E did occur" (p. 132).

Is not, however, the force of this contention of Professor Donagan's derived almost entirely from his taking the word "explain" in a very strict sense indeed? Thus he would have to insist that Thucydides, for example, had nowise explained why the Spartans attacked the Athenians, if the only reason that he could give was that the Spartans had become increasingly frightened at the spectacle of the growing power of their rival. Surely, though, even if this could not be taken to be an "explanation" in Professor Donagan's sense, in any ordinary sense it is not only an explanation but a moderately good one at that.

torical explanation is *sui generis* and hence not like "scientific" explanation, in the sense of either a relating-logic or a what-logic, that still does not mean that so far as a what-logic is concerned historical explanation must ultimately give place to some kind of "scientific"[16] explanation. To be sure, we have maintained, in opposition to Dray, that for a complete intelligibility and understanding of historical events in and through their causes,[17] the statements of such events would need to be formally deducible from other statements expressing the causes of such events. In this sense, and ultimately, the criterion of formal deducibility must be recognized as relevant to explanations in a what-logic, just as it is to explanations in a relating-logic. On the other hand, as we have been at such pains to explain, the very fact that a what-logic stipulates as a further criterion of explanation that the *explanans* must involve a knowledge of real causes both warrants and deter-

16. In the concluding pages of this chapter, we have sometimes put the word "scientific" in quotes, in order to signify that sort of philosophical knowledge of man and of man's situation which, though it may develop out of a study of history, is nevertheless distinguishable from historical knowledge proper, and at the same time is altogether different from scientific knowledge in the modern sense.

17. Once again, we might here make reference to Professor Donagan's article, cited in note 15 above. For Donagan is anxious to give an account of historical explanation that will not commit one to any kind of scientific determinism in regard to the events in history. Thus it is conceivable that he might criticize our treatment of historical explanation on the ground that it would make no difference whether one followed a what-logic and sought to explain events in terms of real causes, or followed a relating-logic and sought to give explanations in terms of mere so-called causal laws; in either case one's explanation would entail a determinism with respect to historical events.

However, we should reply that although in our discussion we did not address ourselves to the specific issue of human freedom, or, as Professor Donagan calls it, "the presupposition of individual choice" (p. 149), particularly as this bears on the logic of historical explanation, still we do not believe that the account which we have given of such explanation in terms of a what-logic is one that need in any way exclude factors such as that of individual choice. Indeed, Professor Donagan himself, in order to incorporate this factor of individual choice into the texture of certain historical explanations, would avail himself of a universal proposition of the following sort to serve as a major premise in such explanations: "All men who resolve to achieve a certain end at all costs, and who judge that only by doing a certain act can it be achieved, will do that act." And to the objection that such a major premise serves as but another instance of a covering law or causal law in historical explanation, Professor Donagan's reply is that such a principle is not a law at all, since laws by definition "must be empirically falsifiable." Instead of being a causal law, the above principle is "an analytic truth" (p. 150).

To this, we need only respond by treating Professor Donagan's principle not as an analytic truth but as a what-statement; and thus, everything that he says about the need to respect "the presupposition of individual choice" in historical explanation becomes not just compatible with, but capable of actually being incorporated into, historical explanation as that is conceived by a what-logic.

mines a characteristic tolerance of explanations that involve no more than a vague recognition of the relevant causal forces or factors operative in the case of a given event, and that consequently do not manage to articulate explicitly the relevant causal principle from which the *explanandum* may be formally deduced. Indeed, it is precisely this situation that prevails with respect both to historical explanations and to explanations in everyday life. Nor is there any reason to suppose that it is a situation that will change very materially in the future, since it is simply a fact that the real causes of things and the real natures of things are largely hidden from us. As a result, "progress" in knowledge as we customarily think of it nowadays is almost exclusively of the sort that the modern sciences have made us familiar with and that in consequence only a relating-logic can vouchsafe for us.

Leaving progress to the sciences, then, and at the same time recognizing that the sort of knowledge that we are able to achieve of historical events and of our everyday world is through real causes and natures that must perforce remain largely unarticulated, does not this very way of characterizing such knowledge determine for us a sphere and a mode of knowledge that are at once basic and indispensable to our very existence as human beings?

In this connection it might be illuminating to recall Aristotle's suggestions as to the respective domains and functions of historical knowledge, "scientific" knowledge, and poetry. In the *Poetics*, it will be remembered, he raises the question as to the difference between history and poetry; and he answers, albeit somewhat cryptically: "It really lies in this: the one describes what has happened, the other what might. Hence poetry is something more philosophic and more serious than history; for poetry speaks of what is universal, history of what is particular." [18] Though seemingly enigmatic, the sort of thing that Aristotle has in mind here is not so difficult to understand. For isn't it a fact that in our lives all of us derive, from history and from our everyday experience, a kind of knowledge and understanding that is scarcely more than ἐμπειρία — that is to say, a kind of experience or wisdom or knowledge of the world in which the universal tends to be neither clearly articulated nor clearly exhibited? Moreover, by "universal" in such a context Aristotle may be understood to mean very much the same as what we have been calling a knowledge of essences and of causes, which is in principle expressible in what-statements.

Nor is such ἐμπειρία to be depreciated, even though it may fall short

18. Quoted in C. M. Bowra, *The Greek Experience* (New York: World, 1958), p. 146.

of bringing the universal to any sort of clear expression. For it is from just such knowledge as ἐμπειρία consists in that the "scientist" or philosopher abstracts his knowledge of the nature of man (in anthropology and psychology, for example, or in ethics and politics), and that the poet fashions concrete representations of the universally human.

Thus in the matter of poetry, Professor Bowra provides the following commentary on the passage just quoted from the *Poetics*:

No Greek poets would have used precisely this language, and most of them would have been surprised to hear their work called philosophical. . . . But Aristotle is right to call it philosophical, because in its own way it is concerned with the revelation of truth. The truth in question, as he saw, is not of particular facts, but of universal principles or tendencies or characteristics. Even if, as is perfectly possible, there was once a historical Achilles, the importance of Homer's presentation of him is irrelevant to his existence. The Achilles whom we know is indeed universal in the sense that he embodies in a convincing and satisfying form qualities which are to be found in many men, but seldom so clearly or so forcibly as in him. To find this universal element the poet must make a severe selection from reality and present it with decisive discrimination. Just as sculptors emphasized what they thought to be the essential characteristics of their subjects at the expense of the incidental and the accidental, so poets emphasized what they thought to be the essential characteristics of human beings and showed how these led to certain kinds of result in action and suffering. They saw too that behind the infinite variety of human behavior and fortune there must be forces at work which could to some degree be understood and presented in a concrete form. Their idea of truth was to find out these principles and forces, which were indeed at work in individuals but could best be grasped if they were abstracted from the particular case and displayed through situations which manifested more clearly their significance and their reality.[19]

Moreover, what Bowra here says of Greek poets and sculptors, in their concern to exhibit the universal as they had come to see it and had derived it from their own ἐμπειρία of history and of everyday life, would appear to be no less true of the figures of a Giacometti or of Michelangelo's Moses, of Shakespeare's Hamlet or of Faulkner's Colonel Sutphin, of Hogarth's "Distressed Musician" or of Dali's "*Le jeu lugubre*." And is it not from just the same sort of experience that philosophers have sought to derive their knowledge of man and of the human situation, and to articulate such a knowledge of the universal in specific what-statements? Surely it was from ἐμπειρία in just this sense that Aristotle derived his principle that the good life for man could only be an intelligent or examined life, or

19. *Ibid.*

that Sartre came to feel that man is but a useless passion, or that Kierke-gaard came to place such stress upon subjectivity as over against objec-tivity, or even, to choose a rather more forbidding example, that Kant concluded that man, being rational, could not but be subject to the moral law.

In other words, human experience as it arises from history and from daily life is the source or seed-bed of philosophy and of all the humanities. More-over, it would seem to be through the operation of a what-logic that our knowledge of the universal comes to be derived from such experience, and that such understanding and explanation of that experience as we are hu-manly capable of comes to be effected and brought about. For as we have been trying to make clear throughout this entire chapter, our experience of historical events and of the everyday happenings in the world about us is already and unmistakably, albeit vaguely, an experience of the causes of such changes and of the natures of the things and events that are caught up in these changes — despite the fact that we may not be able to articulate such knowledge in what-statements or in actual demonstrative arguments.

Clearly, though, with respect to what we might call this characteristically human knowledge as manifested in history and philosophy and the hu-manities generally, a relating-logic is patently irrelevant and out of place. Scientific "explanations" just don't fit, and the use of various substitutes for what-statements, when employed in the context of everyday life, remain strangely opaque as regards the "understanding" and "intelligibility" that we consider to be humanly pertinent. This is not to say, of course, that sci-entific knowledge, such as it emerges from the use of a relating-logic, when applied to the domain of history and of everyday life does not bring with it a kind of intelligibility and understanding all its own. But, clearly, it is of a different kind from that mediated by a what-logic; nor can we legiti-mately consider that the words "understanding" and "intelligibility" are unequivocal as between these two logics, or that it is possible simply to dis-pense with the one kind of intelligibility in favor of the other. On the con-trary, we do so only at our peril and at the risk of a terrible impoverishment of our very human existence.

Thus when a Sir Karl Popper takes a historian's common-sense explana-tion of the first partition of Poland as simply a case of a comparatively weak power being unable to resist the combined power of Russia, Prussia, and Austria, and then construes this explanation as a sort of trivial case of a "law of the sociology of military power," [20] we quite naturally feel that something has gone amiss somewhere. Or when he considers that the attempt to understand Caesar's crossing the Rubicon as owing to his ambition and energy is really no more than an attempt at explanation in terms of "some very trivial psychological generalizations," then again we somehow recognize that Popper's entire enterprise of making historical explanation conform to scientific explanation must surely be wrongheaded. And what is wrong with it? Simply that a relating-logic is hardly the appropriate instrument of explanation in the sphere of the humanities. One can merely shudder at these forcible attempts to impose upon the humanities types of explanation that are proper only to the sciences. Could it be that such attempts are like a recrudescence, right in the twentieth century, of new and rather more insidious forms of barbarian invasion?

20. Cited by Dray, p. 5.

Chapter XII

A Short Digression

from History into Ethics

THE CONTENTION OF THE LAST CHAPTER was not merely that a what-logic is the proper logic to use in the study of history but also that its use in assessing the events of history enables us to arrive at what might be termed a distinctively humanistic, as contrasted with a scientific, knowledge of man and of the world in which he lives. Still, there is much that is wanting in such a contention, or at least in the way we have thus far exploited it. For if it is "the lessons of history" — if we may be forgiven a momentary lapse into an old-fashioned jargon — that the use of a what-logic makes us sensitive to, then we must recognize at the same time that lessons of this sort are not just lessons as to what man is but as to what he ought to be as well. The lessons of history, in other words, cannot be other than ethical lessons; or, in the quaint but elegant language of Viscount Bolingbroke, "History is philosophy teaching by examples how to conduct ourselves in all the situations of public and private life." [1]

Here, though, is a predicament! For how can ethical lessons ever be derived from facts? Even to suggest such a thing is presumably to commit oneself to the whole gamut of fallacies that have been so popularized by English philosophers, lo, these many years — the naturalistic fallacy, the fallacy of deriving an "ought" from an "is," the fallacy of confounding values with facts, etc., etc. Yet are these really fallacies? Could it simply be that the exclusive and uncritical use of a relating-logic is responsible for the seeming fallacy in what would otherwise strike us as perfectly proper inferences? More specifically, could it be that the very sense or nonsense of talking about such things as lessons to be learned from history turns on little more than whether one uses a what-logic or a relating-logic? If the suggestion seems farfetched on the face of it, consider the following.

In a celebrated passage in the *Treatise*, Hume at once confidently poses and provides an answer to a most decisive question:

But can there be any difficulty in proving, that vice and virtue are not matters of fact, whose existence we can infer by reason. Take any action allow'd to be vicious: Wilful murder, for instance. Examine it in all lights, and see if you can find that matter of fact, or real existence, which you call *vice*. In which-ever way you take it, you find only certain passions, motives, volitions and thoughts. There is no other matter of fact in the case. The vice entirely escapes you, as long as you consider the object. You never can find it, till you turn your reflexion into your own breast, and find a sentiment of disapprobation, which arises in you, towards this action. Here is a matter of fact; but 'tis the object of feeling, not of reason. It lies in yourself, not in the object. So that when you pronounce any action or character to be vicious, you mean nothing, but that from the constitution of your nature you have a feeling or sentiment of blame from the contemplation of it. Vice and virtue, therefore, may be compar'd to sounds, colours, heat and cold, which, according to modern philosophy, are not qualities in objects, but perceptions in the mind. [2]

Very well, suppose we let ourselves be convinced by Hume that "vice and virtue are not matters of fact." Still, just what are we to do about counterexamples such as the following? The first is from Jane Austen's *Persuasion*:

1. Quoted in Herbert Davis, *Jonathan Swift* (New York: Oxford University Press, 1964), p. 291. One finds it hard not to comment that in view of Bolingbroke's own character and career, this would seem to be a case where neither history nor philosophy as teachers found an altogether apt pupil.

2. *A Treatise of Human Nature*, ed. L. A. Selby-Bigge (Oxford: Clarendon Press, 1888), pp. 468–69.

Sir Walter Elliott, of Kellynch Hall, in Somersetshire, was a man who, for his own amusement, never took up any book but the Baronetage; there he found occupation for an idle hour and consolation in a distressed one. . . .

Vanity was the beginning and end of Sir Walter Elliott's character: vanity of person and of situation. He had been remarkably handsome in his youth, and at fifty-four was still a very fine man. Few women could think more of their personal appearance than he did, nor could the valet of any new made lord be more delighted with the place he held in society. He considered the blessing of beauty as inferior only to the blessing of a baronetcy; and the Sir Walter Elliott, who united these gifts, was the constant object of his warmest respect and devotion.[3]

As a second counter-example, consider the following character which C. V. Wedgwood gives of James Butler, Earl of Ormonde. Ormonde, it seems, was the man whom Charles I had placed in command of his forces in Ireland during the time of the Civil War, when the fighting in Ireland had amounted to a veritable "fury of destruction and hatred," Irish against English, Catholic against Protestant, Parliament sympathizers against the forces of the King.

The Earl of Ormonde, general of the forces of the Dublin Government, refused to lay waste Irish villages or kill civilians. The greater number of his Norman-Irish family were in sympathy with the rebels; his mother was a Roman Catholic, his brother was in arms with insurgents. He had other anxieties, for the King had certainly communicated secrets to him that he would have been happier not to have known and he, if anyone, knew the extent of Charles's inept tampering with the Irish. His competence and popularity with the Government forces made him indispensable, yet there were those on the Council who suspected him of complicity with the rebels. But Ormonde stood with great steadfastness, for law, order and loyalty to the Crown, and rebutted the whispered slanders: "I will go on constantly," he wrote, "neither sparing the rebel because he is my kinsman, or was my friend, nor yet will I one jot the more sharpen my sword to satisfy anybody but myself in the faithful performance of my charge."

His wife was cut off in Kilkenny Castle with her children and the hundreds of fugitives whom she had received and relieved there. The Irish leaders threatened to destroy them unless Ormonde abandoned his command of the Government forces. The English responded that if the Countess and her children came to harm, no Irish woman or child would be spared. But Ormonde, not slackening his preparations for the spring campaign, proclaimed a different answer. If his wife and children, he wrote, "shall receive injury by men, I shall never revenge it on women and children; which, as it would be base and un-Christian, would be extremely below the price I value my wife and children at." [4]

3. (New York: Oxford University Press, 1930), Chap. i, p. i.
4. *The King's War* (New York: Macmillan, 1959), pp. 79–80.

Now can anyone read accounts of this sort without recognizing that, simply as a matter of fact, Sir Walter Elliott was indeed an ass, or that James Butler was indeed a human being of real nobility of character? How then could Hume have maintained so confidently that virtue and vice are not matters of fact? And how could he have been so explicit in his insistence that you have but to take any action acknowledged to be virtuous or vicious, to examine it in all lights in order to see if you can find that matter of fact, or real existence, which you call *vice* (or virtue), and surely the virtue or vice will entirely escape you, as long as you consider the object? Indeed, one wonders what Hume might have said with respect to the two examples we have cited, where it would certainly seem that one has only to examine the actions of a Sir Walter Elliott or of an Earl of Ormonde, and so far from their virtue and vice entirely escaping him, they cannot but strike one as being the most patent matters of fact, plain and obvious for all to see.

Reading the Facts with a Proofreader's Mentality

Could it be that Hume was looking at the "object," as he called it, through shaded glasses, with the result that various of the features which would otherwise be plainly visible were not visible to him? A better analogy might be drawn from the not uncommon activity that was quite consistently practiced right up to the end of what we are now being told is the but recently terminated "Gutenberg era," viz., the activity of proofreading. We all know that to be a good proofreader a man must so condition himself as to be able to read what is in front of him, but without really paying any attention to the sense and meaning of what he is reading. On the other hand, let him begin to get interested in what he is reading and in what the author is saying, and alas, the typographical errors and the mistakes in spelling and punctuation will tend increasingly to get by him. The situation is such as possibly to prompt a Heideggerian philosopher to add just one more "existential" to the fundamental ontology of our human situation: A human being is such as to be able to appreciate either the sense of a writer or his typography, but not both!

But to return to Hume. Could it be that the virtue and vice of human actions so entirely escaped him simply because he approached them with what might be called a sort of proofreader's mentality? After all, we are only too familiar with the currently elementary cultural fact that the sort of human enterprise that we call modern science is one that is completely and thoroughly value-blind: the physicist, for example, perceives that water flows downhill but not that its doing so is good or bad, or right or wrong. While in such a case it is easy enough to say that the reason the physicist perceives no values in things is that the values aren't there — i.e., they just are not matters of fact — is it always so easy to say this? Can it be said of willful murder, for instance, as easily as it can be said of water flowing downhill? In any case, why not try working on a somewhat different principle from that of Hume? Why not say that the virtue and vice of human actions escape us, not because virtue and vice are not matters of fact, but rather because of the way we approach such actions, the way we look at them. Look at them through the eyes of a what-logic, and the virtue and vice of actions will be readily apparent. On the other hand, look at them through the eyes of a relating-logic, and we will fail to descry anything on the order of virtues and vices, not because such things are not there or are not in their own way as much matters of fact as anything else, but rather because by virtue of our logic we simply have no eye for such things.

Thus suppose we reconsider our examples of Sir Walter Elliott and the Earl of Ormonde. When we say that a man like Sir Walter is simply a stuffed shirt or a pompous ass, just what do we mean by this, if not that he is quite obviously and as a matter of fact a rather poor specimen of a human being? In contrast, a James Butler is recognized as one who has done a rather better job at being a human being than has a Sir Walter Elliott, or even than have most of the rest of us. But does not such a way of putting the matter imply that our judgment as to the virtue or vice of a man's behavior turns entirely on a more basic judgment as to what man is and what it means to be human? In short, is it not something on the order of a what-logic that provides the setting or context that makes possible our seeing moral distinctions, and more generally distinctions in value, simply as matters of fact? Moreover, if such is the case, it takes but little wit to see that given a relating-logic in place of a what-logic, things will not be understood in terms of what they are, nor will they be seen to be either good or bad, right or wrong, virtuous or vicious, or anything of the kind.

The Dependence of Value Judgments on What-Statements

First, though, it behooves us to examine rather more carefully just how it is that in a what-logic judgments of value are determined by what-statements. In the immediately preceding chapters we have been at some pains to consider just how explanations of things and events must be through causes, and ultimately through the *whats* of things. To put it crudely and schematically, in order to understand why *S* is *P*, one must consider what *S* is, viz., *M*. For example, in determining why the Lacedaemonians made war on the Athenians, Thucydides in effect took account of who and what the Lacedaemonians were, and what pertained to them. Having determined that they were a people or a city-state such as to be terrified at the prospect of a rival's growth in power, Thucydides could then assume that it would be understandable why they should have made war on the Athenians. In this case, fear of a rival's growth in power is taken to be a sufficient and proper cause of a certain kind of response. In short, explanation in such a case is what might be loosely called an explanation of a particular response or mode of behavior, in terms of what the behaving thing is, i.e., the kind of being or entity that it is.

But now what about value judgments or moral judgments? Thus far we have done no more than remark on how, in the context of a what-logic, a thing is judged to be good or bad, or a thing's action right or wrong, on the basis of the kind of thing it is and of what is demanded of it by its very nature. Accordingly, the question that presents itself now is how such a justification of value judgments or moral judgments is to be compared with an explanation of why a thing acts or behaves in the way it does in terms of its nature or essence.

To this end, let us invoke by way of example Aristotle's well-known analysis of what happiness or the good life for man consists in.[5] As Aristotle sees it, the happiness or well-being of any thing is to be determined in the light of what he calls that thing's function — that is, its characteristic activity or mode of operation. Accordingly, so far as human beings are concerned, their characteristic activity or function can hardly be regarded as any mere vegetative existence; since even plants are capable of this, there is nothing distinctively human about such a mode of life. Nor is a mere animal existence anything that is distinctively and characteristically human. The way of life that is properly human is what might be called an intelligent or rational life, i.e., a life in which one's actions and choices are guided by knowledge and understanding, or at least by such knowledge and understanding as we human beings have and are capable of. Here Aris-

---

5. *Nicomachean Ethics*. 1. 8. This particular passage from Aristotle, as well as many of the questions and issues raised in this chapter, were discussed in my earlier book, *Rational Man* (Bloomington: Indiana University Press, 1962).

totle has not merely appealed to the nature of man, or to what man is, in order to determine man's proper function or activity; he has also provided a standard in the light of which one can determine whether a given way of life or mode of behavior — say that of a Sir Walter Elliott or an Earl of Ormonde — is truly human, or is perhaps rather less than intelligent and hence less than human.

Likewise, and more generally, a what-logic, through its intention of and reliance upon the *whats* of things, not only has a resource for explaining the actions and behavior of things but also has a means for judging such behavior to be proper or improper, fitting or not so fitting, etc. Thus let us suppose the over-all ontological situation to be one in which things are what they are, and in consequence are ordered to those characteristic modes of existence and to the characteristic functions or types of activity that are proper to the kinds of things that they are. Does it not then become understandable just how through the agency of a what-logic it should be possible to recognize directly, and simply as a matter of fact, that the conduct or behavior of something just is not the conduct or behavior that is appropriate to the kind of thing that it is? Accordingly, recurring to Hume's challenge, it surely is not difficult to see how one has but to examine in all lights an action such as willful murder, for instance, and one will be able to find, in the light of the relevant *what*, precisely "that matter of fact, or real existence, which you call vice." [6]

The Incapacity of a Relating-Logic with Respect to Value Judgments

Now let us abruptly transpose ourselves to the context of a relating-logic. In this new setting, it will be quite as impossible to recognize worth and value as real features of things, plainly discernible in the light of such things' natures or essences, as we earlier found it impossible in the same setting to explain or account for the behavior or properties of things in terms of what they are. For the *whats* of things being systematically excluded from consideration in such a logic, there is no possible way of understanding or explaining why things are as they are, or why they act and behave as they do

6. In two earlier papers I have discussed in more detail just how standards of value and, in the case of human beings, even moral requirements may be derived from a consideration of the *whats* or natures of the things in question. See "Non-Cognitivism in Ethics: A Modest Proposal for Its Diagnosis and Cure," *Ethics*, LXXVI, No. 2 (January 1966), 102–16; "On the Metaphysical Status of Natural Law," *Anglican Theological Review*, XLVII, No. 2 (April 1965), 170–79.

in terms of what they are. Instead, such understanding and explanation as one is able to effect within the context of a relating-logic can only be through devices such as the analytic extraction of features or notes that have previously been arbitrarily and factitiously packed into a conceptual whole, or the logical deduction of conclusions from premises in which they are already tautologically included and into which they have previously been incorporated by some such artificial procedure as that which Professor Hanson called "conceptual construction backwards." When understanding and explanation are effected by these means, it is hard to see how they can quite free themselves from the disabilities of that fallacy which we have labeled "the fallacy of inverted intentionality."

However, it is certainly clear that in a relating-logic it will no longer be possible to ground value judgments in anything like the what-statements of a what-logic, in the manner, say, of an ethics like Aristotle's. To take the case merely of human actions, for the moment, since there is no such thing as a human nature that can be appealed to in a relating-logic, there is no way in which one can determine what man's function is or what sort of activity a characteristically human life must consist in. But then there will be no standard or norm of human conduct with reference to which specific human actions may be recognized either as measuring up or as falling short. In consequence, Hume will be entirely correct in what he says about willful murder, for such an act cannot even be said to be a human act in the sense in which this would be understood in a what-logic. As a result, the standards of what in another context would be recognized as properly human actions would, in a Humean context, have no application or even relevance to an act such as that of willful murder. Instead, considered just in itself and by itself, and since it is not even looked upon as being an act of a human being, willful murder will in such circumstances appear to be neither vicious nor virtuous.

Moreover, considering things still more generally, and going beyond mere human actions, it would seem that value judgments of whatever kind can only be made in terms of what the things that are being evaluated are. For it is only on the basis of this kind of what-knowledge that one can determine what the potentialities and capacities of such things are; then in the light of this knowledge one can go on to determine whether the specific things that one is considering are perfect or imperfect instances of their kind, whether they are fully developed or undeveloped, healthy or diseased, complete or incomplete, excellent or mediocre, genuine or pseudo, good or bad, etc. On the other hand, eliminate all such reference to the *whats* of things, and value judgments will be deprived of what is presumably their only basis in fact. Or, put a little differently, in a relating-logic which systematically excludes all consideration of the *whats* of things, there is no way in which judgments of value can be judgments of matters of fact.

Indeed, considering things even more concretely, it is not hard to reconstruct just how the issue of the ontological status of values might initially present itself when one approaches it from within the context of a relating-logic. For however the primary and original data of experience are to be conceived — whether as sense data or sense impressions, or whether as givens which as such are ineffable, or whether as terms or counters which are inescapably theory-laden — the task which it is assumed is incumbent upon a relating-logic to perform is that of effecting a kind of scientific knowledge or understanding through the relating or ordering of such given elements of experience to one another.

In such a context, so-called values might very well be regarded as just so many more terms or counters or "properties" that must be correlated and put together with other properties to make up the over-all fabric of knowledge. So it was that G. E. Moore began his reflections on the subject of value[7] by asking in effect how so-called value properties might be connected or associated with other properties such as "pleasant," "desired," "more evolved," which he chose to regard as being natural properties. Were such value properties simply to be identified with any of the natural properties, or was the connection between them only a contingent or synthetic connection?

This term "synthetic connection" gives a clue to the entire logical context in which Moore posed his question. For he was seeking to know whether the connection between being pleasant and being good was an analytic or a synthetic one. In other words, nothing on the order of what statements or a what-logic enters into the picture here at all. Rather, Moore is asking whether or not "goodness" is analytically contained in the meaning of "pleasant." And we have already seen how an analytic statement is a horse of an entirely different color from a what-statement — indeed, it belongs to an entirely different logic! Thus in asking whether "to be pleasant" simply means "to be good," Moore was certainly not concerned with anything on the order of what might be called the real nature of pleasure,

---

7. *Principia Ethica*, 1st ed. (Cambridge: University Press, 1903), *passim*.

as if that were somehow to function as a source or cause of goodness, much as the *what* or essence of a thing determines its properties. Rather, Moore was thinking of "pleasant" as if it were a simple property, a veritable logical atom which of course could be related to other properties but which itself, being of no complexity, was literally unanalyzable and hence not even susceptible of being the subject of what we, in the context of another logic, would want to call a proper what-statement.

Against this background of ideas it is not surprising that Moore should have answered in the negative his own question of whether "good" is analytically contained in the notion of "pleasant." Of course it is not, because the only way in which "good" could be analytically contained in another concept would be if it had already been packed into the meaning of a fabricated concept more or less on the order of our earlier example of "logi-milk." Thus if there were a concept put together out of the two notions of "good" and "pleasant" — let us call it "good-pleasant" — then clearly "the good-pleasant is good" would be an analytic truth. In contrast, "pleasant" being a simple or atomic concept, there is no possible way in which "goodness" could be identified with it (or shown to be analytically contained within it). Nor could "goodness" be identified with any other natural property either, and for the same reasons.

Accordingly, if "goodness" cannot be related analytically to the concept of any natural property, the connection between goodness and any and all natural properties can only be synthetic. Moreover, since goodness may not be identified with any natural property whatever, this implies that it is not itself a natural property. Rather, as Moore says, it is "a non-natural property." But if goodness is not itself a natural property, then its connection with such other properties — e.g., pleasant — as are natural cannot be a natural connection. That is to say, it cannot be an observable connection in the natural world. As a result Moore is forced to enunciate the highly implausible doctrine that the only way we ever become aware of any natural property, event, or happening as being good is in virtue of the all too questionable and mysterious faculty of intuition.[8]

From here on, though, the story of the subsequent history of Moorean ethics is a familiar one, which has oft been told and usually at considerable

8. This account of Moore's ethics, as well as the immediately following account of post-Moorean ethics, is highly interpretive and greatly condensed. For a more careful and detailed analysis, see the article mentioned above in note 6: "Non-Cognitivism in Ethics: A Modest Proposal for Its Diagnosis and Cure."

length. Hence we shall give it only very short shrift. For the most part, English writers on ethics coming after Moore found that they could not stomach his notion of a property that was somehow non-natural; nor could they stomach his other notion that the only way anything could ever be seen to have such a non-natural property would be through the agency of some strange faculty of intuition. As a result, nearly all post-Moorean thinkers have followed more or less the same line; not being able to bring themselves to recognize goodness as a non-natural property, they have concluded that possibly it is not even a property at all. Accordingly, in their various ways and in their varying formulations, they have all pretty much come round to a view not unlike that of Hume two centuries before: Because the vice or virtue of actions, or the goodness or badness of things, are not properties of objects, it follows that they are not properly matters of fact at all; instead, "When you pronounce any action or character to be vicious, you mean nothing, but that from the constitution of your nature you have a feeling or sentiment of blame from the contemplation of it." And so it is that through the agency of a relating-logic, values, to say nothing of moral qualities, have tended to be quietly ushered off the stage of the real world or the world of objects altogether. Moreover, in the context of such a logic, even to suppose that values are in some sense matters of fact,[9] or that an "ought" may perfectly well be derived from an "is," is nothing if not fallacious.

Bees and Spiders Again

However, what is fallacious in the context of a relating-logic is certainly not so in a what-logic. On the contrary, the humanist bees, if we may recur to the language of Swift's fable, have only to leave the spider-scientists to their value-blind devices and, availing themselves of their own proper logic, may then quite properly and without the least fear of naturalistic fallacies or other bogeymen, range "through every corner of nature," filling their hives "with honey and wax," and so "furnishing mankind with the two noblest of things, sweetness and light." Moreover, such light, if not such sweetness, will in large measure be in the nature of a moral or an

---

9. It should be noted in passing that in our own insistence that values are indeed matters of fact, we by no means wish to imply that they are therefore properties, either natural or non-natural. Nevertheless, the question as to the precise ontological status of such values, once they are considered in the context of a what-logic, is a difficult and delicate one. See our article on "Non-Cognitivism in Ethics" cited in note 6 above.

ethical enlightenment. For it is just by means of such wide-ranging search through every corner of nature, through the whole of human history, and through all the products of human liberal art that mankind can be brought to a better understanding of what man is and of what man can and ought to be. We might even amend Bolingbroke's enunciation to make it read, "The humanities are nothing less than philosophy itself teaching by examples how to conduct ourselves in all the situations of public and private life." In other words, given their instrument of a what-logic, the humanities prove to be our proper ways and means of learning to be human.

Conclusion:

Epilogue *or* Epitaph?

AN INTRODUCTION and twelve long chapters completed, and what have we accomplished beyond proving, perhaps, that spiders should not try to be bees, or bees spiders! Still, the lesson might bear iteration: A relating-logic just does not operate in the same way as a what-logic; it is not directed to the same end; and the kind of knowledge which one may hope to attain through its use — or to speak rather more figuratively, the picture of the world which it is competent to mediate — is not at all the same. But is this anything more than the elaboration of the perfectly obvious? Doesn't everyone already know that knowledge of the sort that comes through the pursuit of the humanities is quite different from that which is vouchsafed to us through the sciences?

The matter should be, but perhaps is not, obvious, no doubt largely because of the almost complete domination of the current intellectual scene, at least in the English-speaking world, by what may loosely be called the neo-analytic type of philosophy. Nor need we be reminded that the term "analytic philosophy" is not so much a description as a label, which has been used to designate such a heterogeneity of philosophical tendencies and movements — linguistic analysis, conceptual analysis, conceptualistic pragmatism, ordinary language philosophy, positivism, logical atomism, logical empiricism, etc., etc. — that to try to find in all of these a univocal meaning for "analytic philosophy" seems utterly hopeless.

However, in a measure the whole of our foregoing discussion has been directed toward fixing just such a univocal meaning for this term. Neo-analytic philosophy is, in our sense, that sort of philosophy which seeks, in one way or another and in whatever form it may take, to foist upon us a relating-logic as the only proper logic, and to claim for the distinctive kind of knowledge of the world and of the nature of things which results from the use of such a logic that it is the only valid knowledge that human beings are capable of. In consequence, from the standpoint of such a philosophy our everyday knowledge of the world and of ourselves which arises from what Lewin would call the Aristotelian mode of thought, while it may represent an interesting and perhaps even an unavoidable stance which we human beings often assume, can nowise claim to be a properly scientific knowledge of fact or of the way things really are. And with respect to the humanities, while our neo-analytic philosophy may concede them no end of value in terms of the aesthetic, and also perhaps the moral, uplift which those who cultivate them may experience, there must be no pretending that the pursuit of these disciplines can yield anything that in any proper sense may be called knowledge, other than possibly a mere historical knowledge of the particular facts of intellectual or cultural history; anything like scientific knowledge, or a knowledge of the universal, or an insight into the truth of things, such as Bowra talks about, is systematically and in principle denied to the humanities by the high court of present-day analytic philosophy.

We hope that the argument of our book has served not only to show that a logic of the humanities (which we would consider to be properly a what-logic) is different from a logic of the sciences (which we would consider to be properly a relating-logic), but in addition we hope that we have indicated how many of the standard criticisms and objections that have been directed against the legitimacy of a what-logic as a proper mode of knowledge can be refuted or shown to be without foundation. Indeed, we would even go so far as to say that the distinctive issues that are raised in the knowledge claims of a so-called what-logic have never been too honestly faced up to, much less met, by current analytic philosophy — not even when that philosophy is traced back to its origins in such venerated forerunners as Hume and Kant.

A Possible Complementarity of the Two Logics

So be it. But does this not leave us with an even more ticklish question on our hands? For if there are two logics, and if neither is to be simply written off the books in favor of the other — as presumably the humanist-bees may once have thought it possible to do, and as many of the spider-scientists now would seem to want to do — then just how are they supposed to complement each other? To speak as we did in our Introduction of "two knowledges," each of which proceeds from the use of a particular sort of logic, is seemingly to suggest a doctrine of "two truths." Yet the travail of such a doctrine, at least in the middle ages as the historians tell us, lay precisely in the fact that the very same pronouncements that proceeded from Holy Writ in the case of the one truth were contradicted by pronouncements that were based on the supposedly demonstrative evidence of Aristotelian science in the case of the other truth. Following this analogy, then, do we want to say that what we have loosely called the picture of the world or the account of the nature of things that proceeds from the use of the one logic is different from, in the sense of being logically incompatible with, that which proceeds from the use of the other? Surely not. But then what are we to say?

The answer to this question is perhaps implicit in what we hope may have emerged in the course of the foregoing chapters as being the most decisive, over-all characteristic of a relating-logic, in contrast to a what-logic. A relating-logic does not mediate a knowledge of things in terms of what they are and why they are, etc., and in its very unconcern and incompetence with respect to what-questions and why-questions it may be recognized as failing to mediate any sort of picture of the world in the usual sense. It is true that "picture" is a decidedly figurative and misleading term here. Yet if the account which we have thus far given of a relating-logic is at all just, then it would seem that rather than picturing things, or describing them, or giving us any sort of account of how it really is with them, this sort of logic is set up entirely for the purpose of enabling us to "go on" cognitively, to get from one point to another. And in such a cognitive enterprise of merely going on, the points of arrival and departure, if we may so speak of them, are in no sense marks or features of things or of the real world. Nor is there any real or necessary connection between such points, for in the context of a relating-logic all necessary connections involve only analytic truths and reflect nothing of the way things are in fact and in reality; they are, indeed, no more than devices or constructs of our own that enable us to get from one point to another in the cognitive process.

Thus to construe Lewis' example "This is an edible apple" (see pp. 171 ff. above) as a judgment in a relating-logic, it should now be clear how such a judgment is not in the proper sense of the word descriptive of the way anything is in reality at all: it involves us in a network, and not with what the network describes. The "this" turns out to be no more than a point of departure, and to say that it is an edible apple is not to say what "it" or anything else is at all, but only to relate the ineffable "this" as our point of departure to various predicted arrival points — e.g., "round," "ruddy," "tangy," "sweet-smelling," etc.

A comparable analysis holds of each of these arrival points in turn. For taking any one of them — say, a certain tanginess in taste, or a certain roundness by way of visual datum — such an arrival point is not itself tangy or round; in saying that it is round or tangy we do not mean precisely what we say, but rather we mean merely to relate such an "it" to a still further series of possible arrival points in our future experience. In other words, for us seemingly to say what any one such arrival point is just in itself is thereby not to do so at all, but rather to turn our presumed object of description into no more than a point of still further departure.

Moreover, just as a relating-logic does not admit of such experienced departure and arrival points as being in any way describable for what they are, so the operation of this logic rules out the possibility of our considering, if not the points of departure and arrival, at least the relations and connections between them as being of a particular sort or nature. For once more, as we have seen, the connection that holds between the notion of "edible apple" and such verifying notes of the notion as "round," "ruddy," "tangy," etc., is a purely analytic connection. Accordingly, for us to be able to "go on" from one such notion to another does not betoken any describable relation or real connection in the world between the particular relata in question; rather it is only a case of our having related such relata, not of their being so related in themselves.

But if it is no more than "knowledge" in this sense that is mediated by a relating-logic, then it is hard to see how an account of things in terms of the one sort of logic could ever involve any precise or strict incompatibility with an account of the same things in terms of the other sort of logic. Indeed, this should perhaps already be clear in terms of our example of the edible apple. Suppose, just to point the contrast in rather crude, bold strokes, that we take the proposition "This is an edible apple," and construe it first in terms of a what-logic and then in terms of a relating-logic. In the former context, let us imagine that the "this" is taken to refer to a primary substance, and that the predicate is put forward as being descriptive of what such a subject is, both essentially, viz., an apple, and accidentally, viz., edible. In contrast, in the context of a relating-logic, the "this" of the above proposition refers to no more than a cognitive starting point, and the predicates "edible" and "apple" are not at all to be taken as describing what the "this" is, but rather as being mere shorthand for series of possible experiential arrival points to which the "this" is being related through the agency of the proposition.

Surely there is no incompatibility or inconsistency, and in a sense there can be none, between these two alternative accounts or knowledges of the "this," or subject to the above proposition — provided, of course, that when the proposition is construed according to a relating-logic, such a logic is taken as no more than a device for enabling us to keep "going on" conceptually or cognitively, and not at all as an ontology or even as a logic with ontological commitments. For if ontological pronouncements are made — if one says, for example, that the "this" cannot refer to a substance, because there are no substances but only sense data; or that in the real world there are no *whats* of things or natures or essences of things but only relations between bare particulars, and that therefore any logic that seeks to understand things in terms of what they are must be brought under the strictest of interdicts — then there will indeed be an immediate and glaring incompatibility between the respective accounts of things that are mediated through the two different logics.

However, such ontological commitments with respect to a relating-logic would seem to be not only gratuitous and unnecessary but also, in the very nature of such a logic, improper. Briefly, the reason is that an ontological commitment can scarcely be other than a commitment to the existences of certain things or entities, which much be of a certain kind. But to recognize entities as being of a certain kind is to invoke something on the order of what-statements, and immediately one is caught up in a what-logic and has forsaken altogether one's supposed starting point within a mere relating-logic. This is not to say, of course, that one cannot have conflicts of ontologies — goodness knows there are too many of them for the fact of their existence ever to be denied! Yet the point is that any conflict between incompatible ontologies — e.g., between a substance ontology and a logical atomist ontology, or between a Whiteheadian ontology of actual occasions and an ontology such as that of Teilhard du Chardin — must be a conflict which already presupposes a what-logic, and in which the points at issue can only be formulated within the context of a what-logic. For this reason, it can never properly be a conflict arising simply out of the use of a relating-logic as over against a what-logic.

To return to the question which is of more immediate concern to us: Far from there being any incompatibility between the knowledge mediated by the two logics, the use of a relating-logic would in many cases appear to be a decidedly fruitful supplement to the use of a what-logic. For example, one might say that the whole history of modern science could perhaps be read as a progressive supplementation, through the agency of a relating-logic, of what we might call the everyday, common-sense view of the world which emerges from the use of what Lewin would call a more or less Aristotelian mode of thought.

Let us exploit once more our example of "This is an edible apple" to give a crude but readily comprehensible illustration of this. We have noted how, within the context of a what-logic, "This is an edible apple" is used to mediate a knowledge of a certain real thing or substance, the proposition being so designed and structured as to enable us to understand this substance in terms of what it is, both essentially, viz., an apple, and accidentally, viz., edible. Yet how far can such a project of understanding this substance in terms of what it is, of its nature or essence, really carry us? Just how far does knowledge of a thing in terms of its essence enable us to "go on"? The answer is, "Not very far."

Thus with respect to the apple, our knowledge of what it is suffices to assure us that on the generic level — indeed, the highest generic level — it is a substance. And doubtless it may be assumed that we are competent to appreciate the difference between substance and accident. But when it comes to just what particular kind of substance this "apple" is, our what-knowledge begins to falter. We see perhaps that as an organic substance it is different from an inorganic substance; but we are far from sure how such a difference is to be understood and specified. Descending to the still more specific level, we can recognize readily enough that since what we are considering is an apple, it is therefore not a cabbage or a kumquat. But again, as to what the specific difference is that makes an apple precisely an apple and not something else, we cannot say; our knowledge of the *what* just does not extend this far. Indeed, in this connection our earlier discussion of historical explanation may be recalled, in which we pointed out how in the context of its actual use a what-logic enables us to have but a bare inkling of the relevant *what* or essence, without our necessarily being able to specify it further. So in the present case, a knowledge of the apple in terms of what it is essentially and of the causes which account for its various accidental features and of its actual existence here and now is indeed a knowledge which scarcely carries us very far; to use our familiar metaphor, it doesn't enable us to "go on" cognitively for very long.

Having exhausted the resources of a what-logic with respect to a knowledge of the apple, let us shift to a different cognitive apparatus altogether, viz., a relating-logic. In the operation of this logical instrument, as we have seen, one does not proceed — at least not if one uses it properly — by trying to acquire an ever greater empirical familiarity with apples and therefrom to abstract or induce the *whats* and *whys* of apples. Rather one seeks to propound ever more elaborate theoretical constructions, such as, for example, the cell theory in modern biology, in terms of which the various phenomena associated with apples can be not so much explained (for in the usual sense "explanation" suggests causes) as embraced and ordered and fitted into an over-all conceptual scheme or map. Given such a scheme or map, one can indeed "go on" almost endlessly with respect to the countless phenomena that are or may be disclosed, not just through ordinary observation but through the microscope, and not just through the ordinary microscope, but through the electron microscope, etc. Likewise, we do not intend, in employing such a scheme, to represent or picture or mirror or even literally to map the way things are or their relations to one another in themselves and independently of our conceptual scheme. On the contrary, in the context of such a scheme the meaning of the terms and elements is indeed identifiable with their use, and the point of our using them is not in order to know what things are in themselves, or how they are really related to one another, but rather how we may get from one thing to another in terms of the logico-linguistic scheme with which we are operating.

Clearly, though, in any shift from a what-logic to a relating-logic in, say, a consideration of apples, we do not have to suppose that the initial common-sense knowledge of apples from which we started out has now to be given up or considered outmoded. On the contrary, even the most sophisticated scientist in the concourse of everyday life, when he stops to buy apples at a corner fruitstand or afterwards sits down to enjoy them in a pie, surely looks upon apples as being simply apples and consequently talks of them and regards them in the way everyone else does. That is what apples really are, for him just as for everyone else!

However, although such a knowledge of what apples are does not carry the scientist or anyone else very far, and does need supplementation, still the supplement which a scientific knowledge adds to our everyday knowledge does not tell us more about the real nature or essence of apples. It is a knowledge of an entirely different sort, and in a totally different dimension, as it were. For this very reason, as we have already remarked, such a supplementary scientific knowledge need give little or no occasion for conflict with our everyday knowledge and understanding of the real things and events in the world about us — provided, of course, that in the use of a relating-logic we do not consciously or unconsciously slide from the one logical context, in which the meanings of our terms are simply their use or place within a certain conceptual scheme, to that other and very different logical context, in which the meanings of our terms are the very natures and characters and causes of the real things of the world.

A Revealing, if not a Damning, Illustration

We would like to bring forward another example, although an admittedly more dubious and difficult one, to illustrate the way in which a relating-logic can supplement, without displacing, a what-logic. Consider the contrast between the Aristotelian conception of motion and the account of inertial motion as it emerged in the new physics of the seventeenth century. Not only is the story of this contrast one of the classics in the history of science, but it has also served as an ever-ready scourge with which intellectuals for some three centuries have delighted to flay Aristotle and all things Aristotelian. Interestingly enough, though, as our earlier quotations from Lewin have indicated (see p. 205 above), it is precisely Aristotle's account of motion, and not that of the new physics, which would appear to arise directly out of and to be most palpably consonant with our common, everyday observations of the motions and changes in the world about us. For that very reason, this same account of motion provides an excellent example of just the sort of knowledge that the use of a what-logic is able to provide us with.

From our constant experience with the motions and changes of things in the everyday world, it is directly borne in upon us [1] that motion or change is simply a fact, and that it is a fact of motion or change, not of succession. In other words, any supposition or theory to the effect that change or motion is unreal, or that it can somehow be reduced to a series — even a "compact series" of instantaneous moments or events following "densely" one upon the other [2] — is ruled out simply on the basis of our very experience of motion itself. Moreover, if the motions which we experience are changes and not mere successions of discrete events or happenings, then any such motion or change must be the motion or change of something. That is to say, we have to acknowledge that there are things that move, or that undergo change — for example, the leaf that changes from green to yellow, or my friend over there who moves from one side of the room to the other.

Consider, though, what is involved in a fact such as that of a leaf's changing from green to yellow, or of my friend's moving from one place to another. Perforce the leaf that is now yellow must once have been green, and my friend who is now here must formerly have been elsewhere. Moreover, since it is the *change* in the leaf, or the *movement* of the person, that we are now concerned with, and not with the leaf's simply *being* one color at one moment and another color at another moment, or with my friend's simply being in one place now just as he was elsewhere a moment ago, the change or the motion itself has got to be located, as it were, in just this in-between region, i.e., between the time when the leaf was not yellow but only able to be so, and the time when it had finally become yellow and was in process of becoming so no longer. In other words, in the very nature of the case the change or motion can neither be during such time as the leaf actually is yellow and hence is no longer becoming so, nor during such time as it is still able to become yellow but is not actually becoming so; rather the change must be in the time between the potency as such and the actuality as such. Hence Aristotle's definition of change or motion as the

---

1. Needless to say, this is but a figurative way of saying "abstracted from" or "induced from."

2. We are here consciously making reference to Russell's celebrated exploitation of this notion in *Our Knowledge of the External World* (London: George Allen and Unwin, 1922), esp. Chap. 5.

actualization of the potential in respect to its very condition of being potential.[3]

However, such an actualization of that which is merely potential is not self-explanatory. A leaf does not undergo a process of change without there being something to effect that change. Nor does the motion of my friend from one side of the room to the other just happen; either he himself must actively do the moving, or else something else must actively move him. That which is only potentially this or that does not simply of itself, or without any cause, become this or that; it must be made to become this or that; there must be a moving cause or a cause of the change. In short, there is no change without some cause effecting it.

Very well, then, here we have in summary the familiar Aristotelian account of change — an understanding of what change is and has to be, that is mediated by none other than a what-logic, a logic that would appear to render such an account cogent, or even inescapable, directly in the light of experience itself.

But then what happened with respect to this Aristotelian account of change? We all know the story of how such a common-sense understanding of what motion is obviously faltered when confronted with the phenomena of projectile motion. In the case of the latter, just what or where was the moving cause, which, by the requirements of the Aristotelian account of change, had to be continuously operative to keep the projectile in motion, once it had left the hand of the thrower or the mouth of the cannon? Here, quite patently, was a case where a knowledge of *what* did not suffice to explain all of the relevant phenomena; intellectually, scientists simply could not go on from their understanding of the nature of motion to the particular phenomena associated with the motion of projectiles.

What was the result? As a matter of intellectual history, as we all know, the result was largely one of rejecting the Aristotelian account of motion and substituting for it a very different conception of the *what* of motion, as being essentially and by its very nature inertial. Indeed, the new understanding of what motion is might be summed up in Newton's second law: Any body not acted upon by an external force will continue indefinitely in motion or at rest.

Accordingly, some such change in the conception of the nature of motion is what seems to have occurred simply as a matter of history with the rise

3. *Physics* 3. 1.

of modern science in the seventeenth century. But in the light of our analyses of the differing operations of a what-logic and a relating-logic, we wonder if any such change need ever have occurred at all. To be sure, if Newton's law of motion is interpreted as somehow designed to tell us what motion is, then it can only be in terms of a what-logic that the interpretation is possible, since only a what-logic can mediate a knowledge of what things are in their very natures. For that matter, since what-statements, although put forward as necessary truths, can nevertheless be false, there is no reason why, in employing a what-logic, thinkers might not very well come out with conflicting definitions or what-statements with respect to one and the same thing — in this case with respect to motion, as evidenced in the Newtonian definition on the one hand as over against the Aristotelian on the other.

Still our present question is this: Was, or is, such a conflict over the nature of motion really necessary? Suppose that instead of a what-logic we were to avail ourselves simply of a relating-logic in the effort to deal with those particular phenomena connected with motion that seemed inexplicable in the Aristotelian account. In terms of such a logic the question does not even arise — it cannot even properly be asked — as to what motion is, or, for that matter, as to what the causes of motion are. Instead, all that is proper in the context of such a logic is the construction, often in the manner of a *Gedankenexperiment*, of a conceptual scheme that makes it possible to keep going on from phenomenon to phenomenon. It is almost as if one were concerned with something like the plotting of a curve to pass through each item in a vast array of scattered points on a surface. In reality there is no real connection between the points; the curve is just a device that enables us to get from one point to another. In some such way as this, then, one may think of the modern physicist as setting up what might be labeled an inertial scheme for dealing with the phenomena of motion. Not that there *is* any such thing as inertia in the moving bodies themselves; or even that there *are* moving bodies, as over against mere dense series of possible points in the paths covered by the various motions, or real dense series as over against actual moving bodies — these are all questions and concerns that are irrelevant in the context of a relating-logic.

Yet why isn't this the logic that is most fit and proper for the enterprise of what we call modern science? This is not to say that all scientists have clearly and consciously, not to say consistently, operated with just such a logic. Far from it, for in our earlier quotations from Professor Hanson it can be readily seen how in the history of science the scientists as well as the philosophers have been forever inclined, not to say tempted, to invest their logico-linguistic apparatus and their elaborate calculational techniques with an actual ontological status in the nature of things.[4] Even modern analytic philosophers, who have been so largely responsible for the development of such a logic and who have hawked it about as being the only logic there is, have not always seemed to be fully aware, or at least not fully articulate, as to what the use of such a logic would entail in terms of its competence, or rather incompetence, to provide us with anything like an account of the nature of things in the traditional sense.

Now that we are clear as to what is involved, why not take the decisive step and simply identify the so-called logic of the sciences with a relating-logic? This would make possible an ever continuing fruitful supplementation of the limited knowledge that we are able to derive from the use of a what-logic. It would also guard against much of that conflict in modern culture that seems in part to arise because of a supposed incompatibility between the testimony of perennial human knowledge which simply as men we have of ourselves and our world, and the testimony of that rather more sophisticated and fashionable type of knowledge which proceeds from what we so honorifically label "modern science." In short, the proposal is this: Recognize a difference between the two logics and abide by it; it should then be possible to accord a proper status to both that substantive knowledge which we have of ourselves and of the everyday reality of the world and that calculative knowledge which in the sciences enables us so successfully to keep going on from phenomenon to phenomenon.

Some Summary Identifications and a Summary Apologetic

Surely at this point, though, it is time that we stopped for station identification! For throughout this book we have been bandying about a number of contrasts — between the humanities and the sciences, between bees and spiders, between our common-sense, everyday view of things and the radically different scientific world view, between Aristotelian and Galilean modes of thought, between neo-analytic and classical analytic philosophy — and suddenly it begins to appear that we were cavalierly attempting to

---

4. In *The Concept of the Positron* (New York: Cambridge University Press, 1963), Professor Hanson provides confirmation of this point in an illuminating account of a very instructive episode in the history of science; see pp. 34–35.

range all of these various contrasts over a single common denominator, viz., that of our own pet invention of a contrast between a relating-logic and what-logic. Such free and easy identifications call for at least some word of explanation and apology!

Unfortunately, though, at this late stage of the game even our apology must be a bit free and easy. In any event, we have already given an indication in this concluding chapter as to how we propose to make these identifications. In our effort to identify the proper method of modern science with that of a relating-logic, or to identify the procedures of analytic philosophy with those of a relating-logic, we put forward all such identifications largely in the manner of proposals. Wouldn't the procedures of science, that is to say, or the somewhat cryptic theses and claims of analytic philosophy be rendered more intelligible and given a meaningful unity if they were to be understood in terms of a relating-logic? Perhaps "proposal" is scarcely the appropriate word, since it suggests a procedure more akin to the use of hypotheses and the invention of explanatory theories than one of abstraction and induction from the facts themselves. We would like to think that, far from being a mere "free invention of the mind," our account of the sort of thing that is involved in a relating-logic is something that can be read off, as it were, from any close scrutiny of actual scientific procedures or of the actual performances of current analytic philosophy. It is the facts themselves that have brought us to an awareness of their nature, rather than any a priori or transcendental construction that has been imposed upon these facts in order to lend them a more or less supposititious nature.

To move to the other pole in our various sets of contrasts, by what right can we simply identify the program and pursuit of the humanities with the use of a what-logic? Again, rather than through any painstaking process of induction we would seek to point up what is of the essence of the matter here, in terms pretty much of a single question. For supposing, as we have already argued, that the pursuit of the humanities is a pursuit of knowledge and not a mere cultivation and gratification of our tastes, then what is it that we seek to know? Is it not simply a knowledge of man, of human nature, of ourselves, and still more broadly of our human situation and of the real world in which we find ourselves? Surely, it must have been insofar as they were concerned to attain just such knowledge as this that Bowra could say of the Greeks (see p. 17 above) that they "regarded poetry as a rational activity." Moreover, this particular kind of rational activity can only be in association with the sort of thing we have chosen to call a what-logic. For, as Bowra says, it is "the divine laws which operate through human life" which Aeschylus sought to discover and come to understand; and his knowledge of these laws was what "experience has forced upon him."

Here, in the case of Aeschylus and also of Sophocles — at least as Bowra represents them — there is manifested a clear and conscious concern to get at the very *whats* of things, at what is essential and basic in man's situation. Moreover, the procedure followed is the thoroughly beelike one of letting oneself simply be instructed by experience. How patently irrelevant, therefore, in such a cognitive context would be the entire apparatus of a relating-logic. Aeschylus' divine laws were *found*, not constructed spider-like and Popper-like in the course of operating with any hypothetico-deductive method. Or fancy trying to construe such laws as mere analytic truths, as if they could then be classified as purely verbal or linguistic pronouncements. Or again, if one were to consider the way in which Aeschylus would reckon with these laws as being binding upon us as individual human beings, it is scarcely to be supposed that the deductive apparatus by which the universal was applied to the particular could be construed as no more than an exfoliation of a tautology, as a result of which the individual would find himself bound not by any real necessity but only by conventions of language.

Surely, even this brief sketch should suffice to show that with respect to what we choose to call a humanistic type of knowledge, it is a what-logic that is relevant and not a relating-logic. To take an entirely different example — say, Kafka's novel, *The Castle* — it is possible to see how it can only be a what-logic that must have been operative in the production of Kafka's insights and convictions. For supposing that Brod's interpretation of the novel is correct [5] and that Kafka was concerned with what might be called the Kierkegaardian reality of the utter discrepancy of God's ways and man's ways, of the consequent bafflingly tortured and tormented character of the individual's existence, caught up as it is in the regime of such a *deus absconditus*. Once again it must become only too patent how the entire paraphernalia of analytic truths, *Gedankenexperimente*, propositions construed as mere relating devices, hypothetico-deductive demonstrations,

5. Cf. "Nachwort zur ersten Aufgabe," reprinted in Franz Kafka, *Die Romane* (München: S. Fischer Verlag, 1965), pp. 805-11.

theoretical constructs, covering-law models, etc., etc., is palpably and even ludicrously beside the point.

One may counter with the objection that the divine laws that Aeschylus took to be operative through human life are by no means the same as those that Kafka took to be operative, and that therefore it is ridiculous to speak of knowledge in such cases. The answer is the obvious one that the mere fact that authorities disagree does not necessarily mean that no truth or knowledge is attainable. After all, Aeschylus might be right, and Kafka wrong; or perhaps from a recognition of the partiality and one-sidedness of each it might be possible to arrive at a conception of things at once more balanced and comprehensive. Yet what is of importance relative to the main issue under discussion is, of course, not whether Aeschylus or Kafka is right; rather, the pertinent consideration is that when within the context of the humanities it becomes a question of the proper adjudication and assessment of differing views of the nature of man's life and the laws that bind and determine our human situation, it is a what-logic that must be brought into play and not a relating-logic.

Proper and Improper Logics for Science and for Philosophy

Now just see where the course of the present discussion has led us! For has it not begun to be increasingly apparent that what we have been calling a humanistic knowledge and have been associating with the use of a what-logic, so far from being confined just to "the humanities" in the narrow sense in which that term is sometimes understood, is indeed coextensive with philosophical knowledge? In other words, it is philosophy to which a what-logic is appropriate, just as a relating-logic is appropriate to the sciences in the modern sense.

For supposing that in philosophy our concern is, speaking loosely and perhaps a bit grandiloquently, one of knowing not just what man is but what the very nature of things is, then what other instrument would do for this purpose than precisely something on the order of a what-logic? At least, it is obvious that a relating-logic would never do. Or, again, when it comes to adjudicating the claims of divergent philosophies — for example, as to whether it is in substance that we find being *qua* being, or in the Forms or in the One, or in monads, or in actual occasions, or in a Bradleyan absolute — how is the discussion to be carried on, evidence pro and con to be weighed, arguments to be assessed, etc., save in and through and by means of a what-logic? Once more, it is only too patent that the apparatus of a relating-logic just will not work when the what-questions and why-questions of philosophy are at issue.

It is true that in recent years, and particularly among the fashionable English philosophers, there has been no end of talk about just what it is that a philosopher is supposed to do. Thus it is said that one knows what a lawyer is supposed to do, or a doctor, or a scientist, or a butcher, or a baker, or a candlestick maker, or perhaps even — though this is a far more dubious case — what a clergyman is supposed to do. Very well, then, what about the philosopher, what is he supposed to do? The question, of course, is supposed to strike terror into the hearts of the older generation of traditional philosophers. For in this day and age, unless one can stand and deliver when challenged to say just what one's peculiar job or work is, then one may justly be judged to have no sort of legitimate social function, and so be consigned to outer darkness.

Imagine, then, the embarrassment of the poor old traditional philosopher in such a situation. For when asked what he is supposed to do, his first impulse is to say, "To know the nature of things." Whereupon he will be haughtily sneered at and then sternly reminded that that answer "won't do." For if by knowledge one means knowledge of fact and of the real, then in this enlightened modern age of ours it is the scientist, and the scientist alone, who is in a position to vouchsafe to us a knowledge of this sort. Time was perhaps when the philosopher might have said that his job was one of knowing the facts, but that time is long gone in this best of all possible scientific worlds. And so when the traditional philosopher is further pressed with the question, "Just what do you as a philosopher do?", the poor man becomes confused and doesn't know what to say. And with that, some imperious Ryle-like Red Queen is certain to shout, "Off with his head!"

What, then, are our more up-to-the-minute modern and non-traditional philosophers supposed to do? The answer is, "They occupy themselves with language." Indeed, from the current state of English philosophy, it would appear that the new philosophers, having given the world to the scientists, are now bent on claiming the domain of language for themselves. And what remarkable *Fachleute* and technicians they have become with their endless outpourings on such subjects as "If, So, and Because," "A Plea for Excuses," " 'It Was to Be,' " "Moore on Ordinary Language," "Less on Ordinary Language," "Ordinary Language," "Philosophy and Language," "Language and Philosophy," "Logic and Language" (a double dose) "Ethics and Language," "The Language of Morals," etc., etc. Nor can there be the slightest doubt in anyone's mind of the great social utility of such studies, to say nothing of their manifest tendency toward character-building. One can only stand back and, viewing the new-day English philosopher in the light of his work, exclaim, *"Ecce Homo!"*

What, then, is wrong with this picture? Surely nothing save the very conception of philosophy that it represents. Suppose we grant that there is, or ought to be, something that a philosopher does in distinction from other men, and particularly, nowadays, in distinction from the scientist. What is it? Alas, it is in answer to this question, we would suggest, that the traditional philosopher seems to have become confused and to have stammered out the wrong answer. No doubt, he was, like Alice, overawed by the very arrogance of the Red Queen who was confronting him. But what he should have answered was simply that what the philosopher does is to pursue knowledge, and the knowledge which he pursues is indeed a knowledge of facts and of the real things and events of the world — of what they are and why they are and how they are. If the objection is raised, "But doesn't the scientist do this?", the answer is that in one sense perhaps he does, but that insofar as he may be said to strive for a knowledge of fact — albeit in a rather Pickwickian sense — it is through the use of an entirely different logic, with the result that the knowledge which he achieves of the world is knowledge in a radically different sense from that of the philosopher.

Suppose that one is still not satisfied and insists on harking back to that familiar picture of the field of knowledge where the philosopher is represented as having once been the sole occupant and possessor but where the scientists have gradually succeeded in seizing piece after piece of this domain so that they now occupy the whole of it, thus leaving the philosopher completely dispossessed and disinherited. Now to this familiar picture, there is a rather less familiar counter-picture, where the scientists are indeed concerned with knowledge, and in a sense with the real world, no less than are the philosophers. Nevertheless, the logic which the scientist avails himself of is so different from that of the humanist or philosopher that the knowledge which he achieves is scarcely comparable to that of the philosopher, even though it is sometimes a knowledge of the very same things and objects. As a result, so far from having dispossessed the philosopher of his original domain of knowledge, the scientist would seem rather to have left him right where he always was. The sciences, in other words, have one by one, in the course of our Western cultural history, declared themselves independent of philosophy; but so far from this having the result of leaving philosophy with no subject matter and nothing to investigate, it should really be interpreted as having confirmed philosophy in its subject matter more than ever. What philosophy is competent to know as regards man and the nature of things is something that the sciences are totally and in principle incapable of knowing.

It will not be amiss to substantiate this conclusion still further by approaching it now from the other angle, viz., that of the precise nature of the scientific enterprise insofar as this is construed as involving the use of a relating-logic. For just as philosophy, when understood as the characteristic product of a what-logic, may readily be seen to have a characteristic autonomy as over against the various sciences, so when we face directly up to the question, "What exactly is the nature of science?", it will be found that insofar as the proper instrument of science is a relating-logic, then it can in no way trespass upon the domain of philosophy or even challenge a certain hegemony of philosophy with respect to the various special sciences. It is just in this latter respect that our proposal for a division of labor between the two logics and hence of the two knowledges would appear to have got itself into the worst predicament of all. For it must have struck many during the course of our discussion that insofar as we were seeking to restrict the sciences to the use of a relating-logic, to that same extent we were coming dangerously close to depriving science of the right to be considered a knowledge at all. What could this be, if not a specious conjuring trick for transforming modern scientific knowledge into a no-knowledge? As if that very type of knowledge which is, indeed, knowledge *par excellence* and the very paradigm of knowledge, could be discredited by any such trickery as this!

In response to such a challenge, we shall first try to show that a so-called scientific knowledge, even when it is mediated solely by a relating-logic, is indeed knowledge, and a genuine knowledge at that. On the other hand, we shall contest that a knowledge of this sort can possibly be knowledge in any primary sense, much less the paradigm of knowledge. We shall even suggest that considering the exalted position which the sciences enjoy in our modern culture, it is just possible that the tendency to accord them primacy, in comparison with all other types of knowledge, may be a case of confusing social position with genuine merit.

Let us first look more closely into the question of whether scientific

271

knowledge, supposing that it does proceed from the use of a relating-logic, is in any proper sense of the word, a knowledge. It is true, if our earlier analyses are correct, that any knowledge mediated by such a logic will not and cannot be a knowledge either of what things are or of why they are. Consequently, in the context of such a logic the normal understanding of what it means for a statement to be true, or for it to have been proved or demonstrated or explained, will have to undergo considerable overhauling, if not dislocation.

That, indeed, is why neither the Kantian nor the idealistic conception of knowledge is of too much help when it comes to fixing just how the notions of truth and demonstration are to be understood in a relating-logic. For even though a logic of this sort will make no claim to being able to mediate a knowledge of things just as they are in themselves and apart from all operations of the mind and of our human cognitive faculties, still, so far as Kantians or idealists are concerned, they would never wish to deny that knowledge for them is a knowledge of *whats* or of *whys*. They would want to transpose such a traditional type of what-knowledge or why-knowledge from the real world to either a phenomenal or an ideal world. In contrast, a relating-logic does not claim to mediate a knowledge of *whats* or of *whys* at all.

Perhaps, then, something like the distinction between *knowing-how* and *knowing-that* might be relevant when it comes to understanding the sort of knowledge that is peculiar to a relating-logic. Indeed, as we have seen, the concern in such a logic does seem to be simply with a knowing-how in the sense of how to go on. Moreover, this species of going-on is made possible, supposedly, through a relating of things one to another, a relating which we carry out ourselves and which is so conceived as to involve no pre- or post-supposition of the things really being so related. For this reason, one might indeed characterize such a knowledge as being a knowing-how that was nowise based on any kind of a knowing-that.

Nor is it a knowing-how in the Aristotelian sense, in which one may be said to know how to do or to make something, which in turn is something over and above the cognitive activity itself, as, for example, when I may be said to know how to fly-cast, or how to make rice pudding, or how to build a house, or how to live well, etc. In contrast, in a relating-logic, the knowing-how is a knowing-how to go on, and yet the going-on is a cognitive going-on and nothing else. That is to say, the going-on is not an activity or a product over and above the knowing-how; to know is simply to be able to go on, and to go on is to engage in the activity of knowing.

Nor, for the same reason, can one attempt to discredit this sort of knowledge on the grounds that it admits only of a pragmatic justification and is therefore to be called knowledge only insofar as it gets results, as judged, say, by technological advance or the betterment of our human living standard. It is true, of course, that modern science does get results in terms of technology. Yet this by no means implies that those who pursue such science even when it is conceived as but a knowing-how in the sense just specified, may not pursue it simply for its own sake — that is to say, simply for the sake of knowledge and nothing else.

Indeed, we might attempt to illustrate the point in this way. The knowing-how of the scientist is, let us admit, a knowledge that results in true judgments; otherwise, it would not be a knowledge at all. And while these judgments make no attempt to assert that things are thus and so in reality, they do indeed make reference to reality, or, if you prefer, to fact; otherwise, there would be no way in which such judgments might be said to be true. At the same time, the reference to fact which these judgments make is, as it were, always a mere reference, without description. That is to say, although the judgment makes reference to fact, it never gives a description of the fact, but merely orders and disposes the knower toward a going-on to the next fact.[6] Accordingly, it is in this sense that such judg-

6. In an interesting article by James W. Cornman, entitled "Language and Ontology" (reprinted in *The Linguistic Turn*, ed. Richard Rorty [Chicago: University of Chicago Press, 1967], pp. 160–67), the author examines various theories of reference that have been propounded by contemporary logicians, and comes out with the conclusion that "Even for that sense of 'refer' for which we can infer from " 'p' refers to q" that something exists we are ontologically committed to whatever it is that 'p' refers to, *but not to any particular ontological view about what it is that 'p' refers to*" (p. 160, italics added). An even more elaborate treatment of the same topic may be found in Professor Cornman's book, *Metaphysics, Reference, and Language* (New Haven: Yale University Press, 1966).

In other words, here is a very clear and cogent exposition of that curious dissociation of reference from description, or of denotation from connotation, which would seem to be so marked a feature of a relating-logic, particularly when this logic becomes the instrument of modern physics, and indeed of modern science generally. Nor do we believe that it is altogether fanciful to suggest that there may be an analogy between our critical assessment of a relating-logic on this particular score and the criticism which Mr. Yvor Winters has been wont to level against so much of modern poetry, accusing it, as he says, of "pseudo-reference" and of tending to utilize only the one aspect of language, the connotative, and neglecting or impairing the denotative aspect (Cf. *In Defense of Reason*, 3d ed. [Denver: Alan Swallow, n.d.], esp. the study "Primitivism and Decadence"). That is to say, in modern poetry, as well

ments may properly be said to be instruments that enable us to keep going-on from reference to reference in the world of fact, rather than judgments as to how things are in fact.

Thus imagine a situation in which someone might be said to know how to get about in the world, without at the same time having any knowledge of what the character of that world is, or without being able to make judgments of the more traditional sort to the effect that the facts are thus and so. In short, what we are suggesting is that it is just such a situation that the use of a relating-logic places us in, and that it is just this kind of knowledge that science in the modern sense is equipped to provide us with. Surely there can be no denying that a knowledge of this sort is conceivable, and that it is, if not in the usual sense of the word then indeed in some sense of the word, a true and proper knowledge.

The Order and Integration of Knowledge[7]

Very well, then, let us take the question to have been answered affirmatively as to whether modern scientific knowledge, considered simply as a product of a relating-logic, is truly a knowledge or not. A knowledge it certainly is; and yet our entire account points inescapably to the conclusion that it is a knowledge whose role can only be a secondary one, and whose status is perforce one of dependence, not independence. Repeatedly in the foregoing chapters we have sought to bring out how a relating-logic can only yield a knowledge that is severely limited and in a sense insufficient: no knowledge of things for what they are, all necessary truth reduced to mere nominal definition or linguistic truth, no inductive demonstration, no knowledge of things in terms of their causes, deduction construed as mere tautology, etc. For all of these reasons, then, it would seem that if we had to content ourselves with only a scientific knowledge, our human situation would be rendered almost intolerable. A humanistic or philosophical knowledge, as mediated by something on the order of what we have called a what-logic, may therefore be looked upon not just as a possible supple-

---

as in modern science, what seems to count is merely the network or a certain factitious web or structure that makes it possible to "go on"; but as for what the network describes, or what it denotes or refers to — these are all played down, or at least left deliberately vague and indeterminate.

7. William Oliver Martin, *The Order and Integration of Knowledge* (Ann Arbor: University of Michigan Press, 1957). My subhead simply borrows the title of this book.

ment to scientific knowledge, but as an indispensable human need in its own right.

Nevertheless, an existential need does not carry with it any sure guarantee of its own fulfillment. Hence, even supposing that over and above a scientific knowledge, we human beings do desperately need a humanistic and philosophical knowledge as well, is there any such thing? Our answer is that we hope that in the course of our book we have been able to show how the usual skeptical objections that have been raised against the sort of knowledge that proceeds from the use of a what-logic can indeed be dealt with and answered. Yet, in the light of the considerations that have been brought forward in this concluding chapter, we wonder if an even more cogent reason may not be given for the strict logical priority of a what-logic over a relating-logic, and so of a humanistic knowledge over a scientific knowledge. The reason briefly is this: If we are ever to know, much less to weigh and assess, the legitimacy of the kind of knowledge that a relating-logic is capable of yielding, then we must surely avail ourselves of a what-logic. For example, suppose that modern scientific knowledge is essentially a knowing-how, then the knowledge that this is so cannot possibly be itself a case of scientific knowledge, simply for the reason that it consists in a knowing-that and not merely in a knowing-how. More generally, it would seem that while through the instrumentality of a relating-logic we human beings are indeed able to gain knowledge, still if we are ever to know what sort of a knowledge it is that we have got and what the nature and working of the instrument is by which we have got it, then a relating-logic will no longer do, but only a what-logic. It is in just this sense and for this reason that a what-logic, while it need not necessarily be prior to any and all other logics in a temporal sense, can surely be no less than our ultimate human logic, to say nothing of being the logic of philosophy itself.

So, as regards the outcome of the new battle of the books, while it must certainly be conceded that up to now the new analytic philosophy has carried all before it, and the forces of the older and more traditional what-logic are in a seemingly hopeless and utter disarray, still could it be that the outcome is not yet quite final? Would it not be a strange irony if in the end a triumphant analytic philosophy should suddenly discover that only through the agency of a defeated what-logic could it ever hope even to know itself and, as others might hope, to know its place as well? And what goes for analytic philosophers would go no less for spiders, scientists, Galileans, *et al*!

275

Index

277

Index

Family resemblances, 149–53, 233
Formal truth (logical truth), 74–76, 130–31, 211–12, 214–18

Galileo, 191; Lewin-Atkinson interpretation of, 15–16, 204–5
Geach, Peter, Strawson's criticisms of, 66n
Gilson, Etienne, 156n; on essentialism, 154n
Gough, Harrison G., 50n
Graff, Gerald E., 48n
Gram, Moltke S., 98n; on C. I. Lewis, 137n

Hanson, N. R., 131–33, 140n, 177n, 206–10, 264–65; on causation, 127–29; on facts and theories, 181–84
Heidegger, Martin, 23–24
Hempel, Carl G., 211, 214. *See also* Covering-law model
History. *See* Explanation
Humanities: logic of, 11–13, 238–41, 255–56. *See also* Knowledge
Hume, David, 114, 117n, 149, 156, 171–73, 203n; on causation, 161–63; on ethics, 243–46; on impressions, 154–55, 170; on induction, 173–76; on substance-accident relation, 170
Husserl, Edmund, 160n

Induction: and constant conjunction, 173–76; in science, 164–67; Strawson on, 213n; in the two logics, 164–77
Intentions: first and second, 119, 123, 124; inverted intentionality, 118–25, 129, 133, 138, 139, 140, 198, 220–21, 249

Jager, R., 98n

Kant, Immanuel, 113–14, 117n, 156, 163, 165, 167, 169; on analytic truth, 72–76; on "combination," 112n; on concepts, 82–89; on the manifold of experience, 154–55; and modern science, 178–86; on synthetic judgments, 94–95, 101n; on transcendental method, 149, 178–86, 193, 195
Kennan, George F., on diplomacy, 20n
Kepler, on planetary motion, 59–61, 181–82
Kneale, William, 211
Knowledge:
—As correlated with two logics, 46–62 *pas-*

sim, 113–14, 126–44, 177–98, 254–58
—Ethical, 242–53
—Historical, 222–41
—Humanistic and scientific, 16–21, 47, 53, 57–62, 238–41; as mutually supplementary, 256–61, 274–75
—Literature as, 48n
—Philosophical, 254–75
—Scientific, 140–44
—Of "whats," 58
Kuhn, Thomas, 166n; on facts and theories, 182–83

Language games, 193–98, 220–21; contrasted with other games, 129; mathematics, 129–31; and the world, 123–25, 129
Leibniz: on essences, 145–47; on internal relations, 45–46
Lewin, Kurt, on Aristotelian *vs.* Galilean modes of thought, 15, 204–5
Lewis, C. I., 101–2, 126, 160n, 257; on contingent truth, 136–40; on the meaning of concepts, 106–10; on the objectivity of experience, 171–73; use of a relating-logic, 43–45; use of a transcendental principle of justification, 187–89
Logic:
—Alternative logics, 46, 62, 70–71, 254–75
—Bee-logic. *See* what-logic
—"Is"-relationship: in *PM* logic, 29–31, 38–39. *See also* Statements, subject-predicate
—Material (transcendental) logic, 11n
—*PM* logic, 67–71
—Relating-logic, 44, 49–57; and analytic truth, 80; and causal explanation, 204–10; and contingent truth, 134–40; defined, 42; and inverted intentionality, 118–25; and logical necessity, 110–12; in *PM* logic, 67–71; as proper to science, 127–32, 141, 144; the relating in, 140–41, 144n. *See also* Lewis, C. I.; *Principia Mathematica*; Waismann, F.; Ryle, Gilbert; Covering-law model; Wittgenstein, Ludwig
—Spider-logic. *See* relating-logic
—Synthetic-analytic distinction, 93–96, 100–102
—What-logic: and the everyday world, 49, 62, 132–34; and ontology, 258–59; as

278

proper to the humanities, 142n; relation to a relating-logic, 22, 43–44, 61–62, 258–59, 274–75. *See also* relating-logic
Logical atomism: qualities in, 35–41; use of a relating-logic, 34–41

McKeon, Richard, 67n
MacLeish, Archibald, 48n
Marvell, Andrew, 127
Material implication, 69–71
Meaning: of terms, 100n, 101, 134–35; as use, 131, 194–95, 260–61
Metaphysics, 34, 145–48, 180n, 181n, 185n
Moody, E. A., 68n
Moore, G. E., on goodness as a property, 250–52
Motion, Aristotelian *vs.* inertial, 261–64

Nagel, Ernest, 229n; on relating-logic in science, 143–44
Necessary truths, 72n, 84, 93, 97, 110; as capable of falsity, 97–100, 216–17; as synthetic a priori, 77, 101n; about the world, 76–81, 96, 159, 177–78
Necessity, real or logical, 110–14, 117–18, 119, 126, 139–40
Newton, Isaac, 60, 165, 181

Ontology: and epistemology, 157–63; and "is"-relationship, 31–32; in logical atomism, 35–41; and what-logic, 258–59

Parker, Francis, 169n; on the given element in experience, 156
Particulars, bare: relation to universals, 35–36, 38, 267; role in logical atomism, 36–37
Peirce, C. S.: on falliblism, 99; and relating-logic, 42
Phenomenology, 22–24
Philosophy, analytic and neo-analytic, 25, 255, 265, 268–71, 275
Plato, 167
Popper, Karl, 240–41; on essentialism, 154n; on induction, 175–76; on induction in science, 165–67, 175–76; on Kant, 165; on sciences and humanities, 4–10 *passim*; on scientific theories and hypotheses, 189–93. *See also* Covering-law model
Popper-Hempel thesis, 223–37 *passim*
Principia Mathematica, 26–27

Propositions. *See* Statements

Quine, W. V., on logical truths, 212
Quinton, A. M., 194

Realism, in science and common sense, 142–43
Reference, and language, 106–18, 195–98, 220, 221, 273–74. *See also* Language games; Winters, Yvor; Cornman, James W.
Relating-logic. *See* Logic
Relations:
—Internal, 42–46, 93n, 106–12. *See also* Language games
—In logical atomism, 35–36
—As predicates. *See* Statements
—And qualities, 37–41
—Real and logical, 80, 143–44
Rules, of grammar or language, 108–21, 135, 136
Russell, Bertrand, 31n, 163, 202n, 262n; on subject-predicate propositions, 31–34; on substance, 171; on substance-accident, 158–61, 171
Ryle, Gilbert, 122–23, 227n; on "inference-tickets," 115–18

Science: hypotheses and theories in, 165–66; logic of, 11–16, 271–74; relation to philosophy, 268–74. *See also* Knowledge
Shapere, Dudley, 182n
Snell's Law, 56–57
Snow, C. P., on the two cultures, 10–11
Statements (or propositions):
—Function-argument schema for, 29–30, 35–36
—Relational predicates in, 35–36
—Subject-predicate, 27, 28, 30, 64–67; as contrasted with substance-accident, 33, 38–39; "is"-relationship in, 38–39, 67, 103
—What-statements, 27–28, 40–41, 63–89 *passim*; ambiguity in the notion of, 72n; and causal explanation, 202–4; their distinctive import, 91–93; truth conditions of, 68–69, 96–100, 102–5; types of, 72n
Strawson, P. F., 213n; on Geach, 66n; on incompatible predicates, 121n
Substance-accident (thing-property), 27–28,

Index

33, 38–39, 66; Russell on, 158–61. *See also* Hume, David; Statements, subject-predicate

Substantial forms. *See* Essences

Suppositio, Scholastic doctrine of, 85, 96n

Surrealism, and deductive logic, 199–221 *passim*

Swift, Jonathan, 11–14, 92, 252

Synthetic truths: as contingent truths, 136; and what-statements, 90–105 *passim*

Thompson, Manley, 68n

Thucydides, 203–4

Toulmin, Stephen, 56, 213n, 227n; and relating-logic, 42–43

Transcendental method of justification, 179–86

Truth tables, 130–31

Two truths, doctrine of, 256

Universals, in logical atomism, 35–41, 45

Use-mention distinction, 81–86, 115, 118, 119, 122, 123

Waismann, F., 96–97, 135n, 139, 160n, 181n, 185n; on grammatical rules, 108–21 *passim*

Waldberg, Patrick, 200

Warnock, G. J., on visionary metaphysics, 180n

Warren, Austin, 48n

Wedgwood, C. V., 168–69, 244

Wellek, René, 48n

What-logic. *See* Logic

Whitehead, A. N., on internal relations, 45

Winters, Yvor, on pseudo-reference, 273n

Wittgenstein, Ludwig, 75n, 108, 202n; on family resemblance, 149–53, 233; on "going on," 132n, 141, 142, 195, 227, 234–35, 256, 260, 272–74; on language games, 142, 193–98; on "meaning is use," 132–34, 194–95; use of relating-logic, 42

www.ingramcontent.com/pod-product-compliance
Lightning Source LLC
Chambersburg PA
CBHW020213290326
41948CB00001B/29